INDUSTRIAL CONDITIONS
TH DURING THE CIVIL WAR

Corner House Publishers

SOCIAL SCIENCE REPRINTS

General Editor MAURICE FILLER

SOCIAL AND INDUSTRIAL CONDITIONS IN THE NORTH DURING THE CIVIL WAR

BY

EMERSON DAVID FITE, Ph.D.

ASSISTANT PROFESSOR OF HISTORY IN YALE UNIVERSITY

CORNER HOUSE PUBLISHERS

WILLIAMSTOWN, MASSACHUSETTS 01267

1976

REPRINTED 1976

BY

CORNER HOUSE PUBLISHERS

ISBN 0–87928–070–0

Printed in the United States of America

PREFACE

This book is a description of the occupations and pursuits of the North during the Civil War. The histories of the period thus far written seem to leave the impression on the present generation that war and politics were the only topics which then held the attention of the people, or at best to leave a confused notion as to the actual social and industrial conditions of this exciting epoch. An attempt is here made to ascertain what the people at home were doing to gain their livelihood during the memorable struggle; what were their personal interests and pleasures; what attention they gave to other than political and military matters; how far the normal activities of the nation were maintained; how far and in what respects they were changed.

Socially and industrially the North was more active and prosperous than ever before, for the war and war politics did not subvert these phases of the national life. The output of raw material from the farms, the mines, and the forests was unusual, and transportation and manufacturing activity was extraordinary; practically all branches of commercial life flourished. Both capital and labor were alive to their respective interests and made definite advances toward present-day conditions; there was progress in public improvements, while generous contributions for educational, charitable, and religious purposes, and even lavish expenditure upon luxuries and amusements, were not lacking.

In the search for material, sources of every description have been examined, including newspapers, technical and trade journals, United States, state, and municipal documents, reports of various commercial bodies, societies, and institutions, and many special articles and monographs. The subject-matter is treated from the standpoint of the historical student who desires to discover actual conditions. Throughout the work it has been found advisable to take for granted the reader's knowledge of the existence of the shifting paper standard of values, although in some cases especial attention has been directed to the phenomenon.

I wish to acknowledge with sincere thanks my obligations to Professors Edward Channing and Albert Bushnell Hart of Harvard University for their inspiration and suggestion in the beginning of my work; to Professor Oliver M. W. Sprague of Harvard University, and Professors Clive Day and Max Farrand and Mr. Stuart L. Mims of Yale University; to my brother, Professor William B. Fite of Cornell University, and to my wife.

EMERSON DAVID FITE.

YALE UNIVERSITY, NEW HAVEN, CONNECTICUT,
        September, 1909.

CONTENTS

CHAPTER I

AGRICULTURE

ONE of the notable features of the life of the North during the Civil War was the steady growth of agriculture. In spite of the universal enlistment of men in the army and the movement of population to the mines of the far West, bountiful harvests followed one another each successive year. The common fear of failure of crops was discredited; sufficient labor was found to gather every harvest, secession did not cut them off, nor invading armies disturb them. In the leading agricultural centers there was a continued peaceful expansion which in every way compared favorably with that of the previous decade.

In the preceding twenty years the leading crops of the country more than doubled in volume, while the relative position of the states as wheat and corn producers underwent a great change. In the East, in many sections, crops were declining, in the West rapidly advancing; the five states of Ohio, Indiana, Illinois, Wisconsin, and Iowa, which in 1839 furnished one-quarter of all the wheat and corn produced, by 1859 were furnishing one-half of these important crops. The new states, thus so rapidly developed, constituted a new agricultural center of unusual resources and energy; their progress was unprecedented. Conspicuous advance in the size of the cultivated area, the value of the farms, and the volume of the crops was keeping pace with rapidly increasing population.[1] A flood of immigration from the Eastern states and from Europe, accompanied by a

---

[1] For population tables, see *U. S. Senate Executive Documents*, 38 Congress, 1 Session, No. 1; the *Merchants' Magazine*, April, 1861, p. 540.

steady stream of capital for the construction of railroads and other public improvements, was pouring in on its rich lands and producing wonderful activity.

During the years of fighting there was continued progress. Although the crops of 1859 were probably the largest in the history of the country up to that .time, the production of wheat in this year was surpassed in every year of the war. In this record year one hundred thirty-eight million bushels of wheat were produced by the loyal states, in 1862 one hundred seventy-seven million bushels; the leading agricultural states in three years doubled their output. The Western corn crop also showed increase, though that of the country as a whole fell off slightly.[1]

Congratulations over the productivity of the new regions were universal. By all classes of people it was recognized that the United States was a great agricultural nation in a time of prolonged and devastating civil war. "The greatest calamity that could have befallen this nation in its present peril," declared the *New York Independent,* "would have been a deficient harvest. From such an infliction it would have been impossible to recover in many years, and our necessities might have proved fatal to the preservation of our Union and our national existence. It is frightful to think how near we came to such a catastrophe; but happily the time of danger is now past, and whatever other troubles

[1] WHEAT AND CORN PRODUCTION IN BUSHELS

	1839	1849	1859	1862	1863	1864
			ENTIRE UNION			
Wheat . .	84,000,000	100,000,000	173,000,000			
Corn . . .	377,000,000	592,000,000	838,000,000			
			LOYAL STATES			
Wheat . .			138,000,000	177,000,000	173,000,000	160,000,000
Corn . . .			547,000,000	533,000,000	397,000,000	451,000,000
	OHIO, INDIANA, ILLINOIS, WISCONSIN, AND IOWA					
Wheat . .	24,000,000	36,000,000	80,000,000	113,000,000	111,000,000	102,000,000
Corn . . .	86,000,000	181,000,000	309,000,000	361,000,000	237,000,000	346,000,000

— From *Reports of the Commissioner of Agriculture* and *Census Reports.*

may be in store for us, we are saved from the terrible doom of a depleted granary." [1]

Next after the grain crops in importance were the droves and flocks. The sale of hogs was unprecedentedly large; in no year were more than usual raised, but more than usual were put on the market; the number packed almost doubled. [2] Sheep raising made rapid strides. The annual production of wool, which increased but slightly in the previous decade, now quickly rose from forty million pounds to one hundred forty million pounds, the number of sheep from sixteen million to thirty-two million. In Ohio, the leading wool state, in California, Pennsylvania, and Illinois, extraordinary increase was noted; almost all New England became a sheep pasture. "No branch of business increased more rapidly than the domestic wool trade; it grew with gigantic strides." Rarely had the woolgrowers been stimulated to such activity; their new associations and conventions were strikingly numerous; the present society, the National Woolgrowers' Association, dates from this time. [3] Cattle raising was unimportant and cattle packing was in its infancy. [4]

In Maryland, Kentucky, and Missouri, where the system of slave labor was disturbed, the production of tobacco decreased; in the Connecticut Valley it was stimulated. [5]

---

[1] The *New York Independent*, September 8, 1864.

[2] See p. 78. The highest number packed in any year before 1861 was 2,500,000; in 1862 the figure was 4,000,000; and in 1863, 3,000,000. See *Report of the Commissioner of Agriculture*, 1865, p. 373; the *Merchants' Magazine*, May, 1863, p. 400, and May, 1866, p. 376.

[3] *Report of the New York Chamber of Commerce*, 1862–1865; the *Lawrence Sentinel*, Lawrence, Massachusetts, January 2, 1864; *Address before the National Association of Wool Manufacturers at the First Annual Meeting in Philadelphia*, September 6, 1865, by John L. Hayes, Secretary.

[4] *The History of Kansas City*, W. H. Miller, Kansas City, 1881, p. 164; *Report of the Chicago Board of Trade*, 1864–1865, p. 43; *Report of the New York Produce Exchange*, 1873–1874, p. 397.

[5] From 1855 to 1860 the average yearly crop had been 275,000,000 pounds; this was nearly equaled in 1863, but in the next two years the yield was small, at least 100,000,000 pounds below the average. See

The cultivation of the various products attempted as substitutes for Southern cotton and sugar was an interesting development, but did not prove remarkably successful. In California, southern Indiana, and southern Illinois efforts were made to cultivate cotton, and the national government gave assistance, but because of the rigor of the climate only failure attended these efforts. The most prominent substitute sought for cotton was flax; however, all attempts to use it in cotton machinery failed, just as they had failed previously, and no linen was manufactured.[1] For Louisiana sugar the chief substitute was sorghum, recently found in China by a French consul and by him sent to France, whence it was introduced into the United States. The plant in appearance and habits resembled Indian corn, and it was thought that it would grow where the latter grew. So it proved. In 1860 it was raised both in the North and in the South, but more especially in the Northwest, and in the latter region, after the war opened, its cultivation extended very rapidly, but as in the past only syrup was produced from the new cane, no sugar at all. Maple sugar and syrup were consumed in large quantities, while every effort to produce beet sugar failed. And yet, despite all efforts, sugar remained a luxury and was scarce to the end of the war.[2]

U. S. Senate Miscellaneous Documents, 38 Congress, 1 Session, No. 12; *Report of the Special Commissioner of the Revenue*, 1868, U. S. House Executive Documents, 40 Congress, 3 Session, No. 16, p. 6.

[1] *Report of the Special Commissioner of the Revenue*, 1866, U. S. Senate Executive Documents, 39 Congress, 2 Session, No. 2, p. 60.

[2] The *Merchants' Magazine*, January, 1863, p. 17; *Report of the United States Revenue Commission*, 1865–1866, U. S. House Executive Documents, 39 Congress, 1 Session, No. 34, p. 89, Special Report No. 4. For the sugar trade between Louisiana and the Northwest, see *De Bow's Review*, October, 1860, p. 524. The total consumption of sugar, North and South, in 1860 was 415,000 tons; in the North alone in 1864, 220,000 tons. The production of Louisiana sugar was 5000 tons in 1865, 100,000 tons in 1860; the consumption of foreign sugar in 1860 was 296,000 tons, in 1865, 345,000 tons. See *Report of the New York Chamber of Commerce*, 1865–1866, Part II, p. 6.

This scarcity of the products of the South may be readily explained as the natural result of the war; on the other hand, the reason for the abundance of the staple products of the North, wheat, corn, pork, and wool, is not so apparent. How was abundance possible when so many thousands of men were absent in military service? In all the country districts there was this strange characteristic of society, the strong young men were gone. A home missionary in Wisconsin wrote: "In common with all our frontier towns we feel the sad effects of the war. From this town of 250 voters 111 have volunteered, and from Westfield and Ironton about an equal number in ratio of population. In this village of 90 families 20, or more than one-fifth, are those of volunteers." From Illinois another missionary wrote: "I can characterize it [the last quarter] in no other way than by terming it a sad quarter. The call for the last 600,000 was promptly and nobly responded to by our friends. Thirty men, regular attendants on our services, have gone, taking the flower of the community, drawing quite largely on our church roll. The township in which our church is, counts 147 men liable to the draft, and has now in the field or under marching orders 117 of these." Still another declared that "the drain of young and able-bodied men to meet the demands of the army has left farmers very much in need of help, and great difficulty has been felt in securing the crops properly." [1]

A second element, tending to reduce agricultural population, was overland migration to the mines of the far West. There was a steady movement of this nature, especially in the last year of the war, when according to estimate one hundred fifty thousand people crossed the plains to Colorado, Idaho, Nevada, California, and Utah. Many of these adventurers were farmers.

[1] The *Home Missionary*, December, 1862, pp. 90 and 96, January, 1863, p. 212; and December, 1862, p. 196.

Three things saved the harvests the increased use of labor-saving machinery, the work of women in the fields, and the continued influx of new population.

Up to this time the use of reaping machines had been confined almost entirely to some of the large farms of the West; on many farms there and commonly in New York, New Jersey, Pennsylvania, and all New England wheat and oats were still cut in the harvesting bee. Farmers helped one another, each with a scythe and attached cradle cutting his own swath, and by a mighty swing of the body throwing the grain out at the end of each cut. Throughout the East grass was cut in the same slow and laborious way, by the hand scythe. Grain was generally sown by hand. These processes required the work of many men, so that when the able-bodied began to go to war, with large harvests left to garner, new methods and new implements were absolutely necessary if the crops were to be saved.

Immediately interest in labor-saving machinery and in the relative merits of the different machines became widespread, and next to enthusiasm over abounding crops in time of war was the most striking characteristic of the world of agriculture. Scientific papers, like the *Scientific American*, and agricultural papers were filled with the subject, and farmers' conventions discussed it. At the agricultural fairs, both state and county, which were held with almost customary regularity, attended by the usual crowds and meeting with the usual successes and failures, the competitive tests of the rival reapers, mowers, and other implements aroused intense interest; only one other exhibit vied with them in popularity, namely, that of the recently invented sewing machine. It would be difficult to exaggerate the genuine enthusiasm with which the crowd of spectators at the fairs watched these tests. Conservative farmers, who before the war, when labor was cheap and plenty, failed to see the advantage of labor-saving machinery, now, when stared in the face by the possibility of losing their crops for want of labor, looked on with eager interest at machines which with the aid of one man were cutting from ten to twelve acres per day, while they were used in the harvesting bee to seeing one man cut barely two acres. Accustomed to cutting their hay with a scythe at the rate of an acre or so a day, they now saw one man with a mowing machine cutting eight or ten acres. The old apathy was gone; the war suddenly had popularized methods of cultivation in which the agricultural papers had striven in vain for a decade to arouse interest.[1]

The editor of the *Scientific American* bore witness to the efficiency of the new methods in the following words: "In conversation a few days since with a most intelligent Western farmer he told us that manual labor was so scarce last autumn that but for the horse rakes, mowers, and reaping machines one-half of the crops would have been left standing in the fields. This year the demand for reapers has been so great that manufacturers will not be able to fill their orders. Farming is comparatively child's play to what it was twenty years ago, before mowing, reaping, and other agricultural machines were employed. The severe manual toil of mowing, raking, pitching, and cradling is now performed by machinery operated by horse power, and man simply oversees the operations and conducts them with intelligence." [2]

[1] There is a mass of evidence to show the persistence of the fairs; consult especially the files of the *New York Tribune*, the *Springfield Republican*, the *Chicago Tribune*, the *Country Gentleman*, the *American Agriculturist*, and the *Ohio Farmer*.

[2] The *Scientific American*, July 4, 1863. The total number of mowers manufactured increased from 35,000 in 1862 and 40,000 in 1863 to 70,000 in 1864; estimating the number for 1861 at 20,000, this would make the number for the four years 165,000, compared with 85,000, the number made in the preceding ten or twelve years. On these figures, see the *Scientific American*, February 12, 1864, and the *Railroad Record*, May 11, 1865. Of the McCormick reaper, the original, against which patent, according to the commissioner of patents, every other reaper was an infringement, 700 were made in 1848, 5000 in 1858, 6000 in 1864, 8000 in 1868. See *History of Chicago*, Andreas, II, 685.

In appearance the reapers resembled those of the present day. Usually the aid of one man was required to rake the grain off the platform where it was gathered, and to discharge it on the ground in one continuous swath; to complete the process manual labor was required to separate the grain and to bind it into sheaves. In 1862 a device appeared on the McCormick machine to rake the grain off the platform and to separate it automatically into loose untied sheaves before it fell to the ground. The present automatic binder, to bind the grain into firm sheaves before discharging it to the ground, was not perfected till later; this was regarded as the greatest improvement in the process from the time of the original invention in the thirties.[1]

The revolving horse rake was probably in wider use than any other machine on the farm; there were many patents and wide sales for grain drills, two-horse cultivators, and rotary spaders, all of which had been previously used, like mowers and reapers, only in some parts of the West. There were steel plows; neither the sulky plow nor the steam plow was perfected, though the general idea of the construction of both was known. Threshers, small in size and run by horse power, accomplished the same work as now, although imperfectly; the grain was threshed, cleaned, measured, and the straw stacked at one operation.

The work of the new machines was supplemented by that of women in the fields. Said a missionary, writing from Iowa: "I will mention that I met more women driving teams on the road and saw more at work in the fields than men. They seem to have said to their husbands in the language of a favorite song,

> "' Just take your gun and go;
> For Ruth can drive the oxen, John,
> And I can use the hoe!'

[1] During the war, in some parts of the West, binding was done by a separate machine, which tied the sheaf by wire. The automatic binder, at first using wire and very soon twine, dates from 1875.

I went first to Clarinda and the town seemed deserted. Upon inquiry for former friends, the frequent answer was, 'In the army.' From Hawleyville almost all the thoroughly loyal male inhabitants had gone; and in one township beyond, where I formerly preached, there are but seven men left, and at Quincy, the county seat of Adams County, but five." Another from Kansas wrote: "If the war continues, the next year will be a very trying one for Kansas, especially in the back counties, where in many cases the women must harvest the corn and take care of the stock, in addition to their ordinary work." After describing the scarcity of men, another wrote: "We see the practical effect of this state of things. Yesterday I saw the wife of one of our parishioners driving the team in a reaper; her husband is at Vicksburg. With what help she can secure and the assistance of her little children, she is carrying on the farm. In another field was a little boy of ten years, similarly employed; and in another a girl of about twelve, doing the same. Men cannot be found in sufficient numbers to secure the harvest; the wives and children, therefore, are compelled to go into the fields." The same conditions were noted in Ohio, New York, and other states.[1]

Supplementing the aid of labor-saving machinery and the work of women in gathering the crops was continued immigration. "Our state and our village," wrote a missionary from Iowa in 1864, "are filling up with immigrants from the East. Perhaps it is safe to say that at no time since the wild vagaries of 1853, '54, '55, and '56 have we had so many flocking in upon us. There is not a house to be rented in

[1] The *Home Missionary*, January, 1863, p. 209, December, 1862, p. 184, and November, 1863, p. 173; *Report of the Commissioner of Statistics of Ohio*, 1865; the *Working Farmer*, October, 1864; the *Ohio Farmer*, July 23, 1863. The scarcity of young men and the activity of young women in taking their places was further shown by the experiences of the country schools, where the young men, who before the war had done most of the teaching, were rapidly disappearing, the women taking their places. See p. 246.

this place, and when one offers itself there are several applicants ready. What is true of Marion is true of other centers
of population generally." [1] Illinois in the middle of the war,
according to the president of the Illinois Central Railroad,
was still favored by a large immigration and was daily
adding to its numbers and wealth from the substantial population settling in the prairies; the gain in the number of
settlers proceeded uninterruptedly.[2]

One source of the new population was the Border states,
which were harassed by fierce political strife, by the imma-
nence of invading armies, and by constantly recurring bush-
whacking warfare; thousands of their peace-loving citizens,
rather than endure the ordeal, cast in their lot with the
more peaceful Northern communities. The refugees were
generally very destitute, and their migration was assisted by
the national government and by a strong national association,
the National Union Commission.[3]

Many went westward from the Eastern states, where the
farms were at a disadvantage in competition with those of
the West, and where the commercial panic of 1861 and the
later dissatisfaction in the labor world caused greatest inconvenience. The secretary of state in New York, impressed by the shifting of population in that state, near the
close of the war sent out circulars inquiring the probable
causes of the changes, and out of two hundred thirty towns
reporting, although many complained of a loss to the rapidly
growing cities, sixty-five attributed their loss mainly to immigration to the West. The same was noticed in Massachusetts and Rhode Island.[4] The Ohio commissioner of

---

[1] The *Home Missionary*, August, 1864, p. 96.

[2] *Report of the Illinois Central Railroad*, 1863.

[3] *The same*, 1862 and 1863. It was estimated that in 1863 one-third of
the land sales of this road were to people of the Border states. For the
charity to the Southern refugees, see p. 296.

[4] For New York, see *Preliminary Report of the Census of New York*,
1865; for the figures of the other states, see p. 230. In the three states

statistics declared that a commercial crisis always produced immigration from old established communities to new communities and new lands; he believed that Ohio had gained greatly in this way in 1819–1823 and in 1837–1841, as the result of the commercial disturbances of the seaboard cities, and that now she herself, as well as other states, was losing in the same way to the further West.[1]

During the five war years forty-five thousand immigrants from Europe, upon landing at New York, declared their intention of continuing their journey to Illinois, twenty-three thousand to Wisconsin, and smaller numbers to other states. Over eighty thousand of these newcomers were carried inland from the seaboard by a single railroad.[2]

To this immigration, whether from the Border states, the Eastern states, or from Europe, a strong inducement was cheap lands, controlled partly by the national and state governments, and partly by the railroads. The national government, the largest holder, was most generous. In the course of the war itself, after a struggle of forty years or more, the principle of a homestead act, the giving away of farms to actual settlers for a nominal fee, was at last enacted into law; and thus was achieved the most important step ever taken in the public land policy of the nation. The incentive to new settlement was now very strong. Under the beneficent workings of the law in two and one-half years two million five hundred thousand acres of land were disposed of; this represented nearly twenty thousand farms of one hundred sixty acres each and an increase in population of from seventy-five thousand to one hundred thou-

named the farming sections were losing population, and from the case of New York it is fair to assume that in the other two states some of the immigrants went to the West.

[1] See *Report of the Ohio Commissioner of Statistics*, 1861; also the *American Railroad Journal*, February 6, 1862.

[2] *Report of the Commissioner of Emigration of New York State*, 1861–1865; the *Commercial and Financial Chronicle*, December 23, 1865.

sand persons. From the provisions of the act itself most of these were bound to be permanent settlers; absent speculators could not acquire the bounty. The success of the act was its best defense; it induced permanent settlement and developed the resources of the country. Still, inasmuch as the public debt was mounting upwards at the rate of more than $2,000,000 a day, some advocated the repeal of the law and the sale of the public lands in the open market to provide revenue for the payment of the debt. But this was condemned by President Lincoln and others as a short-sighted policy when considered in the light of the future.[1]

The grant of land to agricultural colleges probably did not have much effect while the war lasted, for the reason that the states were slow in accepting the gift and in selecting their lands; little of this land was in the market before 1865.[2] But thousands of acres, previously disposed of by the government for educational and other purposes, were taken up in settlement. Minnesota put her school lands on the market and sold one hundred sixty-five thousand acres; Wisconsin parted with two hundred thousand acres of her school and university lands; and both these states disposed of much of their swamp and overflowed lands. Military

[1] The *Reports of the Secretary of the Interior* show that under this act from January 1, 1863, to July 1, 1863, 140,988 acres were sold; 1863–1864, 1,261,592 acres; 1864–1865, 1,160,532 acres; 7864 of the homesteads were in Minnesota, 2211 in Wisconsin, 711 in Iowa, 1755 in Nebraska, 2067 in Kansas, and a smaller number in other states. The government owned no lands in Illinois, all having been disposed of. New Englanders, ever jealous of the West, and strict constructionists from the South had opposed the measure from the start, but step by step Congress drew nearer to the principle through the preëmption act of 1840, the graduated act of 1854, and special homestead acts for Florida, Oregon, and New Mexico. In 1860 the first general homestead act was passed, but was vetoed by President Buchanan from constitutional motives; President Lincoln quickly signed the measure when it was passed again in 1862.

[2] For a fuller consideration of this act, see p. 235.

bounty lands for the benefit of veterans of previous wars were also in the market.[1]

There were finally the lands of the land-grant railroads, given by Congress to the states to be distributed by them in turn to the various railroads. In this way the Illinois Central received two million six hundred thousand acres of the best lands of the state, and other roads large amounts. In contrast to the military bounty system and to the swamp land grant this railroad policy was a conspicuous success; the military bounty system proved a failure through its inability to attract the old soldiers westward; the states at best were wasteful and extravagant in their use of the swamp lands; but by individual initiative the money-making railroads sold their lands in a businesslike way and attracted a steady stream of settlers. Of these sales, which proceeded in several states, those of the Illinois road were by far the most extensive, and reached a surprisingly large number of people; thirteen thousand persons in the time of the war took over eight hundred thousand acres in all, a sixty-acre farm for each purchaser. In one year alone the road disposed of two hundred fifty thousand acres.[2]

It is evident that from these various sources thousands of settlers found their way to the West, and that through their industry thousands of acres of land were brought under cultivation for the first time. On every side the cultivated area was being extended with apparently as great rapidity

[1] See the official documents of the two states; school and university lands were given to each state by the United States as the states were admitted to the Union; swamp and overflowed lands in each state were given to the states in 1850; military bounty lands, involving fifty million acres, were given to the soldiers by acts of 1847, 1850, 1852, and 1855. See the *North American Review*, July, 1861, p. 13.

[2] From 1850 to 1864 the commissioner of the general land office approved to the states for railroads 19,565,603 acres of public domain. The sales of the Illinois Central were as follows: 102,000 acres in 1861, 87,000 acres in 1862, 221,000 acres in 1863, 264,000 acres in 1864, 154,000 acres in 1865. See the *Reports of the Company*.

as if the country were in a state of profound peace. The actual number of new inhabitants from the outside it is impossible to determine, but probably it reached at least two hundred thousand. The census enumerations, which because of the unusual conditions arising out of the war were taken by almost every state in 1865, are not an accurate guide in the matter, since they do not distinguish between natural increase and increase by immigration; the record, however, is that in Illinois the gain in population was 430,000, in Wisconsin 90,000, in Minnesota 88,000, in Iowa 180,000.

Still another piece of good fortune for the West was the trunk line railroads. These were bands of iron binding the farming sections to the East, helping to hold them in the Union by providing a market for their produce. In the ten years preceding, in the states of Indiana, Illinois, Wisconsin, and Iowa, seven thousand miles of railroad were constructed, provision far in advance of the needs of the country, but, as it proved, a magnificent preparation for the unforeseen strain of war. The Mississippi formerly had been the outlet of these sections to a market, carrying the grain and other produce to New Orleans, whence it was distributed in all directions. After the war closed the river, if the railroads had not been in existence, the West would have been isolated, without a market; and it was believed by some that rather than lose this, the section would have followed its market into secession. According to this view, the Union was saved by the railroads. Others, with less confidence in the roads, or perhaps even ignoring their existence, openly feared the Western secession, and many in the South prophesied it. The most serious test came in the year of the congressional campaign of 1862, when political hostility to the government was the strongest in the North and the crops the largest. Over their material prosperity farmers were highly enthusiastic, but there was discouragement in regard to the military situation, great uncertainty as to slavery, and bitter political strife; if to these unfavorable conditions there had been added widespread discontent over the loss of a market and rotting crops, the opposition at the polls would certainly have been overwhelming, and the government would have lost the elections, a result that might easily have changed the whole course of the war. This the trunk lines, by keeping the Western farmers in touch with a market, rendered impossible.

The new routes of trade to the Atlantic coast were developing rapidly indeed, thanks to the wonderful increase of the crops even more than to the closing of the river. New Orleans had been receiving from the Northwest annually 10,000,000 bushels of all kinds of grain, including flour; this river trade ceased, so that all of the increase of the crops now went eastward over one general route. The receipts and shipments of the port of Chicago grew apace, and were typical of the growth of the new routes eastward. Starting in 1838 with a shipment of 78 bushels of wheat and gradually thereafter increasing her shipments, but never before 1860 sending out over 10,000,000 bushels of wheat and wheat flour, this new city in each year of the war shipped on the average 20,000,000 bushels of wheat and wheat flour; her yearly corn exports, in the past never above 11,000,000 bushels, now averaged 25,000,000 bushels. Her shipments of all kinds of grain doubled. This marvelous increase far surpassed the total amount of the trade acquired from the river,[1] and probably it would have gone on with little disturbance if the river had never been closed; it was mainly the work of the railroads, which were then just beginning to compete successfully with the river.

It was further advantageous to the Western farmers, although manifestly unfair to the railroads, that the transportation rates for grain and other products actually

---

[1] It would be unreasonable to suppose that all of the diverted river traffic went to one city; it was probably distributed to various cities.

declined instead of advancing with the advance of prices in general during the paper money régime. This was due to competition, particularly that of the trunk line railroads with the lake routes. The tramp steamers on the lakes, running wild, without any agreement with the railroads and themselves competing with one another, first made the rate and then on the basis of this rate the railroads made theirs.[1] In 1864, when prices were their highest, the aggregate freight rate, Chicago to New York, via Buffalo, by lake and canal, for a bushel of wheat was twelve cents lower than three years earlier; the rates for corn declined similarly. There was but a slight advance for live-stock. The farmers were reaping undue profits. Points lying on or near the lakes, or on or near the East and West railroads, profited most; on roads with little competition, like some of those entering Chicago, for example the Illinois Central, rates partook of the common advance, and the farther away from Chicago on such a road, the less farmers benefited by the low Chicago-New York rate.[2]

After the Mississippi was closed and while the crops were large, but before the railroads and lake steamers were able to adjust themselves to the new traffic, there was difficulty; even competitive rates were high, slightly higher than previously, although there were new lines in abundance; there were neither enough boats nor freight cars to meet the need, and in other respects the lines were unprepared for the emergency. Much traffic was turned away. It was this

---

[1] *Transportation Routes to the Seaboard*, U. S. Senate Reports, 43 Congress, 1 Session, No. 307, Part I, Volume II, pp. 7–8, 278, 280–281.

[2] *Report of the New York Produce Exchange*, 1872–1873, p. 392; *Transportation Routes to the Seaboard*, U. S. Senate Reports, 43 Congress, 1 Session, No. 307, Volume I, Appendix, pp. 35, 167; *Trade and Commerce of Chicago*, 1861–1865. Undoubtedly at the Chicago Canal Convention in 1863 and at the Detroit Reciprocity Convention in 1865 some discontent was expressed over high freight rates to the East from the West, but this spirit was not common, and the conventions were meetings of special interest, speeches at which must not be taken too seriously.

situation that was the chief cause of the remarkable increase in the number of hogs packed.   In Iowa and those parts of Illinois next to the Mississippi, which had been most dependent on the market down that river, the corn crop in the crisis was unprecedentedly large; prices for corn dropped lower and lower, while rates for freight soared; corn was burned as fuel in unusual amounts, and in unusual amounts fed to hogs.   It was cheaper to fatten and market the hogs than to market the grain.[1]

The question now naturally presents itself, Where and how was the increased production of the farms consumed? What was the new demand?

It must be recognized that the nation was undergoing great progress; in every line there was expansion, not alone in agriculture, but in mining, lumbering, transportation, and commercial life.   This created a demand for more food products.   There were, moreover, the needs arising from the war itself.   Men collected in an army consumed more than when scattered in peaceful pursuits at home; army life was wasteful, and much was either abandoned or lost to the enemy.   This appears specially in the wool industry, the growth of which was greatly stimulated by the demand for army uniforms.[2]

The largest increase in demand came from foreign countries, for in the three years 1860, 1861, and 1862 the harvests of Great Britain were a failure, and in one of the years those of all Europe.   The British deficiency reached its height in 1861, when the crop was 40,000,000 bushels below the average; in the year following this harvest importations of American wheat were 32,000,000 bushels larger than usual. To foreign countries, for ten years preceding, the United States sent 20,000,000 bushels of wheat annually; in the

---

[1] The *Merchants' Magazine*, May, 1863, p. 400, and May, 1866, p. 376.

[2] The scarcity of cotton in the North was another incentive to wool production.

c

second year of the war the total exportation reached
60,000,000 bushels, an increase that equals almost the entire advance of the American output.[1] Plainly the largest
part of the war-time demand for breadstuffs came from
abroad.

To the United States the strong foreign demand at this
time was of peculiar interest and significance, for in the very
year when British imports of wheat from the Northern
states were largest, those of the cotton of the South were
lowest; while the former suddenly increased eight times over,
the latter almost disappeared, falling from two million five
hundred thousand bales to less than seventy-five thousand
bales. It was a tremendous change.

Up to the time of the war the South believed that cotton
was king. One of its senators declared: "Without the firing
of a gun, without drawing a sword, should they make war
upon us, we could bring the whole world to our feet. What
would happen if no cotton was furnished for three years? I
will not stop to depict what every one can imagine, but this
is certain, England would topple headlong, and carry the
whole civilized world with her. No, you do not dare to
make war on cotton. No power dares to make war on it;
cotton is king."[2] But the war came on, and no less an

---

[1] In the loyal states the increase in the total wheat crop was 40,000,000
bushels; the total amount of surplus to be disposed of would be increased
by the cessation of the demand of the Southern states, which in the
decade from 1850 to 1860 had been about 10,000,000 bushels annually
on the average. The British wheat crop in 1858 and 1859 averaged
16,000,000 quarters (a quarter is eight bushels); in 1860 it fell to 13,000,000
quarters; in 1861 to 11,000,000 quarters; and in 1862 to 12,000,000 quarters; in 1863 it reached 14,000,000 quarters; and in 1864, 18,000,000
quarters. See *Report of the New York Produce Exchange*, 1875–1876,
p. 324. Prices per quarter ranged as follows: —

1858	. . . 38s.		1862	. . . 40s. 5d.
1859	. . . 38s. 9d.		1863	. . . 34s. 4d.
1860	. . . 35s. 7d.		1864	. . . 30s. 6d.
1861	. . . 42s. 2d.		1865	. . . 28s. 8d.

[2] *A History of Commerce*, by Clive Day, New York, 1907, p. 523.

authority than the *London Economist*, in the following
words, totally ignored cotton and awarded the kingship to
wheat. It recognized in the development of the external
corn trade of the country "one of the most remarkable,
perhaps the most remarkable, commercial fact of modern
times. As respects the mass of the people, it is little to say
that their comfort is enhanced by these vast importations,
for the truth is that without such importations our people
could not exist at all. If we could not subsist our population without foreign aid in 1847, we certainly cannot subsist them in 1862." [1]

Did Northern wheat prevent British recognition of the
Confederacy? It certainly contributed to this result. The
leading foreign granaries for Great Britain were the United
States, Russia, Prussia, and France, and in the hour of need
only one of these responded. The American harvests were
large in every one of England's three years of scarcity,
while, on the other hand, French shipments to England actually fell off, and those from Germany and Russia remained
stationary.[2] If, when the Southern ports were first block-

---

[1] The *London Economist*, October 25, 1862. On the decline of the English cotton industry, see the *London Economist*, December 10, 1864; the
Merchants' Magazine, April, 1864, p. 277; the *London Times*, April 10,
1865; *Report of the United States Revenue Commission*, U. S. House Executive Documents, 39 Congress, 1 Session, No. 34, Part II, p. 49. The
London Times said, December 31, 1862: "The memory of the year which
ends this day will hereafter be chiefly associated with the American war
and with its consequences at home. No crisis in modern times has been
so anxiously watched, nor has any European war or revolution so seriously threatened the interests of England."

[2] *Report of the New York Chamber of Commerce*, 1878, p. 327, gives an
interesting table on the sources of England's importations of wheat.
England had fears about the security of all her granaries. After the opening of the war in America in 1861, the *Mark Lane Express*, the leading
agricultural paper in England, declared that Britain had "America no
longer to depend on"; "for the present year the American market may
be looked upon as a very limited one." In 1862 it remarked: "As to the
importations, we cannot expect a large amount from the United States.
Not only has war devastated a great extent of the wheat-growing dis-

aded, her Majesty had made a forcible attempt to get American cotton out of the Confederacy, she would have offended the United States and by the resulting war have cut off the importations of American wheat at a time when America was the only country that had grain to spare. The next year there was still little to spare on the Continent, while the United States had a record crop and England was still short. For England to fight the United States at this time was to invite hardship. In the subsequent years, with the improved English crops, there was still need of foreign grain, but the European granaries were threatened by general war over Poland in the one year and over Schleswig-Holstein in the other; if in these two years the queen had interfered for the Confederacy, and thus definitely cut off the American grain shipments, it was a question where her country could obtain the grain previously supplied by America. The Continental supply was liable to be cut off at any time, and it would have been a radical step indeed to cast off the American supply when all other supplies were uncertain.

This importance of American food Englishmen were loath to admit; they recognized its bounteous supply, but were reluctant to admit that it exerted influence in international affairs. Patriotic Americans, on the other hand, were quick to exaggerate this influence, and it remained for a

tricts of that country, but the rural or agricultural population has been so reduced by drafts for the army that in many parts there are not left hands enough to cultivate the land. Such interference with the regular processes of agriculture will have a material effect on production." Constantly throughout the war this was the English expectation. See the *Country Gentleman*, July 9, 1863, and the *Mark Lane Express*, January 19, 1863, January 4 and June 6, 1864. On the fears which were expressed as to the Continental shipments when the Polish question of 1863 and the Schleswig-Holstein question of 1864 became prominent, see the *Mark Lane Express*, March 2, April 6, and December 21, 1863, and February 22, February 29, and August 29, 1864. A file of this valuable paper is in the Yale Library.

leading English Liberal, William E. Forster, debating the celebrated Roebuck motion in Parliament for the recognition of the Confederacy, to state what was probably the conservative view of the matter. "He believed his amendment was proposed with a motive and a view to peace; and in truth, unless the harvest was better than it promised, the sufferings of the countrymen of the honorable member would be great indeed if they were deprived of the American crop of this year. He never would allow commercial considerations to prevent his engaging in a just war, but when they were asked by the honorable and learned member for Sheffield to go to war for merely selfish purposes, to procure cotton, it was allowable to ask, 'What would be the cost of the war in corn?'" He thought that such a war would entail suffering in England, and that this possible suffering was underrated.[1] At this distance it may safely be concluded that while the need of grain would not have prevented England from defending herself from a war of aggression by the United States, it was doubtless one of the factors, and an important one, in preventing aggressive demonstrations by England in favor of the Confederacy and against the United States.[2]

---

[1] *Hansard's Debates*, 3d Series, CLXXI, p. 1813. Anthony Trollope, writing soon after the war scare over the *Trent* affair, declared that a break in the commercial intercourse of the two countries would "rob millions of their bread." See his *North America*, II, 446.

[2] One reason why Americans were glad to export grain was that there was a premium on gold. For imported commodities payment had to be made in gold; paper money, greenbacks, would not be accepted. But gold was an ordinary commodity, to be obtained in the market like any other commodity. Some articles, which Europeans would accept, did not rise in price here so much as did gold; one of these was grain. American importers, therefore, bought wheat in this country and shipped it abroad to pay their debts there; this was cheaper than to pay in gold. But it must be remembered that the United States had plenty of grain to spare and that England was short. This fact stands out. It is incorrect, therefore, to assume that the fluctuations of gold explain the grain exportations. England's need was the main factor.

The foreign demand had of course its natural economic influence in this country; it served to carry off surplus products and to maintain prices. When exportations went on peacefully, prices were high; when rumors of foreign war arose, as, for example, at the time of the *Trent* affair, prices in the West collapsed.[1]

In addition to the size of the crops and the unexpected success in harvesting and marketing them, still other elements contributed to the prosperity of the American farmer at this time. Throughout the country the period was a favorable one for buying land and thus increasing the size of the farms, for, in spite of paper money, prices of land remained almost stationary till the end of the war.[2] Heavy paper money receipts were available for making cheap payments on mortgages previously contracted in gold, and it is a matter of record that the amount of these obligations paid off at the time was very large.[3]

Farmers were accordingly buoyant and prosperous. The mercantile agency of R. G. Dun and Company believed that in the year 1864 the prosperity of agriculture was "immense and general"; it declared that this prosperity was a striking factor in the commercial world of the year, and that the ready money of the farmers and their heavy purchases in the retail trade constituted one of the elements which went to explain the surprisingly small number of commercial failures of the period.[4]

[1] See the *Home Missionary*, April, 1862, p. 295, on the collapse of prices in Iowa at this time; wheat fell suddenly from sixty to thirty-five and forty cents, pork on foot from three to one and three-fourths cents.

[2] See p. 226.

[3] *Recent Financial, Industrial, and Commercial Experiences of the United States*, David A. Wells, New York, 1872, p. 25.

[4] See p. 107. Agricultural prosperity also explains the general increase in the number of business houses in the West, while everywhere else the number was declining; see p. 107. The same prosperity alone explains the subsidence in the last half of the war of the canal agitation in the West which arose during the low prices of 1861–1862; see p. 54. On the growth of the schools in the West, see p. 245.

The picture of war-time agriculture is one of ceaseless activity and progress; of new things and of things done on a larger scale than ever before; of some sacrifices, but yet of general enthusiasm and prosperity. The president of the Illinois Agricultural Society in 1864, referring to Illinois, the center of agriculture, summed up the conditions in that state in the following words: "Look over these prairies and observe everywhere the life and activity prevailing. See the railroads pressed beyond their capacity with the freights of our people; the metropolis of the state rearing its stately blocks with a rapidity almost fabulous, and whitening the Northern lakes with the sails of its commerce; every smaller city, town, village, and hamlet within our borders all astir with improvement; every factory, mill, and machine shop running with its full complement of hands; the hum of industry in every household; more acres of fertile land under culture, fuller granaries, and more prolific crops than ever before; in short, observe that this state and this people of Illinois are making more rapid progress in population, development, wealth, education, and in all the arts of peace, than in any former period, and then realize, if you can, that all this has occurred and is occurring in the midst of a war the most stupendous ever prosecuted among men." [1]

[1] The *New York Journal of Commerce*, September 17, 1864.

CHAPTER II

MINING AND LUMBERING

THE mines were as notably productive as the farms. The output of coal, iron, copper, salt, gold, and silver in most cases surpassed all previous records; many important new mines were opened, and the totally new petroleum industry was developed.

Coal, next to gold, was the most important mining interest in the country. Pennsylvania, ranking first among coal-producing states, produced nine million five hundred thousand tons of anthracite in 1860, ten million tons in 1864, and slightly less in the next year.[1]

The progress of iron mines was represented by the advance in the production of pig iron, from eight hundred thousand tons in 1860 to one million tons in 1864. One-half of the industry, as in coal mining, belonged to Pennsylvania; the most rapid strides, however, were not made in this state but in Michigan, where improvements in transportation, the completion of the Sault Ste. Marie Canal and the Marquette Railroad, had only recently put the mines in communication with the outside world. The results were striking. Shipments southward began with the opening of the canal, but were small till the advent of the railroad, when suddenly

---

[1] The Pennsylvania anthracite statistics, compiled by the *Miners' Journal* of Pottsville, Pennsylvania, were the only completely reliable coal statistics of the time; see the *Statistical Abstract of the United States*, 1902, p. 550; *Report of the American Iron and Steel Association*, 1874; the *Merchants' Magazine*, May, 1865, p. 349, has an exhaustive article on the coal trade. The *Banker's Magazine*, October, 1865, has statistics of New York prices of anthracite coal from 1825 to 1864. A file of the *Miners' Journal* is in the Congressional Library at Washington.

they entered upon an enormous increase that continued through the war period, twice as much being shipped in the closing year of the war as in the first year.[1]

The only considerable source of copper in the East, and in fact in the whole Union, in the first part of the war, and the chief source of the nation's supply after the war tariff decreased that from Chile, was in Michigan. Confined to three districts in the extreme Northern part of the state, these mines produced but little till the construction of the favoring Sault canal and railroad, when suddenly there was an advance till 1860; for the next five years there was no further progress, though the mines continued to produce at their normal rate, six thousand tons per year. During the same years there was a remarkable development of the copper industry in California, and by the end of the war that state was exporting more copper than Michigan. Soon, with the discovery of the Calumet and Hecla mines, Michigan again forged ahead as the leading copper-producing state.[2]

Lake Superior iron and copper, recent if not entirely new productions, served to mark Michigan as a mining community; but a wholly new mineral product of the state, salt brine, attracted wide attention. This was discovered in paying quantities on the eve of the war in the pine forests along the Saginaw River, and was rapidly developed through a liberal system of state bounties as well as by a heavy de-

[1] In 1855, 1445 tons were shipped; in 1859, 67,000 tons; in 1860, 67,000 tons; in 1864, 235,000 tons; see *Internal Commerce of the United States*, 1879, Appendix, p. 208. The Michigan ore came to Cleveland to be smelted there and in the valley towns as far south as Pittsburg; this was the beginning of the iron business of northeastern Ohio. Insufficient transportation prevented the development of the iron mines of Missouri while the war lasted.

[2] Six thousand thirty-four tons of ingot copper were produced in Michigan in 1860, 6246 tons in 1864; 10,234 tons were exported from California in 1864. The *Commercial and Financial Chronicle*, August 19, 1865; *U. S. Senate Reports*, 37 Congress, 2 Session, No. 40; the *Merchants' Magazine*, 1867, p. 156.

mand. Within four years the annual production of the new wells reached five hundred thousand barrels. This was greater advance than had been made on the Kanawha River in Virginia in fifty years, and greater than at the Onondaga works in New York in forty years. On the banks of the Saginaw River, which was twenty-three miles long, in the midst of a lumbering region, three small towns suddenly sprang into prominence, East Saginaw, Saginaw, and Bay City.

The discovery was opportune, for the West had been depending for its salt upon the Kanawha River works, which were soon destroyed by the ravages of war, upon foreign importations at New Orleans, and upon the works in southern Ohio. The smallest supply alone remained. Returning cotton vessels from Europe were in the habit of carrying foreign salt to New Orleans as ballast, and thus was supplied an abundance of cheap salt to the whole Mississippi Valley; when suddenly this exchange ceased and a new supply became necessary, the Michigan product was at hand together with the more distant salt of New York, ready to fill the need, and the loyal part of the valley did not suffer from a scarcity of salt, while competition kept down prices. In a short time, more Michigan than New York salt was used in the meat-packing industry of Chicago, and the Eastern product was prevented from rising to monopolistic prices.

The salt wells of New York, in the vicinity of Syracuse, which were much larger in their output than those of Michigan, for two years experienced remarkable progress, then a rapid decline, owing probably to the competition of the Western product.[1]

---

[1] Nine million bushels of salt were produced in Syracuse in 1862, an increase of more than one hundred per cent over the year 1860. On salt in general, see the *American Railroad Journal*, April 8, 1865; the *Merchants' Magazine*, September, 1862, p. 223, June, 1865, p. 456; *Report of the Cincinnati Chamber of Commerce*, 1861; the *Commercial and Financial Chronicle*, August 5, 1865.

Another new mineral product of the period was petroleum, in the production of which an industry of enormous proportions was soon built up, great fortunes made, and much public interest aroused. Because of its hold on the popular imagination the story may be told in detail.

For many years the existence of this oil had been known. It was occasionally found in drilling artesian wells; it oozed to the surface on the banks of Oil Creek and thus gave a name to that small tributary of the Allegheny River; it was sold in drug stores as liniment under the name of Rock Oil, Seneca Oil, etc. Attempts to secure it in large quantities by digging trenches along Oil Creek, in the hope that in these the oil might collect, proved fruitless; finally wells were drilled after the fashion of artesian wells; and in one of these, in 1859, near Titusville, Venango County, Pennsylvania, oil was struck.

This first successful well, the famous Drake well, though not a flowing one, produced twenty-five barrels of oil per day, worth one dollar per gallon when sold for lubricating purposes; this was a daily income of $1000. "The excitement was very great. Every one who had land in the vicinity of the Drake well made preparations for sinking wells on his own account, or leased to others a right to sink them, on payment of a royalty. Suddenly the whole business was revolutionized by the discovery of flowing wells. The first flowing well was struck on the McIlhinny or Funk farm, and was known as the Funk well. Funk was a poor man when the well was sunk. It was struck June, 1861, and commenced flowing, to the astonishment of all oil-borers in the neighborhood, at the rate of two hundred fifty barrels a day. Such a prodigal supply upset all calculations, but it was confidently predicted that it would soon cease. The oil, however, continued flowing with but little variation for fifteen months and then stopped, but not before Funk became a very rich man. Long before the Funk well had given out there were new sensations, the Tarr farm, yielding two thousand barrels daily, and the Empire well, yielding three thousand barrels daily." [1]

Development was rapid, but not without interruption. Within a year after the first well in the Oil Creek Valley, on the Kanawha River in Virginia, and in southeastern Ohio over two thousand wells were bored, from all of which, however, only nine flowing wells resulted. The supposedly successful refining of the new fluid for illuminating purposes, announced shortly, contributed toward increasing the excitement, which the formation of armies and the news of battle scarcely abated. The progress in this year was on a large scale, but the few heavily flowing wells really embarrassed the trade and brought down prices; when a gusher came, prices at the well went down to five and ten cents per barrel. Heavy production and heavy losses continued the next year. It was more profitable in these months to let the oil run than to gather it; the business was "played out," and the region became a desert, wells, machinery, and all being to a large extent abandoned. Only a few bold spirits held on, to whom the year 1863 brought some improvement and the year 1864 fabulous incomes. Prices in this last year began at $4 per barrel for the crude oil and reached $14 in July; then there was a decline, and a second advance, this time to $12. Profits ranged from $3 to $10 per barrel. [2]

The boring of new wells, which had been suspended for some months, was now resumed with feverish activity, and speculation became rampant. There was the initial excitement over again. The *New York Herald* began now to speak of the petroleum aristocracy, declaring that it had supplanted shoddy aristocracy just as the latter had displaced California

---

[1] The *Resources and Prospects of America*, S. Morton Peto, p. 193, quoting from a work on petroleum wells by J. H. A. Bone.

[2] *Report of the New York Produce Exchange*, 1878, p. 497; *Report of the United States Industrial Commission*, I, 410.

aristocracy; anthracite aristocracy and cod fish aristocracy seemed to be matters of the far-distant past.[1] By the end of this last year of the war one thousand wells were being bored in the vicinity of Wheeling, West Virginia, and many more on the Ohio side of the river; the margin of Oil Creek was again literally covered with derricks for a distance of sixteen or seventeen miles. In other states there was much prospecting. Newspapers were daily filled with announcements of the new discoveries, while long lists of newly incorporated companies were published and their advertisements flaunted before the public in many forms. People had only to invest their money in the stock of a company and a fortune was assured; little attention was paid to the fact that the company often existed only on paper and had neither money nor territory. Seldom has speculation gone to such lengths. Some large fortunes were made, which fact rendered it easy to keep the investing public excited. When the excitement died away soon after the close of the war, one thousand one hundred petroleum companies had been incorporated in the various states with a capital stock of $600,000,000, of which $90,000,000 was paid up. A petroleum stock exchange was opened in the city of New York.[2]

The greatest successes were along Oil Creek, where a number of towns sprang up out of the wilderness as if by magic, Corry, with 10,000 inhabitants in four years and an annual business of over $12,000,000, Oil City, Franklin, Titusville, etc. Venango County had been one of the poorest counties in the state; more than one-third of it could be bought for

[1] The *New York Herald*, October 18, 1864.

[2] On the activity in the year 1864, see *New York Tribune*, September 21, 1864; it then cost $7000 to dig one well, and ten men were employed at each well. On the speculation, see the *Commercial and Financial Chronicle*, October 21, 1865; the *Railroad Record*, November 24, 1864; the *American Exchange and Review*, September, 1865; the *Petroleum Gazette*, September 11 and June 24, 1865; the *New York Independent*, January 19, 1865.

$3 per acre, its best farms brought little over $30 an acre, and its entire industrial product was not worth over $300,000 a year. After the discoveries these lands sold for from $300 to $500 per acre, and some for as high as $45,000 an acre, while 50,000,000 gallons of oil were being produced annually. This was similar to the development occasioned by the occurrence of salt in the Saginaw Valley in Michigan, but much greater, comparable rather in its magnitude to that in the Pennsylvania iron and coal regions.[1]

Speculation partially accounts for the renewed activity in 1864, but there were other fundamental reasons for it. One of these was improvement in transportation facilities. The Oil Creek region at the outset was thirty miles from a railroad, and at first wagons, and wagons only, were used to haul the product to market at Erie, fifty miles away. This was difficult, slow, and expensive, for the roads in the backward county of Venango were poor, but in spite of the introduction of other transportation facilities wagons were even more extensively used at the close than at the beginning of the war. Transportation to Pittsburg from Oil Creek was secured mainly by a thousand rafts and barges, down that stream and the Allegheny. After two years the first railroad reached the wells, the Oil Creek road, built by the owners of the wells themselves and connecting with Erie and the West. Soon came the Atlantic and Great Western, with connections for New York. Within a year the latter road reached Cleveland in its gradual extension westward, and within two years the former reached Philadelphia. Thus Erie, New York, Cleveland, and Philadelphia in turn secured rail connections with the new fields; a direct line to

---

[1] One hundred twenty-eight million gallons of petroleum were produced in 1862, 109,000,000 in 1863, 88,000,000 in 1864, and 104,000,000 in 1865; 30,000,000 gallons were exported both in 1864 and in 1865; see *Report of the United States Revenue Commission*, U. S. House Executive Documents, 39 Congress, 1 Session, No. 51, p. 33.

Pittsburg was not finished till after the close of the war. On all these roads iron tank cars soon appeared, and thus shipment in barrels was gradually done away with; iron tank steamers came into use at about the same time.[1]

Pipe lines were another expedient used in getting the oil to market. These failed to work when first tried, but were finally successful, one satisfactorily performing service over a stretch of five miles; it carried eighty barrels an hour, and in ten hours did the work of three hundred teams; it further had the advantage over teams of doing its work continuously without intermission day or night. Numerous strikes against the introduction of the new device all ended in failure. Boats, railroads, iron tank cars, iron steamers, and pipe lines, therefore, were gradually supplanting wagons and solving the difficult problems of petroleum transportation.

Another cause for the renewal of interest in petroleum in 1864 was improvement in refining. The excitement in 1861 following the first announcement of what was styled successful refining proved but short-lived, for the refined product was found to be unsatisfactory. Numerous explosions of the volatile fluid and fires shook the confidence of the public and of the insurance companies, which was not restored till new methods were put into operation in the middle of the war. As an illuminating fluid refined petroleum, commonly termed coal-oil, or kerosene, was superior to the other illuminants then on the market. These were whale oil and lard oil, both of which were rapidly declining in use, burning fluid, which was a volatile and dangerous combination of alcohol and spirits of turpentine, and coal-oil. The last, the most recent and the safest of them all before the introduction of petroleum, was extracted from coal by a process introduced from Europe; its popularity was rapidly extending, and it was bidding fair to possess the whole market; but it was expensive, costing from $1.25 to $1.50 per gallon. All these

[1] The tank cars appeared in 1865.

fluids cheap kerosene at once displaced. In towns unsupplied with gas the characteristic kerosene glass lamp came to be well-nigh universally used. Refined petroleum served also as a substitute in mixing paints, while the unrefined product was found useful as a lubricant.[1]

The mines of the precious metals were as active as those of coal, iron, copper, salt, and petroleum, and in three widely separated regions new deposits of the precious metals of great riches were developed.

In 1859 on the eastern slopes of the Sierra Nevada Mountains, in what was soon to be organized as the territory of Nevada, the famous Comstock Lode was discovered, an immensely valuable gold and silver mine, the first large deposit of silver found in the history of the country. For a few months only a small amount of ore was produced, but the output rapidly increased and soon amounted to over 400,000 tons annually, worth when refined $15,000,000; the value of the first six years' output was $52,000,000. The deeper this lode was worked, the greater and more wonderful were the riches disclosed. Numerous mining towns sprang up, the chief of which, Virginia City, quickly attracted a population of eighteen thousand.

Again in 1859, a few months after the discovery of the Comstock Lode, the great Gregory Lode was discovered in Colorado and a beginning made in gold mining in that region; in five years there was deposited in the mints of the United States from these mines $11,000,000 worth of gold, probably about one-half of their total output. The mines here, although not so rich as those in Nevada, attracted fully as much attention, and the growth of the community went on at a rapid rate. The territory of Colorado was at once or-

---

[1] Refined petroleum was called coal-oil because it was thought that in some way the original product came from coal deposits; this use of the term must not be confused with the coal-oil distilled from coal, which kerosene, or the new coal-oil, displaced.

ganized, but the offer of statehood by the national government was refused; Nebraska refused the same dignity, the only territory to become a state at this time being Nevada.[1]

During the progress of the war gold was discovered in what was at first organized as the territory of Idaho, but was later divided into the two territories of Idaho and Montana.[2] The leading town in Idaho was Bannock City, in Montana Virginia City. In three years these mines deposited $7,000,000 worth of gold in the mints and probably produced $14,000,000 worth.

The older gold mines of California fell back considerably, although the state itself was gaining both in population and in the size of its agricultural output, and although the leading city, San Francisco, was growing very rapidly. The high water mark of California gold, a yearly production of $65,000,000, was reached early in the fifties; thereafter decline set in which steadily increased from year to year and was especially noticeable after the discoveries in Nevada and Colorado. In ten years it amounted to over fifty per cent.

But in spite of this falling off, the total production of precious metals in all the Union during the war advanced $10,000,000.[3]

[1] The census takers found in Colorado in 1860 32,227 people; by 1864 the population was variously estimated at from 75,000 to 100,000, although there was one estimate of 25,000 and another of 16,000. In Denver, the chief city, a mint was opened in 1862, and one in Carson City in Nevada in 1863. The expense involved in setting up the new state governments was probably the reason for the refusal of Colorado and Nebraska to accept statehood; taxes were too high to warrant the additional expense. The Democrats in the three territories opposed the step for political reasons, not caring to further Lincoln's war policy.

[2] In 1864, before the arrivals of that year, the United States marshal's census found there 33,000 people. The discovery of gold was in 1862.

[3] On the Nevada mines, see *United States Geological Survey Monographs*, IV, *Comstock Mining and Miners*, by Eliot Lord; for the mines of Colorado and Idaho, see the newspapers of the time; the *Report of the New York Chamber of Commerce* published figures as to the amount of pre-

This bare enumeration conveys but little impression of the strong hold of the Western mines at this time upon the public mind, of the boastings of the newspapers, the excitement among capitalists, and the mania for mining speculation. In San Francisco, after the fever of speculation had been running for some time, an authoritative list was printed containing the names of over two thousand mining companies with offices in the city, most of which were formed in one year. In Denver excitement was intense. Much of the mining property in that vicinity was bonded for sale in New York, where large amounts of it were sold. "The mountains have been prospected anew," said one account from Denver, "and many rich lodes discovered. The recorder's office is crowded every day by those who are entering new claims, and looking up their old and hitherto worthless property. How long the excitement will continue, it is impossible to say." When the craze struck the East, speculation in mining stocks and the formation of new speculative companies was extensive, but not as common as in California; in a short time over forty such companies were formed in New York and three hundred in all the Eastern cities, with a capital on paper of $90,000,000, all inviting the people to "get rich quick" on mining stocks. It was similar to the excitement over petroleum a few months later, though not so intense.[1]

The movement of population over the plains to the mines

cious metals received into the mints; for California, see *Statistical Abstract of the United States*, 1902, p. 61. This last publication, p. 63, gives statistics that differ from those given in the text, taken from Lord. In the production of lead there was no advance; foreign importations were here largely relied upon. See the *Merchants' Magazine*, June, 1864, p. 428; *One Hundred Years of American Commerce*, Chauncey M. Depew, Editor, II, 436.

[1] The *Mining and Scientific Press*, August 10, 1863; the *American Exchange and Review*, March, 1865; the *Railroad Record*, April 24, 1864; the *Commercial Bulletin*, April 30, 1864; the *Congregationalist*, May 20, 1864.

was constant. Throughout the Mississippi Valley interest in the discoveries, especially in those in Idaho, the most recent, held a large place in the popular interest. It was not so much the interest of speculators as that of hardy adventurers, who sought personal exploits and new conquests. The newspapers were filled with maps of the far Western country, suggested routes, warnings of evils to be avoided, and descriptions of mining life, while occasional arrivals of the precious metal increased the interest. The adventurous, restless class was attracted; some sought to escape the dangers and disorders of life in the Border states, and others from the South fled from the ignominy of defeat by Federal arms. Still others fled from the draft; the governor of Iowa on one occasion even went so far as to assume by proclamation to forbid any leaving that state until after the draft, and it was reported that in some cases Federal marshals guarded the ferries over the Missouri. These various motives, together with the love of gain, led on the vast throng. The great farming districts, already depleted by the formation of armies, still submitted to this further drain and at the same time succeeded in harvesting the crops.[1]

[1] It is impossible to tell the exact destination of the immigrants just as it is impossible to tell the exact population of the mining districts. Mining population is very unstable; it tends to move off to the newer mines. Many miners left Colorado for Idaho, — one thousand, it was estimated, in the short space of three months. A regular coach was established between Denver and Bannock City, and a brisk intercourse between the two places sprang up. There was the same vigorous communication between San Francisco and Virginia City in Nevada. The gain in population in Utah may be measured by some quite accurate statistics. On their arrival in New York between eleven thousand and twelve thousand immigrants declared their intention of going to that territory. Every year large companies of the Mormons came, mostly peasants from England, Scotland, and the north of Europe, and every year a large caravan set out from Utah to meet the newcomers on the frontier, and to conduct them to their destination. They moved as one large organized body, men, women, and children walking, with only the baggage in wagons; it was a true pilgrimage; every morning and every evening the whole body reverently engaged in prayer.

The migration was shared in alike by Nevada, Colorado, Idaho, Montana, and California; as an isolated community, without connection with the agricultural centers farther east but contributing by its agriculture and domestic manufacture to the support of all the surrounding mining regions in every direction, Utah must be added. Not a mining section, it was still a part of these communities, trading with them and competing with them for settlers.

A continuous caravan, in May and June of the first year of the war, journeyed westward from Fort Kearney;[1] for several weeks from twenty-five to one hundred teams daily crossed the ferry at Omaha, Nebraska, bound for California; five thousand Mormons passed that point for Utah, two thousand of them direct from Europe.[2] At Omaha, the next year, there was an "immense number" of immigrants passing to California, and a "very large number" to Utah. In 1863 the road at Omaha was covered most of the time with the wagons of those bound for Colorado, California, and Oregon; one train of nine hundred wagons was noted, another of twelve hundred.[3] On the Kansas route this year a traveler from Colorado, sixteen days on the road, met on an average five hundred wagons a day going to Colorado and California, two-thirds of them to California.[4] Fifteen thousand people, according to the toll-gate statistics on the South Fork of the Platte, entered Colorado this year.

Of the movement in 1864, which was larger than that of any other year of the war, there were some striking descriptions. The Rev. Jonathan Blanchard, president of Wheaton College in Illinois, traveled over the Omaha

[1] The *Knickerbocker* or *New York Monthly Magazine*, August, 1861, p. 117; this is a good description of the overland passage.

[2] The *Home Missionary*, October, 1861, p. 41, and November, 1861, p. 165.

[3] The *Watchman and Reflector*, September 17, 1863.

[4] The *New York Journal of Commerce*, January 7, 1864.

route to Idaho and sent back several valuable letters. From Council Bluffs, Iowa, he wrote: "The one all-absorbing, master passion of the whole region is that in which all human evils take root. The immigration is said never to have been exceeded. When you approach this town, the ravines and gorges are white with covered wagons at rest. Below the town, toward the river side, long wings of white canvas stretch away on either side, into the soft green willows; at the ferry from a quarter to a half mile or more of teams all the time await their turn to cross. Myriads of horses and mules, the largest and finest I ever saw, drag onward the moving mass of humanity toward the setting sun; while the oxen and cows equal them in number. A large ferry, plying rapidly all the day long, makes no diminution of the crowd, though twenty or thirty animals are carried over at once, and trips take but a little time. As my inquiries run, not one-half are for Idaho. California, Denver, Arizona, Oregon, are receiving multitudes; and most of them have their families with them to settle there. The motives which propel this living mass are, of course, various. Old Californians, who many times cursed their folly for starting, and who thought on their former return that they would never leave home again, missing the interest and terrible stimulus of a mining life, have sold out their farms and are off for a better climate. The golden dreams of all, the real success of a few, the fabulous sums made by merchandise and speculation, goad on a mixed multitude of jobbers and traders, while the ubiquitous liquor seller, and the smooth, quiet black-leg, with his lizard eye and countenance, bring up the rear. The result is, realms are being peopled as if by magic. The great majority are going the way whence they will never return, many because they cannot, many more because they will not, and a few because they will do well and will not wish to return. The result will be—nations."[1] Later, resting on the

---

[1] The *Home Missionary*, July, 1864, p. 81.

Platte River, opposite Fort Kearney, he wrote: "The immigration is enormous. Wisconsin and northern Illinois and Iowa are largely represented; and a sprinkling of good men are among them. But coppers from southern Illinois and Missouri are here in large force."[1] Further on he wrote: "Such is the region over which two thousand six hundred wagons had preceded us to Fort Laramie, averaging four horses, mules, and oxen to each. If an equal number have come up on the road south of the Platte, and about the same number from California and the West, nearly eight thousand wagons and twenty-four thousand men, with a sprinkling of women and children, have already preceded us, two-thirds to Idaho, the rest to Colorado, California, Nevada, and Oregon. It is guessed that three-fourths of this year's immigration is yet to come, and if so, the whole will foot up to a hundred or a hundred and twenty-five thousand people. But the route will breed pestilence with dead animals, before such a number can get through. Day after day they trudge on, with sand in their eyes, sand in their ears, sand in their hair, neck, bosom, boots, stockings, hats, clothing, victuals, drink, bed clothes; their bed is sand."[2]

An engineer of the Union Pacific Railroad, who observed the migration at another time of the year, wrote: "Four thousand wagons and six thousand tons of freight have crossed the Missouri River at Omaha since April first. There is now a daily movement of two hundred teams, three hundred tons of freight, and one thousand persons. The teams are equally divided between those drawn by horses and those drawn by five yoke of cattle. No immigration has ever been known to bear any comparison to this. The line of teams waiting ferriage reaches nearly to Council Bluffs, or three

---

[1] The *Home Missionary*, August, 1864, p. 103.
[2] *The same*, November, 1864, p. 174.

miles in length. This rush will undoubtedly continue to the middle of June. The ferry boat runs night and day. This does not include government transportation." [1]

The movement of the same year, 1864, through Kansas and Colorado was also noteworthy. A certain judge, journeying from Fort Kearney to St. Joseph's, declared that he was never out of sight of a wagon, and that on one day he met four hundred.[2] Another traveler estimated that there were ten thousand people on the road between Denver and the Missouri.[3] Many took the river up the Missouri from St. Louis, St. Joseph's, and other points.[4]

It was estimated that the migration in 1864 from the one town of Omaha amounted to 75,000 people, 22,500 tons of freight, 30,000 horses and mules, and 75,000 cattle, while all authorities seem to agree that the total migration from all the Missouri River towns, through Kansas and Nebraska, by all routes, equaled 150,000 people.[5] Judging from the amount of freight dispatched, the movement of this year was much larger than that of 1860.[6]

The manner of life in the Western towns was as picturesque as it was wild and dangerous. Virginia City, Montana,

[1] *U. S. House Executive Documents*, 38 Congress, 1 Session, No. 55, p. 210.

[2] The *Daily Missouri Republican*, St. Louis, June 10, 1864.

[3] The *Boston Journal*, July 13, 1864.

[4] The shipping news of the St. Louis papers contains material on this river traffic.

[5] *U. S. Senate Executive Documents*, 38 Congress, 1 Session, No. 55; the *Philadelphia North American and United States Gazette*, November 1, 1864; *Report of the Secretary of the Treasury*, December 6, 1864, Enclosure "T"; the *National Intelligencer*, December 3, 1864.

[6] In 1860, 36,000,000 pounds of freight were carried over the plains, in 1864, 63,000,000 pounds. See *Report of Lieutenant James H. Simpson, Corps of Engineers, U.S.A., on the Union Pacific Railroad and Branches*, etc., in the Report of the Secretary of the Interior, December 4, 1865, p. 885; the *History of Kansas City*, W. H. Miller, Kansas City, 1883, p. 105; *U. S. Senate Executive Documents*, 38 Congress, 1 Session, No. 55; *Board of Trade Statement of the Trade and Commerce of Buffalo*, 1865.

may be taken as a typical settlement. Here the first buildings were erected in 1862, and in two years there was a population of from ten to fifteen thousand; in one year more than
five hundred buildings were put up. There was the usual
number of gambling and liquor saloons; the Sabbath was
almost habitually desecrated; prize fights, bull fights, and
drunkenness were common. Desperadoes, gathered from
every quarter of the globe, at first carried everything with a
high hand, threatening to overthrow all morality and setting
at defiance all law. But by 1864 the better elements arose
in their might, and formed a vigilance committee, inevitable
in such communities, which in one night arrested one of the
leading criminals, and tried, condemned, and hung him on
the spot. "In the first three days of the acts of this committee forty persons were arrested, tried, condemned and
executed, among whom were the sheriff and one or two of his
deputies, several other county officers, and men of apparently
good standing, many of whom confessed their guilt before
death. This summary proceeding sent terror to the hearts
of all who belonged to the gang, and they fled to parts
unknown. About sixty persons in all had been executed up
to the first of October, 1864. Law and order have since
prevailed, and the vigilance committee still hold their councils, ready at all times to bring men to justice, not without
examination and trial, but without delay, bribery, or corruption on the part of the culprit or his hirelings." [1]

Although without the novelty and excitement of many of
the mining activities lumbering played an important part in
the nation's development through these years. The amount
of lumber surveyed at Bangor, Maine, more than doubled in
four years; in New York state at all points on tidewater, the
receipts by canal of board and scantling were larger in each
of the last three years of the war than for many years; [2] in

---

[1] The *Boston Review*, May, 1865, p. 277, and March, 1865, p. 128.

[2] Amounting in 1860 to only 377,000,000 feet, in 1864 to 495,000,000 feet.

Chicago lumber receipts practically doubled,[1] while those of shingles and lath greatly increased. The figures for Chicago in 1865 were the highest ever reached in the history of the city up to that time. On the Great Lakes and the New York canals the transportation of lumber was second only to that of grain in magnitude and importance. This meant extreme activity in all the lumber camps, in Maine, New York, Michigan, and Wisconsin, for the importations from Canada did not materially increase, while receipts from the South ceased altogether.[2]

In time of war the country's mineral and lumber resources seemed almost inexhaustible; they were numerous and progressive, safe within the bounds of the Union and undisturbed by war. Not only were the old mines and forests abundantly productive, but many new mineral deposits were opened up, iron, copper, and salt in Michigan, petroleum in Pennsylvania, gold and silver in Nevada, and gold in Colorado, Idaho, and Montana. As in the case of agriculture such abundance in war time and sufficiency of labor in spite of military demands demonstrated the nation's wonderful vitality.

[1] From 262,000,000 feet in 1860 to 501,000,000 feet in 1864.

[2] Four hundred million feet of lumber were cut in Wisconsin in 1860, with a constant increase thereafter up to 1867, when 800,000,000 feet were cut. In the valley of the Saginaw River in Michigan, the seat of the salt industry, also the leading lumber section of the state, 135,000,000 feet were cut in 1863, 215,000,000 feet in 1864, and 250,000,000 feet in 1865. In the whole state of Michigan 390,000,000 feet had been cut in 1854, 620,000,000 feet in 1864. For the statistics of the Chicago lumber trade, see the *Reports of the Chicago Board of Trade;* for those at Albany, *Trade and Commerce of Buffalo,* 1869; for those at Bangor, the *New York Observer,* January 16, 1862, the *Boston Shipping List,* December 7, 1864; for those of Wisconsin, *Transactions of the Wisconsin Board of Agriculture;* for those of Michigan, *American Annual Cyclopædia,* 1865, article on "Michigan," also *Trade and Commerce of Buffalo,* 1869.

CHAPTER III

TRANSPORTATION

THE prosperity of agricultural and mining industries was naturally reflected by the transportation lines, both canals and railroads. During the four years of war there was heavy traffic on these lines, unprecedented activity, and a surprisingly widespread public interest in transportation questions. At the close of the year 1861 the *American Railroad Journal* declared: "The year has been on the whole a very favorable one for the Northern railroads. Their earnings for the present year greatly exceeded those of 1860. Their traffics have immensely increased to supply the foreign demand for breadstuffs. It is consequently a somewhat remarkable fact that in a period of civil war the value of railroad property should have improved while that of all other kinds has greatly deteriorated." [1] Of 1862 the *Railroad Record* said: "But the year 1862 will ever be remembered in railroading as one of the most prosperous that has ever been known. The railroads never earned so much in the whole course of their existence as they have during this much-dreaded year. Railroad stocks and bonds never were regarded with so much favor, and very justly, because they have demonstrated their value by actual earnings." [2] The first-named journal, reviewing the year 1863, declared: "The railway system has greatly flourished the past year. The companies have got out of debt, or largely diminished

[1] The *American Railroad Journal*, January 4, 1862.
[2] The *Railroad Record*, January 8, 1863.

their indebtedness, their earnings are increasing, their dividends have become regular and inviting. The past year has been, therefore, the most prosperous ever known to American railways."[1] According to the same journal, the roads during the next year were used to their utmost capacity.[2]

Of the various railroads those in New England, almost shut off from grain movement and army transport service and largely restricted to the distribution of manufactures, showed the least advance over their previous condition, which in fact had been flourishing; those in Pennsylvania prospered with the growing output of iron, coal, and petroleum which they carried; those in the West, built in the previous decade far in advance of immediate needs, were now for the first time used to their utmost capacity in carrying the crops, which but for them could scarcely have reached a market; the north and south lines, such as the Illinois Central and the Cleveland, Columbus, and Cincinnati, which hitherto had the reputation of never making money, throve on army business and to some extent on the movement of the crops. The most prominent and probably the most important roads were the three trunk lines, the Pennsylvania, the Erie, and the New York Central, which were continued westward by the Pittsburg, Fort Wayne, and Chicago, the Michigan Central, and the five lines later consolidated into the Lake Shore and Michigan Southern. Farther north the Grand Trunk reached the lakes in Canada; to the south was the Baltimore and Ohio, for a part of the time within the war zone.

During the period of the war the growth in freight tonnage and in the number of passengers carried on such leading roads as the Illinois Central, the Erie and the Pennsylvania, and on many other lines, amounted to as much as one hundred

---

[1] The *American Railroad Journal*, January 2, 1864.
[2] *The same*, December 31, 1864.

per cent, and there was a corresponding gain in the number of freight cars on hand.[1]

Railway stocks, which before the war had generally been low, quickly rose. Some, like Erie and Hudson River, which had never paid a dividend, by the end of the war were above par and were paying 8 and 9 per cent, respectively; Erie in three years rose from 17 to 126½, Hudson River from 31½ to 164. The stock of every important road was above par by the end of the war, of many nearer 150 than 100, and all dividends were "regular and inviting." Dividends in stock were often declared.[2]

It had been the fears in regard to the approaching presidential election of 1860, coming soon after extensive construction and the panic of 1857, the secession of the Southern states which followed the election, and the actual blows of war, that had kept these stocks at the previous low quotations, and it was the growth of traffic that was the solid foundation of their advance, although the spirit of speculation and to a much less extent increase of freight rates were

[1] The freight tonnage on the Pennsylvania from 1860 to 1865 increased from 1,346,525 tons to 2,798,810 tons, the number of passengers from 1,203,444 to 2,861,836, and in this interval the road acquired 3133 freight cars and 147 engines. It was approximately the same on many roads. See the *Commercial and Financial Chronicle*, March 10, 1866, February 24, 1866, December 23, 1865, and June 9, 1866. Throughout 1865 and 1866 this paper published statistics of many of the leading roads. For the gain in the number of freight cars and engines, see the weekly tables in the *American Railway Journal*.

[2] Cleveland and Pittsburg and Illinois Central had never paid dividends, but in 1863 each paid 4 per cent and in 1864 8 per cent; in the latter year the highest quotation of the one was 138, an advance from 52½ in 1861, of the other 132, an advance from 6½ in 1861. Cleveland and Toledo, and Philadelphia and Reading were below 30 in 1860, in 1864 above 150; Chicago and Rock Island and Michigan Central, below 40 in the one year, were above 149 in the other. The Pennsylvania paid a stock dividend of $15 per share in 1862, the Chicago, Burlington, and Quincy one of 20 per cent. See the *Merchants' Magazine*, September, 1868, p. 207, on the enormous stock dividends during the war of the Cleveland, Painesville, and Ashtabula.

factors of some influence. For almost two years, while the business world was recovering from panic conditions, and while there were but few chances for good investment, railroad securities were the leading ones on the market, in fact almost the only desirable stocks for investors, and many millions of them changed hands. Their place of prominence in the world of speculation was then shifted first to mining shares, then to those of the petroleum companies. It was estimated early in 1864 that up to that time the stocks habitually on the New York market in two years had risen in value $200,000,000; the stock of sixteen railroads, worth $126,000,000 at par, had increased in market value from $70,000,000 to $150,000,000. Thus great fortunes were made.[1] Increase of freight rates contributed but little to the advance;[2] for grain these rates actually went down, while, as a result of competition between roads, the average rate on all articles in 1864 was less on most lines than in 1856 and 1857.[3]

Traffic by water progressed as rapidly as that by land. The various meat products shipped eastward from Chicago passed over the railroads, especially over the Pittsburg, Fort Wayne, and Chicago, but most of the grain took the lake route to Buffalo and other lake ports, to be forwarded thence by rail to New York and Boston.[4] The lake routes secured much more business than the competing land routes. In the second year of the war five thousand more vessels entered and cleared the port of Buffalo than in any year before that time, while the grain receipts of the city, including flour, almost trebled; the traffic in lumber was also very

---

[1] The *Merchants' Magazine*, March, 1864, p. 217.
[2] See p. 16.   [3] See p. 161.
[4] *Report on the Internal Commerce of the United States*, 1879, p. 100; in the middle of the war 99 per cent of the wheat, 95 per cent of the corn, and 81 per cent of the flour shipped from Chicago were dispatched by the lakes.

heavy.[1] The tonnage carried by the Erie Canal greatly exceeded that of the Erie and the New York Central railroads together.[2] Never had the New York waterway performed such services; in the middle of the war it accommodated one million tons more freight than in any previous year; on its waters, which were free to all who would navigate a boat there, the number of boats rose from three thousand to six thousand in three years.[3]

Activity in boat building was correspondingly conspicuous. Not since 1847, the year of the heavy exportations of grain to famine-stricken Ireland, were so many vessels built on the New York canals as now.[4] There was the same activity on the Northern lakes and Western rivers.[5]

It is interesting to note the agitation of the time by the various cities in favor of increased transportation facilities. One searching the contemporary newspapers, the commercial periodicals and trade journals, the reports of chambers of commerce and boards of trade, is strikingly impressed with the widespread peaceful warfare among competing centers of

[1] The *Merchants' Magazine*, March, 1865, p. 239. See also pp. 41 and 215 of this book.

[2] *Report on the Internal Commerce of the United States*, 1879, p. 109.

[3] The *Commercial Bulletin*, Boston, February 22, 1862; the *New York Tribune*, May 22, 1863. All the canals of the state delivered at tidewater in 1862 two hundred per cent more wheat than in any year before 1860.

[4] *Report of the Auditor on the Tolls, Trade, and Tonnage of the Canals of New York*, 1864. In 1844 in New York 378 canal boats were built; in 1847, 1466; after this year the number fell to an average of about 300 per year up to 1860; in 1860, 403 vessels were built; 1861, 619; 1862, 850; 1863, 771; 1864, 399. But the total tonnage in 1862 was 142,470 tons as compared with 110,745 tons in 1847; the average tonnage of the boats in 1847 was 76 tons; in 1862, 154 tons. This was a sudden increase from 98 tons in 1859.

[5] *Statistical Abstract of the United States*, 1887, p. 160. One hundred and eighty two vessels were built on the Great Lakes in 1857 with a tonnage of 51,498 tons; in 1863, 476 vessels with a tonnage of 67,973 tons. On the Western rivers in 1857 there were 244 vessels built with a tonnage of 51,498 tons; in 1863, 476 vessels with a tonnage of 67,972 tons.

trade. Formerly the South had been the largest market of the Northeast, now it was the West; but the existing lines of communication, east and west, were inadequate, and the new market was expanding. Every sound consideration of business called for more roads and canals, and in the effort to meet the demand there was great rivalry among the cities.

Of the competing points New York, with the Hudson River Railroad, the New York Central, the Erie, the Hudson River itself, and eleven transatlantic steamship lines, all meeting on the finest harbor of the Continent, possessed the best facilities. Her exports of wheat, wheat flour, and corn rose suddenly from nine million bushels to fifty-seven million bushels annually, while those of Boston never got beyond two million bushels and those of Philadelphia never beyond five million bushels. New York's total foreign commerce was nine times the value of that of the one city and twenty times that of the other.[1] Neither Philadelphia nor Boston had regular lines of steamships to Europe; the former had one trunk line leading to the West, but Boston was dependent on the lines terminating in other cities. On the north Boston had a rival, small but growing, Portland, the terminus of the Grand Trunk; on the south Philadelphia was opposed by Baltimore, but this Border city was too harassed by war to be formidable while hostilities lasted.

In the West the most fortunately situated city was Chicago, which as the converging point of a magnificent network of railroads covering the whole West, whence three trunk lines and the Lakes led eastward, constituted the collecting and distributing point of a vast area. This post Milwaukee sought to wrest from her, while the honor of being the gateway between the East and the West was contended for by four cities, Buffalo, Oswego, Cleveland, and Erie. St. Louis and Cincinnati each possessed favorable transporta-

---

[1] *Report on the Internal Commerce of the United States*, 1879, p. 119.

tion facilities, although, like Baltimore in the East, they were too near the seat of war to obtain much share in the growing trade; all three Border cities had difficulty in holding their own. Most of the new business went to Chicago in the West and to New York in the East, and the Chicago-New York route was the most important highway of commerce.

The attempt to improve water communications between these two points, or more properly between the Atlantic and the Mississippi, began as soon as the war closed that river. The freights of the river sections, which were diverted to Chicago, in addition to the city's ordinary traffic, at once choked all land and water routes eastward; and still many points in Illinois, Wisconsin, Iowa, and Missouri, unable suddenly to establish that connection, were practically without a market. Freight rates went up, prices went down. To this extraordinary situation the Illinois and Michigan Canal, which in continuation of the Illinois River led from the Mississippi to Lake Michigan at Chicago, might have afforded relief if only it had been wide enough and deep enough to allow the Mississippi commercial fleet to bear its commerce through to the Lakes; but it was inadequate. Immediately a demand arose for an enlargement of the canal, and the national government was urged to do the work. The West seemed to be at the mercy of the transportation lines, which had a monopoly acquired under very extraordinary circumstances, and to break the monopoly, to reduce rates and raise prices, the Mississippi and the Lakes must be adequately connected. The demand was not new, but it was now made more urgently than ever before.[1]

To the argument of commercial advantage the war scare over the *Trent* affair added the argument of military necessity. War with Great Britain loomed in the distance, but there was no avenue by which to introduce gunboats from

---

[1] The *Chicago Tribune*, March 29, November 8, December 1, and December 4, 1861, and April 18, 1862.

the interior of the country to the Lakes for service against an enemy there, while British and Canadian gunboats, over the Canadian canals, could easily reach these waters during a half of the year at least. The British boasted of the predicament of the Americans, and of their own facilities. The *London Times* declared: "As soon as the St. Lawrence is opened again there will be an end of our difficulty. We can then pour into the Lakes such a fleet of gunboats and other craft as will give us the complete and immediate command of these waters. Directly the navigation is clear we can send up vessel after vessel without any restrictions, except such as are imposed by the size of the canals. The Americans would have no such resource. They would have no access to the Lakes, and it is impossible that they could construct vessels of any considerable power in the interval that would elapse before the ice broke up. With the opening of spring the Lakes would be ours, and if mastery of these waters is indeed mastery of all, we may expect the result with perfect satisfaction." [1]

These boasts were repeated throughout the United States, and to those who were searching for arguments in favor of national improvement of waterways they afforded sudden capital. Later on in the canal controversy the argument was undoubtedly pressed into service for purely selfish reasons, but in the early part of 1862, for some months after the *Trent* affair, it was most sincerely advanced to remedy what seemed to be a glaring military need.

Thus the Illinois and Michigan Canal, widened and deepened, was urged as an outlet for Western products and in case of the sudden emergency of war as a channel for gunboats from the interior to the Lakes. Extensive reports on the plan, with estimates and specifications, were made to the Secretary of War and to Congress, and three different

[1] *U. S. House Reports*, 37 Congress, 2 Session, No. 114; the *Merchants' Magazine*, July, 1862, p. 43.

bills were introduced in Congress on the subject, but no action resulted.[1]

At the same time the state of New York was aroused over the inadequacy of her accommodations for Western traffic, although after twenty-seven years' work and an expenditure of $40,000,000 she was just bringing to conclusion an extensive enlargement of the Erie Canal. If the increasing Western crops were to be handled, the canal would have to be further improved. Here again the *Trent* affair brought into the discussion the military argument; but the state was unwilling to tax itself again for the purpose, and if the work was to be done, Congress might furnish the money. Congress held back. New York plainly was blocking Chicago, and Chicago New York.

Few anticipated the next step. Chicago business men held a mass meeting, and within less than six months transformed their local scheme into an almost national demand, with the hearty coöperation not only of New York but of many other parts of the Union. It was a fine illustration of the sway of the Western market over all sections. To bring New York to terms, Chicago, ignoring for the moment the military argument, held up the rival route seaward of Canada and the St. Lawrence, appointed committees and secured the appointment of others in various parts of the West, which in person urged upon the Canadians the improvement of the Canadian waterways. Canadian boards of trade, newspapers, and parliamentary committees argued and reported in favor of similar schemes, as they had done in the middle fifties at the same solicitation until the crisis of 1857 interposed, setting forth the advantages of a route by Lake Michigan, Georgian Bay, a short canal thence to the Ottawa River, and on to the St. Lawrence and to Europe, with

[1] The *Chicago Tribune*, January 7, 1864; the *Merchants' Magazine*, April, 1862, p. 337.

a considerable saving of distance over the Erie Canal route.[1]

Canada was in earnest, and New York and New England aroused. At the psychological moment, in response to a call signed by fourteen United States senators and eighty representatives, a great ship canal convention assembled in Chicago at the invitation of her board of trade.[2] The Vice President of the United States was in the chair, representatives from every section were present, strong Eastern delegations coming from Portland, Boston, and New York. Although some cities refused to send delegates, there were yet two thousand delegates in all, over one thousand from Illinois. It was one of the largest commercial conventions ever held, at the time often compared with the river and harbor convention held in Chicago in 1848. All agreed that the Western trade must not be allowed to go through Canada. In the convention many interests were represented. There were urged a canal around Niagara Falls, and around the rapids of the Mississippi, the improvement of the St. Clair Flats, and of the Fox, Wisconsin, and Hudson rivers, a canal between lakes Cayuga and Ontario, and the improvement of all the Ohio canals. These plans were allowed to be presented in order to placate the various localities, but the dominant, overpowering interest was that of the Chicago and New York delegates, and the final resolution by a mass vote was that the national government be requested to improve both the Illinois and the New York canals, a measure, said the resolutions, "demanded alike by military prudence, political

[1] The *American Railroad Journal*, March 14, April 18, June 6, and November 14, 1863; the *Railroad Record*, April 16, 1863; the *Commercial Bulletin*, June 6, 1863.

[2] The call in part read, "Regarding the enlargement of the canals between the valley of the Mississippi and the Atlantic as of great national and commercial importance and as tending to promote the development, prosperity, and unity of our whole country, we invite a meeting of all those interested in the subject in Chicago, on the first Tuesday of June next." See the *Tenth Annual Report of the Boston Board of Trade*.

wisdom, and the necessities of commerce." A special committee was appointed to lay the memorial before the President and before Congress, and the President favorably referred to the petition in his next annual message.[1]

The desired bill after over a year passed the House, but no action was secured from the Senate, for the opposition was very strong. Philadelphia, Pittsburg, Cincinnati, and Milwaukee sent no delegates to the convention, and bitterly, though not always consistently, denounced the whole plan. Canals were out of date, they declared; where railroads had not already superseded them, as, for example, in New York, nothing but state taxation could keep the water routes alive. The relief must be immediate, but to complete the improvements proposed would require many years. Chicago and New York were using the cloak of military necessity to conceal local and selfish designs which it would be unwise for the government to gratify when so many other communities were clamorous for their special claims.[2] Parts of Iowa, Wisconsin, and Minnesota based their opposition on the ground that for them the Illinois and Michigan Canal was roundabout, and in the Northwestern Ship Canal Convention, held in Dubuque, Iowa, a memorial to the President and to Congress was framed, advocating the improvement of the Fox and Wisconsin rivers and the construction of a short canal between these two rivers; this, the memorial urged, would give a desirable route from the Mississippi to Lake Michigan which for their sections would be more direct than the Illinois canal. Little public attention was paid to the suggestion, and no aid was given by the general government.[3]

[1] *Tenth Annual Report of the Boston Board of Trade; U. S. House Executive Documents*, 38 Congress, 1 Session, No 1.

[2] The *Railroad Record*, June 11, 1863; the *Scientific American*, April 25, 1863; *Report of the Philadelphia Board of Trade*, 1862; the *United States Economist*, May 10, 1862.

[3] *U. S. House Miscellaneous Documents*, 38 Congress, 2 Session, No. 23; *U. S. Senate Miscellaneous Documents*, 37 Congress, 3 Session, No. 19.

Cities on the Ohio River, Louisville, Cincinnati, and Pittsburg, jealous of the rapidly growing Lake routes and heartily supported in their position by Philadelphia out of jealousy of New York, preferred the improvement of the Ohio River to other schemes, and a small convention in Louisville framed a petition to Congress for that claim, but even less public attention was given to it than to the Fox and Wisconsin project.[1]   Others would have the much discussed boats reach the Lakes by way of the canal between Cincinnati and Toledo; a few renewed the plan of connecting Lakes Michigan and Erie by a canal west from Toledo. Oswego, in northern New York, jealous of Buffalo and its possession of the leading western outlet of the Erie Canal, advanced the old scheme of an American canal around Niagara Falls, the route for which had been surveyed a number of times, and for this proposition they found strong support in Philadelphia and the West.   Western interests contended that this plan, by providing for the passage around the Falls, would enable some of their grain to take the Canadian or St. Lawrence route to the sea, and thus by creating a rival route to the New York canal, would lower tolls on that canal.   In spite of this possibility, however, Oswego yet believed in the project and thought that thereby she would attract to her port some of the traffic, to be shipped thence to Albany over the Oswego branch of the Erie Canal; but Buffalo, foreseeing in the new canal inevitable decline for her commerce, offered most strenuous opposition.   Much pressure was brought to bear upon New York City to secure its support, which was never given; Congress was besieged in the ordinary way and the House of Representatives passed the desired bill, but there the matter rested."[2]

[1] The *Louisville Daily Journal*, January 13, and February 25 and 26, 1864; *U. S. Senate Miscellaneous Documents*, 38 Congress, 1 Session, No. 16.

[2] *U. S. House Reports*, 37 Congress, 3 Session, No. 53; *U. S. Senate Miscellaneous Documents*, 38 Congress, 1 Session, No. 91; *Reports of the New York Chamber of Commerce* and of the *New York Produce Exchange*, 1861–1865.

For a period of over two years all these plans were widely discussed in the newspapers and magazines, and at the Chicago convention the enthusiasm, which had been gathering gradually up to that date, reached its height; after that event interest in waterways gradually declined, and the subsequent conventions aroused no enthusiasm whatever. The railroads and the water routes were now successfully adjusting themselves to the new demands upon them, and the Westerners were actually privileged to enjoy the spectacle of the railroads and the water routes rivaling one another in making low rates. Times had changed since 1861. Farmers in the middle of the war felt prosperous, and in their prosperity complaint and agitation died away. Little was practically accomplished for waterways; no new ones were dug, and no important improvements made.[1]

Much more was accomplished by competing cities in expansion of the railroads than of the canals. Public interest in railroads was as great as in canals and probably more widespread, for every city had its rail connections to improve. The roads themselves felt spurred to the greatest activity in the endeavor to hold their own against the canals.

New York was foremost. She secured a new trunk line to the West, the Atlantic and Great Western, now a part of the Erie system, running from Salamanca in the state of New York to Cincinnati; in the East the Erie furnished connections with New York, in the West the Ohio and Mississippi with St. Louis. This, the longest railroad constructed during the war, had been planned in the early fifties, when the other trunk lines to the West were constructed; only a little was

[2] In the world at large there was much interest in canals at this time. The French were building the Suez Canal, which they formally opened in 1869, and English and French interests were negotiating for concessions for the Panama and Nicaragua routes between the Atlantic and the Pacific, interest in which projects was renewed by the presence of the French in Mexico.

accomplished then however; reverses came, and operations were not again actively resumed till the sixties. After the war began, in the darkest days of the struggle, $25,000,000 for the enterprise was raised in Great Britain, as well as smaller amounts in Germany and Spain. Fifteen thousand laborers were sent over from Europe to build the road, five thousand of these from England, and although on account of military bounties and the attractions of army life, it was difficult to hold the men to their task, the construction was pushed steadily westward, rapidly as railroad building then went, a mile a day, over western New York, the oil fields of Pennsylvania, the Western Reserve of Ohio, and on to Cincinnati. The line helped to solve the transportation problems in the Oil Creek Valley, and afforded to the city of Cleveland direct, unbroken connection with New York, rousing in that port of Lake Erie the hope that now a part of the Chicago-New York traffic, which was then transshipped almost wholly at Buffalo, would be diverted to her, to go eastward by the new road. A special excursion, triumphal arches, fireworks, and a large banquet celebrated the completion of this part of the road. A few months later, when the first train arrived in Cincinnati by the new route, New York shipments, which formerly had taken thirty to forty days, began to come through in less than a week. In Cincinnati, St. Louis, and in all the Southwest, merchants were delighted beyond expression, all believing that now a road had been built with which they might wage a more successful warfare on Chicago and the Lake route.[1]

These rejoicings were greater as people realized the significance of the contribution which the new road made toward

---

[1] The *Railroad Record*, June 23, 1864, and March 31, April 13, and June 1, 1865; the *American Railroad Journal*, November 28, 1863; the *Portland Transcript*, December 12, 1863; *First Annual Report of the Commissioner of Railroads and Telegraphs to the Governor of the State of Ohio*, 1867; the *Commercial and Financial Chronicle*, August 5, 1865.

the solution of the complicated problem of railroad gauge. An obstacle to traffic in all parts of the country was the different gauges of the railroads. On the New York and New England roads the rails were laid 4 feet, $8\frac{1}{2}$ inches apart; in Ohio, the West, and south of Philadelphia, 4 feet $8\frac{1}{2}$ inches and 4 feet 10 inches; in Canada and some parts of Maine 5 feet 6 inches; in some special cases 6 feet. There were at least eight different gauges in the several states. In no direction could cars run long distances without changes and delays. The Hudson River and the New York Central cars passed directly from New York to Buffalo, but could not run to Chicago over the Lake Shore route without changes on the five lines between Buffalo and Chicago; they could not go through Canada over the Grand Trunk and strike the Michigan Central without similar obstacles to overcome, and if they proceeded over the Ohio lines to Cincinnati, there were the inevitable changes; Grand Trunk trains suited to the Canadian gauge could not reach Boston from Portland, nor Chicago from Detroit, without the delay. In the opening months of the war, when the government made requisition on the railroads for cars, this condition of affairs caused confusion; the response of the roads could not be immediate, and after the cars were once delivered there was the delay of fitting them to the Southern tracks. Ingenious expedients were resorted to. Some roads availed themselves of a new patent wheel, extra wide, designed to run on different gauges; others built cars with an adjustable axle, of a "compromise gauge." In many cases two roads of a different gauge were made continuous by building a third rail. Where none of these adjustments were made, as was too often the case, trains had to stop while the freight was loaded into cars waiting on the next track.

The Atlantic and Great Western, by establishing a single gauge between the far distant points of New York and St.

Louis, attracted the attention of the general public because it offered by far the longest unbroken journey then possible, a distance of over one thousand miles. Ordinarily an inland city like Cleveland, which had already two seaboard connections, would not have felt so jubilant over the acquisition of a third; it was the continuous gauge that merchants appreciated. The undertaking, however, in so far as it sought to establish the broad gauge as the standard, was a failure, for the already widely accepted narrow gauge of 4 feet 8½ inches was soon to be adopted by all roads.[1]

In addition to the new connections in the Southwest New York profited by other improvements. It was to her advantage that the Erie, gaining possession of two small roads in western New York, entered Buffalo and thus started competition with the New York Central in taking the Lake shipments received at that point. Thenceforward Buffalo instead of Dunkirk was considered the western terminus of the road.[2] The city was further benefited by the

[1] The *Christian Advocate*, New York, August 11, 1864; *Eleventh Annual Report of the Boston Board of Trade;* the *American Railway Times*, March 7, 1863; the *Railroad Record*, April 20, 1865. There was a standard gauge of 5 feet in the Confederate States. Eleven railroad presidents were asked to recommend a gauge for the Union Pacific, and of these seven recommended 4 feet 8½ inches, two 5 feet, one 5½ feet, one 6 feet. President Lincoln finally fixed this guage at 5 feet, but was later forced by public opinion to change it to 4 feet 8½ inches; the President's defense of his original action was that the ferry would necessitate a break at the river anyway, but it was pointed out to him that the ferry was no real break because it carried the cars directly across. The Atlantic and Great Western entered Cleveland from Leavittsburg, and Cincinnati from Dayton, by a third rail. It may be of interest to add that the railroads of Great Britain were originally built on many different gauges, and that at the present the same lack of a standard gauge hampers the development of interurban electric cars there; these lines do not afford a common gauge for long distances, and are therefore not continuous, as in the United States. There is now a break in gauge on all roads as soon as they cross the border line from the rest of Europe into Russia.
[2] *Between the Ocean and the Lake; The Story of the Erie*, Edward H. Mott, New York, 1900, p. 137 ff.

improved service on the two rivals of the Erie-Atlantic and and Great Western route, namely, the New York Central and Hudson River Railroads. The river at Albany, after many years of successful opposition on the part of Troy and other near-by towns, was finally spanned by a great iron bridge two thousand feet long. This was a revolution in American railroading and attracted universal interest. A ferry had previously been used, while in the winter passengers rode across the ice in sleighs or walked; if the ice was soft, there was a plank to walk on. In this ridiculous fashion the jealousy of Troy and Albany and the latter's reluctance to lose the business of transshipment were allowed to balk America's greatest railway. Double tracks were put through between New York and Albany, and Albany and Buffalo. The Great Western in Canada was induced to build a third rail to allow the New York cars to run over that route to Chicago. Cars of a compromise gauge were built to run over the Ohio tracks to compete with the Atlantic and Great Western at Cincinnati, and the same expedient was adopted by the five roads continuing the Central from Buffalo to Chicago.

Connections between New York and Washington, which were important not only for commercial but also for military reasons, were hampered by a giant monopoly, the Camden and Amboy Railroad, running across New Jersey from New York to Philadelphia. This was the only direct line between these two points, but in spite of public outcry the monopoly succeeded in maintaining its position while the war lasted.[1]

In continuation of the route from Philadelphia to Washington there was only a single track, with breaks at Philadelphia, Havre de Grace, Maryland, where there was a ferry over

---

[1] It seems best to postpone the consideration of this monopoly till the chapter dealing with monopolies and combinations in general. See p. 169.

the Susquehanna, and at Baltimore. Changes at these points caused many delays; oftentimes the regularity of the mails was disturbed, and the business of the government hampered. Freedom from competition on this southern part of the line gave rise to an odious monopoly. If in one point the connection was broken, as when, for example, Baltimore was controlled by a mob, or when the freezing of the waters of the Susquehanna stopped the ferry at Havre de Grace, Washington was isolated. Few cities had such poor railroad facilities as the national capital, yet changes came slowly. Threatening congressional action and perhaps also the crush of business led to such improvements as double tracks, a common gauge, and a bridge over the Susquehanna; but while the war lasted continuous connections in Philadelphia were not secured; that city, like Albany, was reluctant to give up the business of transshipment, and no competing line was constructed.[1]

The competition with New York, offered by Philadelphia, was vigorous. There was here the same reaching out to the West, the same improvements of gauge, the same construction of double tracks and new bridges, and the same process of consolidation of competing lines.

For many years there had been a demand for a railroad to run northwest from Philadelphia, but little was done on the project till after the petroleum discoveries, when the Pennsylvania got possession of the unfinished road, and during the excitement of the presidential election of 1864 the Philadelphia and Erie was completed to Philadelphia. Like the Atlantic and Great Western, it ran through the new oil fields, and in further imitation of the latter road tapped the Chicago-

[1] The complaints about the service between Philadelphia and Washington were much the same as the complaints against the Camden and Amboy; the two lines formed one continuous monopoly. For the attitude of Philadelphia, see a pamphlet in the Boston Public Library (4478.22, No. 14), entitled *Improved Railway Connections in Philadelphia*, Philadelphia, 1863.

New York Lake route by a line of uniform gauge direct to the seaboard; the port of Erie now, like Cleveland, was prepared to rival Buffalo as a gateway between the East and the West. Philadelphia appreciated the advantage and hoped that as the ocean terminus of the new route she would be enabled to wrest from New York some of that city's commercial prestige as a depot for western products. The governor of the state left off making campaign speeches for Lincoln and Johnson in order to join in an excursion in honor of the event. The port of Erie, however, for various reasons, never met expectations, and Philadelphia profited little by the connection.

Other measures in her interest were more successful. By the construction of short connecting links in Ohio and Indiana a second and a third western connection were established, the one a uniform gauge route to Cincinnati *via* Pittsburg and Columbus, the other a new connection with Chicago *via* Columbus. The city's most important connection with Chicago and the West, the Pennsylvania Central, improved its service in the usual ways, by consolidations, new bridges, double tracks, and improvements in gauge. Of especial importance was its control of the Pittsburg, Fort Wayne, and Chicago, acquired in the first year of the war, and the consolidation of the latter with the Cleveland and Pittsburg. One burden which the New York Central had been rid of for a number of years, the tonnage tax, the Pennsylvania Central did not shake off till the opening year of the war. Every bushel of wheat carried across the state was taxed two cents, every bushel of flour seven and one-half cents. It was the country interests in the Legislature that blocked the reform.

But awakened as Philadelphia was, one step forward she did not take; she was without a steamship line to Europe, and throughout the war, in spite of great efforts, she did not succeed in establishing one. The need was great; it would

avail little to bring Western grain to the city if there were
no steamers to carry it to Europe. Moreover, she alone of
the Atlantic ports retained the half-pilot tax, which was a
decided restriction.[1]

New York on the north had another rival. Boston, the
metropolis of New England, shut off in a corner away from
the rest of the country, conscious that she had been comparatively indifferent in the past to the trade of the West, and
that she was consequently losing her hold there, was aroused.
Massachusetts had spent only $5,000,000 on Western connec-
tions, and individuals in the state together with the city of
Albany $11,000,000 more, while the state of New York
had spent $65,000,000 for the same purpose, Pennsylvania
and Philadelphia $40,000,000, Maryland and Baltimore
$12,000,000, individuals in these states and cities $17,000,000,
and Canada $75,000,000. Boston saw that she must exert
herself to meet the occasion.[2]

It was vexatious to Boston to be dependent to so great an
extent for Western trade upon a single line, the present
Boston and Albany, then consisting of two roads, the Boston
and Worcester and the Western, which line was often overcrowded, and without a rival save indirect routes through

[1] For Philadelphia's connection with Cincinnati *via* Pittsburg, see the
Commercial and Financial Chronicle, December 2, 1865; *First Annual
Report of the Commissioner of Railroads and Telegraphs to the Governor
of the State of Ohio*, 1867. For the connection with Chicago, see the *American Railroad Journal*, May 27, 1864. On the tonnage tax in Pennsylvania, see *Annual Report of the Philadelphia Board of Trade*, 1861 and
1862. On the half-pilot tax, see the *Philadelphia Inquirer*, April 6, 1864;
if a ship did not hire a pilot from the capes of the Delaware to Philadelphia, but was piloted by the captain himself, it must still pay one-half
of the regular pilot charge of $400. The custom was as old as 1793, when
the pilot society was formed, and the money from the tax was paid to this
society for the benefit of its needy members. Boston, New York, and
Baltimore had done away with the tax. It was a hindrance to Philadelphia, for it tended to keep ships away.

[2] The *Merchants' Magazine*, May, 1863, p. 410.

Canada, liable to charge high rates.   All interests demanded
a new Western road, but while it was commonly agreed that it
was impracticable to build a new one through from Boston to
the West, and that some existing line should be tapped and
traffic diverted, there was no unanimity as to the manner in
which this was to be accomplished.

The Grand Trunk, the New York Central and the Erie
Canal, and the Erie Railroad were considered as possible
outlets for Boston.   Negotiations to draw the terminus of the
Grand Trunk from Portland were repeated each year of the
war, but with no result beyond exciting ill-will between
the two cities.   One obstacle to be overcome if the Canadian
cars were to be run through to Boston on the existing roads
was the gauge of the Grand Trunk, different from that of
any other line entering Boston.   There were two plans suggested for striking the Canadian road before it reached Portland, one suggested by Canadians and not then acted upon,
the completion of the Connecticut and Passumpsic northward to Canada, thus to connect the Grand Trunk with
Boston *via* that valley line to Springfield, and thence to
Boston; the other a Boston scheme, and carried through, the
consolidation of the seven existing lines leading in a continuous route from that city to Ogdensburg, New York, in the
hope that thereby Boston might tap the Grand Trunk across
the St. Lawrence at that point.   This, when completed, was
judged to be Boston's most effective stroke in achieving new
Western connections, but little came of it, for the Grand
Trunk traffic managers looked with little favor on the plan
of diverting any of their through traffic before the real terminus of the road was reached and thus rendering the last one
hundred miles of the track almost useless.[1]

South of the Grand Trunk were the New York Central and
the Erie Canal, which might be met at Albany by a new line

[1] *Report of the Boston Board of Trade*, 1863; the *American Railroad
Journal*, June 13, 1863.

parallel to the existing Boston-Albany route. Forty years before, when the great New York canal was completed, Boston merchants planned and advocated the Hoosac Tunnel as a canal route to connect with the new water route west. Nothing then resulted, and soon, after railroads began to supplant canals in public favor, the Troy and Greenfield Railroad was chartered and given seven years in which to build the road and the tunnel. There was delay in raising money, and finally state aid was secured. The tunnel was begun, but although the company availed itself of state aid a second time, little was accomplished, and finally it abandoned the task. In 1863 the state took up the unfinished work and pushed it vigorously throughout the war as a state work with Boston's most hearty support, and in another decade the tunnel and the connecting Fitchburg Railroad were opened to traffic. This tunnel was one of the most substantial public works of the period, rivaling the Atlantic and Great Western and to some extent the Pacific Railroad in general public interest, and comparable to the contemporary undertaking of tunneling Mont Cenis for the first railroad between France and Italy. Governor Andrew, of Massachusetts, took the ground that it was necessary to support public works of this kind as far as possible in order to keep up the courage of the people; to occupy their minds with such matters was the surest way to preserve them from the doubts and fears that naturally arose from the war. For the same reason he was one of the most ardent supporters of the Pacific Railroad.[1]

The two connecting roads between Boston and Albany were far from being as effective as possible because of contin-

---

[1] The *Commercial and Financial Chronicle*, September 23, 1865, and scattered references in the Boston press. The Hoosac Tunnel was 4¾ miles in length and was completed in 1874, nineteen years after the beginning of the undertaking; the Mont Cenis Tunnel was 7⅝ miles long and was completed in fourteen years, in 1871.

ual quarrels over division of profits.   These quarrels were as old as the roads themselves; agreement after agreement had been made only to be broken, but when it came to getting an act for consolidation through the Legislature, the city's commercial interests could not carry the rest of the state with them.   The people were jealous of large corporations; the capital stock of the two companies, if combined, would be $15,000,000, and this large sum would be a danger to politics.   In some states there were corporations with a capital as high as $40,000,000, but in the opinion of many the tendency was a harmful one that should be checked. Not till two years after the war was over was the desired combination effected.[1]

Farther south than the New York Central was one of the Eastern termini of the Erie, at Newburgh, New York, opposite Fishkill, to which point Boston capitalists secured a charter for a road, designing to use some small existing lines and to build the necessary connecting links.   This was to be called the Boston, Hartford, and Erie, and a great future was predicted for it, since it would establish direct communications without change of cars with Cincinnati and St. Louis, and would further have the advantage of delivering its freight by the side of the ships themselves, whereas the Boston and Worcester delivered the Western grain at its terminus on the Charles River, whence cartage was necessary across the city to the ocean.   Despite all considerations the road was not finished for twenty years.

In addition to its lack of trunk lines, Boston, like Philadelphia and in strange contrast to New York, lacked the regular steamship line to Europe, which was necessary to make the port a desirable one for the West.   As in Philadelphia, subscription papers were opened for such an enterprise,

---

[1] On railroad consolidation, see p. 159; see also the *American Railway Times*, February 18 and March 12, 1864; *Annual Reports of the Boston Board of Trade*.

and the daily papers gave wide publicity to the movement, but the expense and the fear of the rebel privateers thwarted all plans. Baltimore in this respect was more successful than either Boston or Philadelphia, for there the progressive Baltimore and Ohio Railroad inaugurated a steamship line of its own to Liverpool. New York had no incentive to build such lines for the reason that eleven foreign lines were already performing this service for her.

Cincinnati, St. Louis, and Chicago, and other Western cities were as active as the seaboard cities in reaching out for more trade. In Cincinnati there were many who believed that a line through Kentucky and eastern Tennessee would be more profitable to that city than the Eastern connections established by the Atlantic and Great Western; they argued that the latter road would take away more trade than it would create. Spurred on by jealousy of the Louisville and Nashville, then recently completed to Louisville, they renewed Cincinnati's old plan for the Southern road, and persisted in their agitation till the Cincinnati Southern, a municipal activity which is almost unique in American history, was completed in the early seventies. In his first annual message President Lincoln had urged the building of such a road by the military power of the government as the due of the loyalists of eastern Tennessee, and he never lost interest in the project. But Congress would do nothing. In further extension of the plan for Cincinnati's expansion southward was the displacing of the ferry over the Ohio by the construction of the suspension bridge at that point, one of the great suspension bridges of the world.[1]

[1] On the Cincinnati Southern, see *The Cincinnati Southern Railway, a Study in Municipal Activity*, Johns Hopkins University Studies, Twelfth Series, I–II, by J. H. Hollander; for the President's attitude, see *U. S. Senate Executive Documents*, 38 Congress, 1 Session, No. 40; *U. S. Senate Miscellaneous Documents*, 37 Congress, 2 Session, No. 14. The bridge was in a class with similar structures at Lewiston over the Niagara at

St. Louis, like Cincinnati, secured the Atlantic and Great Western, but aside from this line the interests of the two cities lay in different directions; St. Louis turned to the West as Cincinnati to the South. The prize in the West for St. Louis was the transportation business over the plains.[1] If this growing trade could be securely won for the Missouri city, it was hoped that the temporary loss of the river trade to Chicago might thereby be compensated for. St. Louis was desperately in earnest. The state Legislature passed favoring legislation, the county of St. Louis loaned its credit to the extent of $700,000, and, thus assisted, an unfinished road across the state from St. Louis to Kansas City was taken in hand toward the close of the war and rapidly brought to completion. It was the shortest route between the two cities, and as it was enabled to reach farther and farther over Kansas by the gradual construction westward of the Kansas branch of the Union Pacific, its value to St. Louis increased. The road was also prepared to join the Atchison, Topeka, and Santa Fé, whenever that long-discussed line, endowed by rich land grants from Congress, should begin to traverse the old Southwestern Trail. Thus St. Louis anticipated Chicago in gaining a through line to one of the great routes over the prairies.

The other insistent demands voiced almost daily in the St. Louis press in the struggle with Chicago were not as promptly realized; one, for a bridge over the Mississippi, the ferry companies succeeded in postponing for ten years longer. Furthermore, the city was without grain elevators. To the commercial world the spectacle was almost pathetic, to be-

---

Niagara Falls, and over the Ohio at Wheeling. It was begun in 1856, but work was soon suspended because of the panic of 1857 and not resumed till 1864; the engineer was J. A. Roebling, who had built the bridge at Niagara Falls, and who also during the war had plans projected for suspension bridges at New York and St. Louis.

[1] For this trade, see p. 39.

hold a city without these elevators assuming to compete with Chicago for grain trade.[1]

The efforts to increase the trade of Chicago by means of railroads, as befitted the largest railroad and commercial center of the West, were many and diverse and of more practical value than the movement to improve the canals, though attracting less public attention. This city had the unique distinction among the growing Western cities of possessing no railroad indebtedness and no tax for railroad indebtedness, while her rivals, St. Louis, Milwaukee, Detroit, and some smaller cities, weighed down by debts to obtain the few railroads they had, were even compelled to call upon their respective states to issue many millions of dollars of bonds in their aid. The railroads created Chicago, not Chicago the railroads.[2] It was a natural trade center, to which in the short space of ten years seven new trunk lines from the South, West, and North were built, and from which three trunk lines and the Lakes led eastward. As late as 1850 the city celebrated the arrival of its first train; in 1864 it was entered by over ninety trains daily. The city's participation in the overland Kansas trade and in the business of the Kansas branch of the Union Pacific, although not then completely realized, was made more nearly possible of realization after the war started by the acquisition of the Hannibal and St.

[1] In 1864 these two demands of the St. Louis press were particularly incessant.

[2] Pittsburg, which originally owed $1,800,000 for railroads, still owed $400,000 in 1864; San Francisco gave $600,000 to the Central Pacific; Indianapolis in 1865 voted $200,000 for certain roads; Cincinnati in 1865 owed over $1,000,000 on railroads; Milwaukee in 1865 owed $750,000; St. Louis loaned $700,000 to the Missouri Pacific; but Chicago, aside from small gifts to the Galena, the first road entering her boundaries, and to the Northwestern, gave nothing. Of the $150,000,000 necessary to build the more than 4500 miles of road tributary to her, the roads themselves, that is, outside capital, furnished almost every cent.

Joseph by Chicago interests. On the overland Nebraska route, which was growing more rapidly than that through Kansas, her hold was strengthened by the consolidation of various roads under the spreading influence of the Chicago and Northwestern, though Omaha was not reached till a few years later.[1] This line was further improved by the construction of a bridge over the Mississippi, the second bridge completed over that river south of St. Paul. The achievement aroused much enthusiasm.[2] Under the influence of the Chicago and Northwestern, also, the Peninsular Line was built across the upper peninsula of Michigan, and connections thus secured with the iron and copper mines there; it was an expansion that resembled that of the Eastern roads in their endeavors to reach the oil regions of Pennsylvania. Plans in Chicago's interests were made for a new line to St. Paul, Minnesota, and a new road was constructed to Madison, Wisconsin.[3]

While this reaching out to the Southwest, the West, and the North was strongly supported by the business men of the city, Chicago's deepest interests lay in the direction of the East. Everything that the Eastern cities and the roads leading thither attempted for the improvement of their Chicago communications was followed in the Western city

[1] In 1862 the Galena and Chicago Union perpetually leased the Chicago, Iowa, and Nebraska, leading to Cedar Rapids, and the Cedar Rapids and the Missouri River, leading from Cedar Rapids to Council Bluffs, opposite Omaha, but then completed only to Boonesboro, one hundred thirty miles from Council Bluffs. In 1864 the Galena and Chicago Union consolidated with the Chicago and Northwestern.

[2] The first bridge over the Mississippi was completed April 1, 1856, on the Chicago and Rock Island, at Rock Island. The one completed in 1865, begun in 1864, was owned by the Chicago and Northwestern. A large excursion celebrated the event; this bridge was 3650 feet long, and an island divided it into two parts. It stretched between Fulton, Illinois, and Clinton, Iowa.

[3] This road to Madison was *via* Beloit, and obviated the necessity of the journey to Milwaukee when traveling between Madison and Chicago.

with the heartiest coöperation. One new connection in this direction was secured, that with Philadelphia *via* Columbus, already mentioned; another was planned before the war was over, the extension to her limits of the Grand Trunk across Michigan from Canada.

West from Chicago was the small but progressive city of St. Paul. The Chamber of Commerce there declared that the city's whole commercial future was projected with the far Northwest in view; her hopes were centered in the development of the distant British possessions. Especially was she desirous of securing for herself the fur trade of the Hudson Bay Company in the valley of the Red River of the North, which region, it was believed, would soon be converted into a crown colony and thrown open to settlement.[1]

These rivalries over transportation facilities were not the subordinate interests of a few men but the prominent interests of whole communities. They were discussed in the newspapers by leading editorials day after day, and at great public meetings; in many cases the same paper that detailed the incidents of battles described, now the public rejoicing

[1] The leading settlement of the Hudson Bay Company in the valley of the Red River of the North was Selkirk, a town of 10,000; the trade of the company was worth $1,000,000 per year in exports and $500,000 in imports. This trade St. Paul would win away from the two difficult routes, one *via* Hudson Bay and Nelson River, the other west from Lake Superior along the international boundary; the city would establish a new trade route west from her own boundaries and thence north on the Red River of the North. A railroad to this river was planned, and, aided by British capital, partially built, and American steamers were already running on the Red River. A reorganization of the Hudson Bay Company in 1863 seemed to portend the throwing open of the company's lands for settlement. In furtherance of her plans St. Paul was seeking a road to Lake Superior, and as an inducement to the company that would build such a road voted a bonus of $250,000. However, Indian massacres prevented much railroad building in the state while the war lasted. See *U. S. Senate Miscellaneous Documents*, 37 Congress, 2 Session, No. 55; 37, 3, 8; 38, 1, 38; 37, 2, 26; 35, 2, 44; *U. S. Senate Executive Documents*, 38 Congress, 1 Session, No. 55.

over the completion of some new road, now the adoption of some improvement, voiced the common demands of the community for the completion of a new road, or chronicled the progress of a road, bridge, or tunnel. To share in the wonderful trade expansion, to gain advantages over rivals, evoked public interest which the war never suppressed.

The Union Pacific Railroad in which the cities of the Middle West felt especial interest, but in which, in fact, the whole country was interested, was the realization of public discussion extending back for thirty years. The national government incorporated a company to build the road through the public lands from the wilds of Nebraska to the eastern border of California, with a number of branches in the Mississippi Valley and one in California.[1] The location of the route was determined by the existence of frontier settlements in both Nebraska and Kansas and by the thin strip of settlements extending across the continent in Colorado, Utah, and Nevada. Congress pledged itself to subsidize the line with thirty-five million acres of the public lands and $50,000,000 in government bonds.[2]

Many men of national prominence were numbered among the incorporators, General John A. Dix, Mayor Updyke of New York, A. A. Low, president of the New York Chamber of Commerce, William E. Dodge, and others, who after a meeting in Chicago easily secured the $2,000,000 necessary to proceed with the work. Arguments in favor of the undertaking were numerous. California must be drawn

---

[1] The government charter applied only to regions over which the government had full power, that is, to the territories, and not to the states. See the *Federal Power over Carriers and Corporations*, E. Parmalee Prentice, New York, 1907, p. 152. See p. 169 of this book for the efforts made to induce Congress to assume power over railroads running within the states themselves.

[2] Poor's *Manual of the Railroads*, 1869–1870, p. 403; the *Methodist Quarterly and Review*, July, 1863; the *Northern Monthly*, December, 1864.

more closely to the Union, her trade retained, and her secession made impossible; the nation's influence in the Pacific and its share in the growing commerce of China and the East must be advanced; the movements of the French and English in Mexico and Central America for short isthmian railroads and canals must be checkmated; Western mining and agriculture must be fostered; great public works, like this road, the Atlantic and Great Western, and the Hoosac Tunnel, must be pushed for the sake of their encouraging influence on the public mind; and the rapidly increasing passenger and freight traffic to California and the West, then struggling across the plains or over the water route and the Isthmus of Panama, must be facilitated.[1]

Only a few miles of track for the road were constructed while the war lasted, but that little aroused much interest, especially the laying of the first rails in Kansas, Nebraska, and California. The Northern Pacific, to which attention was drawn by the discovery of gold in Idaho and Montana, received a government charter at about the same time,

[1] See p. 39 for the record of this traffic across the plains; the *Merchants' Magazine*, February, 1867, p. 146, gives the following table of travel to California : —

	By Isthmus		Other Routes		Totals	
	Arrive	Depart	Arrive	Depart	Arrive	Depart
1863	24,337	9,505	7,568	4,225	31,905	13,730
1864	24,622	14,529	4,963	5,643	29,585	20,172
1865	18,510	21,517	5,589	3,746	24,099	25,340
1866	20,962	17,895	4,656	4,040	25,618	21,935

Peto, *Researches and Prospects of America*, p. 242, gives a report of the Panama traffic of 1861–1862; 21,456 people crossed the isthmus from the Atlantic to the Pacific, 9796 from the Pacific to the Atlantic. The total value of the Panama trade of this year was $82,622,049, of which $57,829,620 was inward, $24,795,428 outward.

together with a subsidy of forty-seven million acres of public land, but no bonds.[1]

Until these roads could be completed the government was bound to protect in every possible way the enormous traffic of the plains from the Indians of Indian Territory, New Mexico, and Arizona, who were hostile throughout the war, as well as from the Sioux and other tribes on the plains of the North. In an uprising in Minnesota the Sioux butchered over eight hundred men, women, and children, and destroyed property to the value of $5,000,000; escaping punishment here, they pillaged in the valley of the Missouri, attacking especially the immigrants. The latter were forced to move in large bands under the escort of soldiers, and in three years this protection cost the government $20,000,000 and required the services of five thousand soldiers.[2] The usual number of treaties were made with the Indians, as many as was usual in past times, providing for the extinction of the land titles of the Indians, requiring their removal from the line of overland travel, guaranteeing the safety of the new railroads, etc. Wagon roads leading to the mines were constructed by the government in Nebraska, Dakota, and Idaho.[3]

While the country was devoting itself to these practical questions of transportation, although some important lines were built, the total construction was not large; while 2000 miles on the average had been built in each year of the previous decade, only 650 miles were built in 1861, and 738 miles in 1864. After the war the increase in construction

[1] Poor's *Manual of the Railroads,* 1869–1870, p. 421.

[2] The Minnesota massacre was in 1862; see the report of the government commissioners sent to inquire into the disaster in the *New Haven Palladium,* January 9, 1864.

[3] *Indian Laws and Treaties,* U. S. Senate Executive Documents, 58 Congress, 2 Session, No. 319; this is a collection of all the treaties between the government and the Indians from the beginning of the government to the present time.

was rapid.[1] The decline following the heavy construction of the fifties was perhaps natural, and war prices may also have kept down the total figure. There was much improvement, however, of the existing facilities and methods of operation; much attention was given to the vexatious problem of railroad gauge, consolidation of competing lines went on rapidly, many new bridges were built, and many double tracks and grain elevators constructed. Almost every road was unfavorably affected by the absence of a standard gauge, and almost every road suffered from immoderate competition. The nuisances of changing cars and crossing ferries were wide-spread, but desirable as bridges were, they were bitterly opposed by the ferry companies and by rival cities. Yet many were built, and the old wooden bridges, cheap but dangerous, easily burned by a hostile party, were fast disappearing; the new bridges at Albany, Havre de Grace, Cincinnati, and over the Mississippi were notable structures.

The building of grain elevators as auxiliaries to transportation was extensive. Some cities, like Detroit and Erie, during the war secured their first elevators; New York, where but little grain was stored, and where large amounts were loaded for foreign shipment, near the beginning of the sudden increase in exportations of grain acquired her first floating elevators to lift the grain from the lighters and canal boats to the steamers. But the chief centers of elevators were Chicago and Buffalo, and nothing more clearly shows the growth of Lake commerce in grain than the doubling of the capacity of the elevators in both these cities.[2]

Besides these improvements there was a heavy consumption of rails in the renewal of tracks, and a large increase in the number of freight cars; yet the advance in these

---

[1] Three thousand five hundred miles were built in 1856, 834 miles in 1862, 1050 miles in 1863, 1177 miles in 1865, 4600 miles in 1869.

[2] See p. 197.

respects, though great, was not commensurate with the growth of traffic, and by the close of the war the rolling stock, tracks, and bridges were badly worn out. Terrible accidents were frequent. Toward the close of the war the *New York Sun* said: "Unless the war has blunted the public sense of the value of human life, the recent series of railroad disasters that culminated on Tuesday morning, in the awful slaughter upon the Philadelphia and Trenton Railroad, must produce a profound impression on the community. Fifty persons were either killed or injured, in a moment, by the neglect of the most ordinary precautions of safety. The fact that the victims were chiefly soldiers who had earned a furlough by distinguished services in battle and were on their way to their homes to enjoy a brief visit with their families, only aggravates the disaster. . . . But this accident is only one of many that tend to force the conviction upon the public mind that railroad traveling has at last become dangerous to life and limb, and that every one that purchases a ticket subjects himself to a needless risk of a deadly and awful fate. It is only ten days since a gentleman of western New York was roasted to death in a railroad car in Pennsylvania. On Friday last five persons were killed and twelve injured, some of them fatally, upon the Pennsylvania Central. We could name half a dozen railroads upon which a man has less chance for life and limb in a fifty-mile trip than our soldiers had in the battles of the Wilderness. We know some lines upon which a regular trip on time has not been known for four months. Passengers calculate beforehand upon being detained, frozen, and starved, and consider themselves fortunate if they escape with nothing worse. Since New Year's not less than four hundred persons have been killed and maimed by railroad accidents. Every day the columns of the *Sun* present one or more evidences of the danger of railroad traveling. 'Awful railroad disaster' is now the standing headline in all the newspapers that faithfully chronicle the events of the day. These events show that a thorough reform in our railroad management has become a pressing necessity. The railroad companies have been in too great a hurry to grow rich, and have suffered their engines, rolling stock, and tracks to deteriorate. The accommodations have not kept pace with the increased demands for passenger and freight traffic. The consequence is, that carelessness of management, old clumsy engines, rickety cars, and rotten railroad bars are now the rule upon the majority of our railroad lines." [1]

Passenger cars on a few of the roads were lighted by gas, although as a rule oil lamps furnished the only light. There was no steam heat on any cars,[2] but instead the unevenly distributed heat of the wood stove, itself always a source of danger in case of accidents. The modern dining car was unknown.[3] Commonly there were stops for meals at the station dining rooms, so that it was hailed as a great improvement when on the road between Philadelphia and Baltimore a lunch counter was partitioned off in one corner of the smoker, and orders for meals solicited through the train by a waiter. Then as now the newsboy hawked his papers and books, gumdrops, water, apples, and tobacco; Americans on the passenger trains, so it appeared to the *London Times* correspondent, lived on these things, especially on gumdrops, and to judge from the condition of the car stove the majority of male passengers were addicted to the use of tobacco.[4] Foreigners were further impressed by the republican simplicity and equality of American travelers, all sorts and conditions of whom they found crowded together in the same car. The English preferred to be locked up in small boxes away from the crowd, with no connection even

---

[1] The *New York Sun*, March 9, 1865.
[2] The *American Gaslight Journal*, November 2, 1863.
[3] The *Railroad Record*, February 16, 1865.
[4] The *London Times*, February 19, 1862, and November 3, 1863.

with the train officials, but Americans, who had heard of the horrible crimes committed on the English cars, liked their own democratic cars and boasted of them.[1] For those desiring a mild kind of seclusion there were provided sleeping-cars with their convenient washing and lounging rooms; these were in use before the war, but they were still for the most part made-over passenger cars, crude affairs compared with the modern palaces.[2] The station was generally a light wooden building of temporary nature.

The rate of passenger trains was slow, the average speed on the leading lines being somewhat less than thirty miles an hour. Expresses, leaving New York at seven in the morning, arrived at Pittsburg at one the next morning; leaving Albany at twelve-forty, they arrived at Buffalo at eleven-thirty the same day, twice the time now required; all this in case the trains were on time, which was seldom.[3] There were no limited fast mail trains. On the arrival of the passenger train in the city there was delay and confusion, occasioned by the fact that steam engines were not allowed to run in the city streets. The Pennsylvania traversed Market Street in Philadelphia for a mile, but all cars, passenger and freight, were drawn through the street by mules; gangs of muleteers, with a dozen mules each, constantly passing through the street with a single car, were that city's remedy for the smoke and other nuisances of railroad engines. It was the same in New York,

---

[1] The *Merchants' Magazine*, September, 1863, p. 203; this gives a typical example of the crimes on the English cars. See the *New York Spectator*, August 5, and September 22, 1864.

[2] *Illinois Central Railroad, Fiftieth Anniversary*, Chicago, 1901; the *Railroad Record*, July 11, 1861; the *New York Tribune*, May 29, 1861, October 9, 1862, and March 31, 1864; *Transportation Routes to the Seaboard*, U. S. Senate Reports, 43 Congress, 1 Session, No. 307, Volume I, Appendix, p. 150. The first Pullman cars were put on the market in 1863.

[3] The *United States Mail and Post Office Assistant*, October 18, 1875.

Boston, and Baltimore. These delays at the end of the journey were "unspeakable."[1]

In spite of all inconveniences, such as varying gauges, single tracks, and ferries, the story of Civil War transportation is one of remarkable growth and prosperity, of extraordinarily heavy traffic, great profits, and many improvements in equipment; of hard wear on every part of the roads, but of little actual construction of new lines. It was an era of decided public interest in transportation questions, of keen competition between rival cities to secure additional facilities. Far from checking their development, the war worked to the advantage of the canals and railroads.

[1] The *Railroad Record*, October 24, 1861, January 30, and July 17, 1862; the *American Railroad Journal*, July 12, 1862; the *American Railway Times*, May 21, 1864.

CHAPTER IV

MANUFACTURING

THE consumption of the abundant raw materials supplied from the farms, the mines, and the forests, and thence distributed by the railroads and canals, occasioned unprecedented activity in manufacturing. Never before was the total manufactured product so large.

Progress in hog packing was centered chiefly in Chicago. The industry here had been progressing slowly for almost thirty years, when suddenly as the result of the unusual transportation conditions arising out of the closing of the Mississippi River the yearly output rose from two hundred seventy thousand hogs in 1860, the largest number packed in any one year before the war, to nine hundred thousand, and one-third of the whole packing business of the West was gathered in the one center; in the revolution St. Louis, Louisville, and Cincinnati as pork-packing centers were left far behind, the last-named city losing forever to its rival on the Lakes the proud title "Porkopolis of the West." In a single year eight large packing houses and twice that number of smaller ones were erected in Chicago, thus doubling the city's packing capacity; also, in the same period, her grain elevators doubled their capacity. Well might the Board of Trade declare, "While our city has thus been cut off from some of its commercial points, it is generally conceded that we are the gainers by the internal troubles that afflict the country." The great Union Stock Yards were established at this time.[1]

[1] These yards cost $1,500,000, covered 300 acres, and had pens for 10,000 cattle and 100,000 hogs, the most extensive cattle yards in the world.

This rapid centralization of what previously had been a domestic industry, carried on by farmers themselves on the farms, was a marked change in the industrial life of the country; if the business was to be conducted on a large scale, it was found that the product was not so saleable when packed in the country as when packed in the larger plants of the cities.

Cattle packing was carried on in only a few cities, principally in Milwaukee and Chicago, and in each place on a comparatively small scale. In Kansas City the war crushed out the industry that had sprung up there in the late fifties, supplied by cattle from Texas.[1]

In the East the cattle market was quite as important as in the West, though for a different reason, for here animals were killed for immediate local consumption and not packed for foreign shipment; more were slaughtered annually in New York than in Chicago.[2]

In every city, both East and West, the omnipresent slaughter-house was a constant menace to public order and health. In New York there were two hundred of these institutions, scattered in different sections of the city; the cattle were driven to them in large droves through all the principal streets, sometimes causing distressing accidents and always a

[1] In no year in Milwaukee were more than twenty thousand head of cattle packed, while in Chicago the number increased from fifty thousand in 1859 to ninety thousand in 1865. In 1857 the overproduction of Texas cattle began to be driven overland northward to Kansas City and to Chicago, chiefly to the latter city; the number was rapidly increasing when the war intervened to stop it. But in 1866 the overland drive was again started, and from that time onward the Kansas City cattle market has been important. See the *History of Kansas City*, W. H. Miller, Kansas City, 1881, p. 164.

[2] Nearly two million animals were received annually into New York for slaughter. For the New York cattle market, see the *New York Tribune*, January 18, 1864; for that of Philadelphia, the *Philadelphia Inquirer*, January 1, 1864; for that of Buffalo, *Board of Trade Statement of the Trade and Commerce of Buffalo*, 1869.

source of confusion. Occasionally companies of volunteer firemen, with dozens of pieces of apparatus, amid deafening noise and commotion, on a run to a fire encountered a drove of a hundred or more steers in a narrow street. Bone boiling, fat rendering, and the other accompanying processes caused a multitude of smells, which permeated widely. Chicago felt the nuisance especially. Here the filth and refuse of the slaughtering establishments continually found their way to the river, whence they were carried into the lake, the source of the city's water supply, and not only the air that was breathed, but the water that was drunk, was saturated with decomposed animal matter.[1]

Flouring mills in St. Louis, Cincinnati, Chicago, Milwaukee, and Buffalo, and smaller centers, abundantly supplied with grain, maintained their normal output, while exportation of flour to foreign countries was quickened.[2]

Sugar refining, in spite of the fact that the general consumption of sugar declined, grew apace under the fostering influence of the tariff; many new refineries sprang up, and their product rapidly took the place of the raw, unrefined sugars theretofore common. Formerly in few hands and but little known, by the end of the war the industry, using chiefly foreign raw material, was one of the largest in the country, especially important in New York, where six new refineries were erected. Profits were large, and for a time undoubtedly equaled two to two and one-half cents per pound. After the war increase in the number of refineries continued unabated, and in a short time the business of sugar refining

---

[1] The *American Medical Times*, April 23, 1864.

[2] From 1850 to 1860 the country had sent on an average one million five hundred thousand bushels of flour to Great Britain and Ireland; in 1861 and 1862 this was almost doubled. See *Report on the Internal Commerce of the United States*, 1879, Appendix, p. 227; *Report of the New York Chamber of Commerce*, 1866–1867, p. 109.

ranked ninth in value of manufactured products among the large manufacturing industries of the countries.[1]

The manufacture of whisky was intimately bound up with the system of internal taxation. This tax was first twenty-five cents per gallon, and was then rapidly raised to sixty-five cents, to one dollar and fifty cents, and finally to two dollars. As the rate advanced, prices rose and consumption declined. In 1860 ninety million gallons of whisky were produced, in the middle of the war as much and even more annually; so abnormally heavy did production become that when the one dollar and fifty cent tax went into effect there was on hand in storage sufficient whisky to satisfy the needs of the country for from twelve to eighteen months. This extraordinary result was due to speculation. For months before, in anticipation of the increase of the tax, the distilleries had been pushed to their utmost capacity, and speculators strove to accumulate as much whisky as possible under the old tax in order to take advantage of the increase in price that would result under the new rate. In furtherance of these plans it was necessary in Congress to block the proposition of those who favored making the new levy apply to the whisky on hand as well as to that to be manufactured in the future, and after a long, bitter struggle, by dint of much lobbying, log rolling, and probably, to put it mildly, as much corruption as was ever practiced in the halls of Congress, the whisky on hand escaped the tax; Congress seemed to be legislating directly in the interests of the speculators. Profits made in the transaction were without parallel in the history of speculation or commercial transactions in the United States up to that time, and cannot have

[1] *How Congress and the Country deal with a Great Revenue Problem*, David A. Wells, New York, 1880; the *Sugar Industry of the United States and the Tariff*, David A. Wells, New York, 1878; *One Hundred Years of American Commerce*, Chauncey M. Depew, Editor, New York, 1895, II, 597; *Report of the United States Revenue Commission*, U. S. House Executive Documents, 39 Congress, 1 Session, No. 34, Special Report No. 4.

been less than $50,000,000; on all the immense stock of whisky on hand the rate of profit ranged from ninety cents to a dollar and forty cents per gallon, while one firm stated that for several weeks prior to the imposition of the tax it manufactured or secured by contract an average quantity of thirty thousand gallons per day, and held most of it till after the two dollar tax. After this tax the distilleries remained idle for many months.[1]

High excise and high prices led to reduced consumption of whisky among the poorer classes, and to a pronounced increase in the consumption of beer, the brewing of which was stimulated.[2]

Commercial alcohol, like whisky, was seized upon by speculators as each new tax loomed in the distance, and its manufacture carried on far in advance of the needs of the country, although actual consumption was rapidly decreasing.[3] Another case of the continued manufacture of an article, the actual consumption of which was falling off, was that of cigars, seventy-five million of which were stored at one period in New York in anticipation of increased taxation; likewise, the stock of matches, accumulated while

---

[1] *Report of the United States Commissioner of the Revenue,* U. S. House Executive Documents, 39 Congress, 1 Session, No. 62.

[2] The amount of beer manufactured was estimated to have increased from 5,375,000 hectoliters in 1860 to 8,500,000 hectoliters in 1865; see *Annuaire des deux Mondes,* 1864–1865, p. 772. A hectoliter is 26½ gallons.

[3] When the tax advanced in the middle of 1864, there were stored at least 40,000,000 gallons, or enough to supply the country for one year. The decreased consumption of alcohol was very pronounced. The first and largest cause of this was the growing disuse of burning fluid as an illuminant, in the manufacture of which alcohol had its largest commercial use; refined petroleum as an illuminant was driving out the use of the burning fluid. In mixing paints and varnishes products of petroleum and naphtha displaced alcohol; it was supplanted in the manufacture of enameled ware, pots, kettles, etc.; it was less used for fuel and for dyeing, cleansing, bathing, lacquering, and for making soap, patent medicine, perfumery, various proprietary articles, and fluid extracts.

taxes were low, satisfied the needs of the country for two years after additional taxes went into effect.

One of the most thriving branches of manufacture was that of making woolen cloth, which was in especial demand both to furnish army uniforms and to serve as a substitute for cotton. At first uniforms were very scarce; in the various United States garrisons, when the war came, there were only enough on hand to accommodate the regular army of thirteen thousand men, and but few factories were fitted for making cloth suitable for military purposes. Although under these circumstances the woolen factories were the first to open their doors after the general business depression that attended the opening of the war, and although many cotton factories were at once converted into woolen factories, at the coming of the first winter of the struggle there was actual suffering among the soldiers for want of uniforms as well as for blankets, undergarments, and overcoats. The newspapers took up the subject and printed letters from the front in description of the situation; complaints were frequent; fear was expressed that enlisting would be unfavorably affected; and yet when the war department made heavy purchases of army cloth in England and France in order to meet the crisis, the almost savage cry arose in some quarters, "Patronize home industries." Seldom has the home market agitation appeared in such an unenviable light. When later, driven by the force of selfish protectionist criticism, the department attempted to conciliate dissatisfied interests and bought any kind of cloth in the home market, cloth of all colors, designed for domestic use, dyeing some of it the regulation color and in the emergency leaving some of it undyed, just as bitter criticism of a different nature arose, for in the thick woods on the field of battle the Northern soldiers, clad in uniforms of different colors, fired on one another, mistaking their comrades for the enemy. There was the satisfaction to the manufacturers of knowing that those motley uniforms were bought in the home market.

In the succeeding years the woolen factories were able to cope with the situation, and no more complaints were heard; the millions of soldiers were clad in products of the country's own mills. The annual military consumption of wool in the height of the war was 75,000,000 pounds, for domestic purposes 138,000,000 pounds more, a total consumption for all purposes of over 200,000,000 pounds, against 85,000,000 pounds in times of peace.[1]

The progress of the woolen factories, most of them located in New York and New England, was enormous; every mill was worked to its fullest capacity, many working night and day, Sunday included. In all 2000 sets of new cards were erected, representing many new mills.[2] As the report of the New York Chamber of Commerce said, the progress seemed scarcely credible. Profits were enormous, thanks to the high prices of government contracts and to the scarcity of cotton. One manufacturer, a few months after the war opened, declared to the correspondent of the *London Economist* that up to that time he had already made $200,000; another was making $2000 per day; equally high rates of profit were common throughout the trade. With the recurrence of each new year one of the usual items of news in the daily papers was the list of heavy and increasing dividends of the New England manufacturing concerns, many of which were woolen mills; dividends of 10, 15, 25, and even 30 and 40 per cent were frequent. The conventions of the wool manufacturers, their contentions with the woolgrowers and with Congress over the tariff, and their signal prosperity

---

[1] In 1862, 51,000,000 pounds of wool were used in making 21,000,000 yards of kersey cloth for uniforms, 61,000,000 pounds in 1863 to make 20,000,000 yards; in addition to this there was the amount used in making blankets, flannels, etc.

[2] There were 3000 sets of cards in 1860, 5000 in 1865.

were quite as characteristic a feature of the times as was the part played by the woolgrowers; at this time the present powerful organization, the National Association of Wool Manufacturers, was formed.[1]

It cannot be claimed that the products of the woolen mills were by any means entirely satisfactory. The soldiers received many poor uniforms, and it was openly and bitterly charged that these uniforms were often made not of wool but of shoddy, a material which consisted of rags of all colors and descriptions, cut into pulp and pressed into cloth by a process similar to that used in making felt; such cloth had no resistance, it easily fell back again into rags and pulp, and the sunshine or rain was wont to bring out its true nature very quickly. Shoddy quickly became the popular synonym for fraud and corruption, and was applied to all government contractors alike; the shoddy aristocracy were those who got rich by cheating Uncle Sam and the people; their profits were too large to be honest. Other articles than clothing soon were shoddy; there were shoddy shoes, hats, stockings; as the prices of raw material went up for the manufacturer, everything was liable to become shoddy; the tendency is usually observed in times of rising prices, for the manufacturer skimps in every possible way before he will raise the price of the finished product to the consumer.

The contrast between woolen and cotton manufacturing was striking. The former before the war, while making some progress, did not enjoy a reputation for money making, while the latter was much larger, was growing more rapidly, and was in a condition that was generally recognized as

[1] The *United States Economist*, September 9, 1865; the *Commercial and Financial Chronicle*, September 23, 1865; *Address before the National Association of Wool Manufacturers at the First Annual Meeting in Philadelphia*, September 9, 1865, by John L. Hayes, Secretary; the *Boston Shipping List*, March 5, 1862, and January 2, 1864; *Reports of the Boston Board of Trade; Martin's Boston Stock Market;* the *London Economist*, December 14, 1861.

flourishing. Both industries were hampered by the commercial panic of 1860–1861, but whereas that of woolen goods revived almost at once and enjoyed unheard-of prosperity as soon as the war afforded the stimulus of government contracts, that of cotton, suffering from diminished supply, was seriously curtailed.

The suffering from the curtailment of the cotton industry in New England, where two hundred thousand workers were employed, was not, however, so serious as in England, where four hundred thousand were employed; in both countries the mills were to a large extent closed, but in the latter country the male operatives, dismissed from work, could not avail themselves of military service as a new occupation, but were thrown on charity for support, while here thousands of the class withdrew to the army.[1] Furthermore, many of the women and children, who together constituted a large percentage of all employed in the mills, in New England withdrew to the country homes from which they came; but in England, where the manufacturing class was more highly organized and less mobile than in the United States, this was impossible. In America there was no army of unemployed, no great national charity for unemployed cotton operatives, no harassing tales of suffering. Wherever the papers mentioned New England manufacturing, it was generally to chronicle its unexampled prosperity.

In the first year the American mills ran on two-thirds time, the next year on from one-quarter to one-half time, in these two years consuming cotton that remained over from the heavy purchases of 1860, made when the crop was large and the prospects for the immediate future seemed poor. Soon a considerable amount of cotton began to find

[1] On this point, see the *Scientific American*, June 21, 1862; the *New York Herald*, January 13, 1862; the *New York Independent*, May 2, 1861; the *Boston Shipping List*, January 1, 1862; the *New York Tribune*, July 15, 1861.

its way north through the permitted trade with the South under the regulations of the United States Treasury, through the shipments from the confiscated and abandoned plantations in the hands of the United States, and to some extent through shipments from Europe, so that in the last year of the war the cotton mills gradually increased the scale of their operations. But generally, notwithstanding the diminished production, profits were large. The *New York Herald*, after a year of war, declared that the manufacturers up to that time had made $20,000,000 as the result of the enhanced value of the cotton on hand. In Providence the cotton manufacturers were never more prosperous than while the war was going on, declared a correspondent in the *Scientific American;* a certain company in that city on a capital of $200,000 in one year reaped a gross profit of $97,000, and a net dividend of thirty per cent. Some of the heavy manufacturing dividends declared in Boston belonged to the cotton mills. The New England Cotton Manufacturers' Association, which was later merged into the National Association of Cotton Manufacturers, was now formed.[1]

Emphasis perhaps should be laid on the fact that the lack of cotton goods did not constitute an irremediable situation, for there were many substitutes for cotton. The rich man could afford cotton at any price, and for those of moderate means there were woolens, silks, and other fabrics. Naturally fabulously high prices were paid for a cotton dress, and this fact is often cited to prove that war times were

---

[1] *U. S. House Executive Documents*, 37 Congress, 2 Session, No. 116; United States Census, 1860, volume on Manufacturing, *Introduction; Report of the United States Revenue Commission*, U. S. House Executive Documents, 39 Congress, 1 Session, No. 34, Special Report No. 3; the *New York Herald*, January 13, 1862; the *Scientific American*, May 6, 1865; the *Journal of the Franklin Institute*, Volume 72, p. 119; *Martin's Boston Stock Market; Reports of the Boston Board of Trade*. The New England Cotton Manufacturers' Association was an outgrowth of the Hampden County Cotton Spinners' Association.

"hard"; but these high prices denote nothing else save that this particular material was scarce and difficult to obtain.[1]

Cotton thread continued to be used, with the more or less complete substitution of American-made for the English-made product, which had been almost the only thread sold before the war. Through the influence of the heavy war tariff three-fourths of the market came to be supplied from home. The advance in the price of "Coates," which finally reached four times its old value, created a chance for American manufacturers, which was readily seized upon, and a vast new industry sprang up; the Willimantic Company, with a new plant worth $1,000,000, Green and Daniels, and other firms appeared. At Newark, New Jersey, an English firm built a very large plant to manufacture their product on this side of the tariff wall and thus reap its advantages.[2]

Aside from woolen and cotton manufacturing there were no other important textile industries in the country; silk was made on a very small scale and linen not at all, so that foreign importations were here relied upon. In Ireland linen manufacture was greatly stimulated.[3]

The ready-made clothing industry was as necessary for clothing the army as were the sheep farms and the woolen

[1] In the search for substitutes for cotton goods, paper string came to be used for cotton string; straw, wood pulp, and even corn husks came to be used as a source of paper after cotton rags became expensive. But despite the difficulty of securing materials for manufacture the paper industry remained throughout the war probably one of the most profitable of all industries. See *Report of the Special Commissioner of the Revenue*, U. S. Senate Executive Documents, 39 Congress, 2 Session, No. 2.

[2] *Annual Report of the American Institute of the City of New York*, 1864–1865, p. 405; the *Lawrence Sentinel*, Lawrence, Massachusetts, December 10, 1865; the *Scientific American*, November 26, 1864, and January 27, 1866; the *Chicago Tribune*, February 1, 1865.

[3] The *Scientific American*, February 4, 1865, p. 81, gives many interesting statistics on the growth of the Irish linen industry. This contrasts with the depression of the cotton industry, and may be compared with the growth of woolen manufacturing in America and of the sugar industry in Cuba.

mills. Called into existence a few years before 1837 for the purposes of the Southern trade, destroyed by the panic of that eventful year, thereafter gradually recovering and soon reaching out for the Western trade, the developed business in the hands of German Jews in the four cities of Boston, New York, Philadelphia, and Cincinnati comprised a capital of $40,000,000. The development was fortunate. Not only did the trade thus created supplant importations from the East Side of London, but it was at hand when armies began to gather, fully organized and equipped, prepared to make soldiers' uniforms. Some of the cloth for these uniforms came at first from abroad, but by the middle of the war the importations ceased, and then the country succeeded in clothing its army of over a million men almost entirely by native industry, not only furnishing a large percentage of the wool and manufacturing all the cloth, but making the uniforms.[1]

Much of this success was doubtless due to the sewing machine, then but recently invented. This machine was the invention of Elias Howe and was by him put on the market in 1849, one year after the appearance of the McCormick reaper; the two machines were developed in the following decade, the sewing machine more rapidly than the reaper; both had a large influence on the fortunes of the country during the war, and the manufacture of both during the period proceeded very rapidly, that of sewing machines practically doubling in five years. The manufacture of clothing was greatly stimulated. Men's shirts, which required fourteen hours and twenty minutes for making by hand, by the machine could be made in one hour and sixteen minutes; with the machine drawers could be made in twenty-eight minutes,

[1] *U. S. House Executive Documents*, 37 Congress, 2 Session, No. 116; *Report of the Commissioner of Statistics of the State of Ohio*, 1860; the *United States Economist*, August 9, 1862; the *New York Independent*, April 7, 1864; the *London Times*, October 20, 1863.

and night shirts in one hour and seven minutes, tasks which by hand took four hours and six minutes and ten hours and two minutes, respectively.[1]

The shoe industry likewise benefited by the sewing machine, in fact was converted by it from a system of household manufacture to the modern factory system. As shoe manufacturing was formerly conducted, no expensive buildings or outlay of capital were required; nothing but labor. "Every little shoe shop by the wayside is alive with the cheerful voices of the journeymen as with nimble fingers they pierce the sole, or draw the thread. Every crossroad leading to the large manufactories is dotted with people seeking fresh work, or returning with the products of their labor." Shoe factories there were, but they were mere storerooms or salesrooms, or central points where the raw material was cut out and the finished product received and polished for the market. Women in their homes or perhaps at the church sewing circle or missionary meeting bound the uppers and sent their work to the central depot, and this part of the work, together with the soles and insoles, the men carried to their little shops, where they sewed or nailed the uppers to the soles. Boys cleaned the finished product with pipe clay and blacking and put in the findings. There had been no material change in the process for hundreds of years; from time immemorial the awl, bristle, thread, lapstone, and hammer had been in use. The first

[1] In 1853 the total number of sewing machines manufactured up to that time was 2500; in 1860, 116,000. The rate of increase in manufacture during the war may be represented by the business of the two largest companies; Wheeler and Wilson made 25,000 machines in 1860, 40,000 in 1864; Singer, 13,000 in 1860, 23,000 in 1864. In the latter year 50,000 machines were exported. In 1864 Wheeler and Wilson erected a very large factory in Bridgeport, Connecticut. In all ten firms were in competition, each paying a license to Howe. See the *American Railroad Journal*, June 28, 1862; the *Scientific American*, May 16 and August 16, 1862; *One Hundred Years of American Commerce*, chapter on Sewing Machines.

indication of change came with the slow adoption in the fifties of pegging machines, followed soon by sole-cutting machines, and machines to bind the uppers, none of which wrought revolutionary changes. The honor of revolutionizing the business belongs to the McKay sewing machine, a mechanical device for sewing the uppers to the soles with great rapidity, first patented by L. R. Blake, later purchased, much improved, and made practical by Gordon McKay and by him put on the market in the second year of the war. One man with the aid of the new machine could sew several hundred pairs of shoes a day, a process approximately one hundred times faster than that formerly in use. There was need of the improvement, for without it the large contracts then coming in from the army, calling for hundreds of thousands of pairs at one time, could never have been filled in this country, while with it they were easily filled and importations rendered unnecessary, so that the shoes of the soldiers as well as their uniforms were supplied by home industry.

By applying steam power many of the new machines could be set to work at one point; economy both of time and expense dictated further that the other processes of manufacture should be carried on at the same point, and that under the same roof, too, the raw materials, the separate parts, and the finished products should be housed. As if by magic the little shops by the roadside disappeared, and great factories took their place. The *Lynn Reporter*, Lynn, Massachusetts, declared: "Operatives are pouring in as fast as room can be made for them; buildings for shoe factories are going up in every direction; the hum of machinery is heard on every hand." In Haverhill, Danvers, and other towns in eastern Massachusetts, as well as in Lynn, the erection of the new factories proceeded rapidly. Other centers of the business were Philadelphia and New York, although more than one-half of it was centered in eastern Massachusetts.

Seldom have such immediate triumphs been achieved by
one invention, and seldom has an inventor reaped such profits.   A great industry had been revolutionized and wonderfully quickened.   The first year after the machine came into
general use more than one million five hundred thousand
pairs of shoes were manufactured, double the number manufactured in any previous year, and this activity continued to
increase in the following years.   Each machine sold for $500,
and a royalty was paid to McKay, which soon amounted to
$750,000 a year.[1]

Naturally there was advance in the leather trade for the
purpose of supplying not only the shoe factories, but also
the saddlery and harness works, which were pressed hard to
equip the artillery, the mounted troops, and the immense
army trains.[2]

The progress of manufactures involving the raw materials
of the mines was marked.   Iron was used in all branches of
manufacturing, and its growing consumption was an indication of general industrial progress.   The progress of the
business is indicated by the increased production of pig
iron, confined almost entirely to the three states of Pennsylvania, New Jersey, and New York, particularly to Pennsylvania.   Of all the flourishing centers of iron manufacturing Pittsburg was the largest; here in one year six extensive
iron mills were erected, and in the last year and a half of the
war $26,000,000 worth of iron and steel were manufactured.

[1] In this way was built up the great fortune recently bequeathed to
Harvard University for purposes of science.   On the changes in the shoe
industry, see the *Shoe and Leather Reporter*, Annual, 1891 and 1897;
U. S. House Executive Documents, 37 Congress, 2 Session, No. 116; the
Ohio Farmer, January 23, 1864; the *Lynn Reporter*, Lynn, Massachusetts,
February 28, 1863; *Fourth Annual Report of the Boston Board of Trade*,
1858; the *Scientific American*, November 9, 1861, quoting from the *Shoe
and Leather Reporter*, August 16, 1862, and November 14, 1863; *the same*,
July 3, 1863, quoting from the *Lynn Reporter*.

[2] The *Scientific American*, November 26, 1864.

The iron manufacturers, in imitation of the policy of the woolgrowers and of the proprietors of the woolen and cotton mills, formed their national society, the American Iron and Steel Association.[1]

The steel industry was small, although for thirty years or more many attempts had been made to establish it on a sound basis. Bessemer steel had been made in small quantities, but numerous new steel works now sprang up, and shortly after the war the first Bessemer steel rails were produced in this country, the beginning of a great industry. Although it was already apparent that the iron rails in use on the railroads were too soft and that their too rapid deterioration was the cause of many accidents, their production year by year throughout the war surpassed the figures of all previous years, while importations fell off.[2]

Petroleum refining, within two years after the first successful establishment of the business, was extensive in such cities as Cleveland, New York, and Pittsburg, so that when the total production of petroleum averaged a little over one hundred million gallons per year, probably somewhat over one-half of this was refined; the total yearly value of Pittsburg's oil trade reached $15,000,000 in 1864. Important

---

[1] In the Lehigh district of Pennsylvania the production of anthracite pig iron rose from 173,075 tons in 1860 to 214,093 tons in 1864; in the Schuylkill district from 92,345 tons to 112,800 tons; in the Susquehanna district from 101,246 tons to 118,615 tons; in the Upper Susquehanna district from 69,698 tons to 101,644 tons; in the Eastern district, embracing New York, Massachusetts, Connecticut, etc., from 88,167 tons to 130,140 tons; the total increase of anthracite pig iron was from 524,531 tons to 684,319 tons, 80 per cent of it coming from Pennsylvania.

[2] In 1860, 205,000 tons of iron rails were made in the United States, the largest amount ever made in any one year up to that time ; 187,000 tons were made in 1861, 213,000 tons in 1862, 275,000 tons in 1863, 335,000 tons in 1864, and 356,000 tons in 1865. In 1853 importations reached 358,000 tons, the highest figure reached in the fifties ; 146,000 tons were imported in 1860, 89,000 tons in 1861, 10,000 tons in 1862, 20,000 tons in 1863, 146,000 tons in 1864, and 63,000 tons in 1865. See *Report of American Iron and Steel Association*, 1871.

subsidiary industries were the manufacture of barrels, glass lamps, and glass chimneys.[1]

The manufacture of equipment for the mines and for the petroleum and salt interests must have been enormous. Derricks, pipes, and numerous other implements, in all of which millions were invested, were supplied to the oil regions. Less equipment was needed in the salt business. Machinery was required for the growing mines of coal, iron, and copper in Pennsylvania and Michigan, and for the new mines of the precious metals in the West; a large part of the freight sent westward from the Missouri River was reported to be mining machinery. The activity in the lumber camps had its counterpart in that of the sawmills and planing mills.

For the overworked transportation lines, aside from the supply of rails, there was considerable manufacturing, as, for example, that of the hundreds of new engines and thousands of new freight cars,[2] while even more extensive was the manufacturing required by the water transportation lines; on the seaboard, the canals of New York State, the Great Lakes, and the interior rivers almost every shipyard was busy as never before.[3]

The impression of extensive manufacturing, conveyed by this survey of special industries, is corroborated by certain statistics of a general nature. In Philadelphia, which was

[1] Oil refineries were then very small, employing on the average ten men each; there were 30 of these refineries in Cleveland in 1865, 25 in New York, and 85 in Pittsburg, nearly 200 in the whole Union.

[2] One hundred and fifty engines and 3000 freight cars were made for the Pennsylvania, for the Erie 100 engines and 2000 freight cars, and for the Illinois Central 50 engines and 1000 freight cars; for the other leading roads in like proportion.

[3] Throughout the United States in 1857, 1434 vessels, with a tonnage of 378,805 tons, were built; from that time the number decreased rapidly up to 1863, and in 1864, 2366 vessels were built, with a tonnage of 415,741 tons. This percentage of increase was maintained on the seaboard, the New York canals, the Mississippi, and the Great Lakes. See *Statistical Abstract of the United States*, 1887, p. 160.

perhaps the largest center of manufacturing in the country, 58 new factories were erected in 1862, 57 in 1863, and 65 in 1864; and the building inspectors reported that those erected in the last-named year were generally very large. In the small city of New Haven, Connecticut, in one year 6 large factories were built. Striking figures were given out for Chicago, showing that the grain and cattle center of the country was progressing in general manufacturing. In 1864 in this city there were 9 agricultural implement factories, compared with 2 in 1857, and in the same interval breweries rose in number from 19 to 27, distilleries from 7 to 21, grain elevators from 7 to 18, packing houses from 13 to 60, iron foundries from 18 to 19, machine shops from 17 to 28, tanneries from 4 to 21, carriage and wagon factories from 43 to 54. Beyond a doubt a large part of this progress was achieved during the war period, for in these years the city's consumption of coal almost trebled.[1]

If to the foregoing there are added the total general consumption of coal, iron, and lumber, and the unprecedented consumption of water and gas, the conclusion is again irresistible that manufacturing in the time of the war was enormously active.[2] In some lines there was decline, as in the carriage industry in New England, and in certain small in-

[1] For the statistics of Philadelphia, see the *Scientific American*, October 5, 1861, and the *Reports of the Building Inspectors*, in the City Documents; for the statistics of New Haven, the *New Haven Daily Palladium*, June 4 and July 12, 1864; for Chicago, Halpin's *Chicago Directory*, 1864; for Massachusetts, the *Growth of Manufactures*, Horace G. Wadlin, Boston, 1890; for Rhode Island, *Rhode Island Census*, 1865; for Illinois, the *American Annual Cyclopædia*, article on "Illinois," 1866; for the coal statistics of Chicago, see *History of Chicago*, Andreas, II, 673. One hundred and thirty-one thousand tons of coal were received into the city in 1860, the largest amount received in any one year, except one, after 1852, 184,000 tons in 1861, 218,000 tons in 1862, 284,000 tons in 1863, 323,000 tons in 1864, and 344,000 tons in 1865; shipments from the city were inconsiderable.

[2] On the consumption of water and gas, see pp. 216–218.

dustries dependent on highly taxed and therefore high-priced alcohol, but the total result was of unusual proportions. Furthermore, the new activity characterized all the important industries with the single exception of that of cotton goods.[1]

For this progress of manufacturing there were many reasons. First, the ordinary needs of the country were greater than usual, since the market was somewhat depleted of goods because of the suppressed manufacturing consequent upon two bad commercial panics; in the natural course of events, after these crises, one of which followed so closely upon the other, the country was bound soon to demand more goods for its daily needs. Then the paper money régime was in full swing, and money was plenty and prices soaring. There was, too, the incentive of the tariff, not a session of Congress passing without some raising of these bars to foreigners. Every manufacturer, great and small, was conscious of more buoyancy and freedom as he realized that under the cloak of the supposed needs of revenue with which to wage the war he was rapidly dispensing with foreign competition with all its attendant risks; examples of industries benefited in this way were sugar, thread, iron, steel rail, and woolen manufacturing. But greatest of all incentives were government contracts, which generally have a way of bringing higher prices than ordinary sales, and which at this time became more and more lucrative as foreigners were effectu-

[1] *The Census of* 1870, III, 395, ranked the various manufacturing industries of the country according to the value of the manufactured product as follows: (1) flouring and gristmill products; (2) sawed lumber; (3) boots and shoes; (4) cotton goods; (5) men's clothing; (6) woolens and worsteds; (7) carpentering and building; (8) forged and rolled iron; (9) sugar. Only one of these industries was seriously impaired during the war, that of cotton goods; another, carpentering and building, was perhaps slightly impaired, but only slightly, as will appear on page 224 of this book; all other lines flourished, and the decline in the two lines was more than compensated for by the remarkable advance in all the others.

ally barred from competition. Fortunate the manufacturer who had such contracts, and small the number who did not have them. Contemporary opinion plainly inclined to the view that a government contract was the manufacturer's greatest opportunity.

To a limited extent the government itself engaged in manufacturing. These activities included, first, those in which the government had long been engaged, coinage, ship building, and the manufacture of implements of war. The mints were less busy than formerly, though their operations were not so much curtailed as the disappearance of gold and silver from circulation would lead one to expect, falling off only about twenty-five per cent.[1] The navy yards at the outset were fitted for building wooden vessels only, so that new plants had to be installed suitable for building ironclads; and in these near the close of the war two hundred vessels, iron and wooden, had been built, together with many more in private yards.[2]

In the government armory at Springfield, Massachusetts, where 3000 men were employed, 350,000 rifles were turned out annually, 1000 per day, while twice as many were made in private establishments.[3] A rifle manufactured by the government at Springfield cost $9, made by the contractors, $20; the lowest grade made by the contractors cost the government $16. This represents the usual rate of profit made by a government contractor. This matter of too large profits was one of the justifications of the charges brought against the shoddyites. At first almost a third of the muskets in use were bought in foreign countries, and foreigners furnished a large part of the carbines, pistols, sabers, and

[1] *Statistical Abstract of the United States*, 1902, p. 531.

[2] There were then in the navy seven hundred seventy-one vessels in all.

[3] The other government armory, that at Harper's Ferry, was destroyed to prevent its falling into the hands of the enemy.

swords, a situation that to the protectionist, jealous of the home market, appeared as an abomination, just as did the foreign purchases of army cloth.   In the second year of the war the foreign contracts ceased, though consignments on the previous contracts continued to arrive for many months.[1]

There were certain new manufacturing ventures on which the government embarked. The Government Printing Office was established just as the war came on, and from year to year extended its operations till it expended a million and a half of money annually and employed eight hundred people.   The Bureau of Engraving and Printing in the Treasury Department began its work at this time, a mammoth factory employing five hundred people, set up by Secretary Chase at a cost to the government of $600,000, for the purpose of engraving and printing the national currency, the greenbacks, the fractional currency, and the bonds.   In Cincinnati there was a government clothing factory, in New York, Philadelphia, and St. Louis government laboratories for the manufacture of drugs and medicines, in Louisville and at other points in Kentucky, and in Knoxville, Tennessee, government meat-packing establishments.   A resolution was introduced in the United States Senate providing for a national foundry for the manufacture of cannons, projectiles, etc., but failed of enactment. People were not ready to extend indefinitely the policy of the government's going into business; private contracts were too lucrative, and touched the interests of too many people.

Diversion of activities from private to public demands occasioned many changes.   Cotton mills and carpet mills were changed into woolen mills, machine shops into gun

[1] The *Atlantic Monthly*, October, 1863; *U. S. House Reports*, 37 Congress, 2 Session, No. 43; *Springfield Directory*, Springfield, Massachusetts, 1864.

factories, saw factories into saber factories, jewelry factories into brass button factories, etc. At the same time the factory system was extended, as, for example, in meat packing, in the manufacture of clothing, and in the shoe industry.[1]

Further light is thrown upon the progress of manufactures, and incidentally upon the general social and domestic conditions of the time, by a study of the patents of the period. The war stimulated rather than stifled inventive genius. More patents were issued in the height of the war in the North alone than ever before in the whole Union, over 5000 in 1864 compared with 4778 in 1860, which was the greatest number ever issued in any year before the war. Secession did not take inventive genius out of the Union, for labor-saving devices were never consonant with the system of slave labor. In a typical year of the fifties, to citizens of Massachusetts 421 patents were issued, or 1 to 2362 inhabitants; to citizens of North Carolina 14, or 1 to 62,064 inhabitants; to citizens of South Carolina 12, or 1 to 55,708 inhabitants; and in one year of the war the Commissioner of Patents of the Confederate States granted 42 patents for the whole of the Confederacy.[2] Inventive genius was fostered by free labor only, and the period of prolonged war, with its ardent national pride, scarcity of labor, abnormally active production, and the creation of new industries stimulated inventiveness to the highest pitch. Inventors had never found such strong incentives. Entire new industries had to be provided for, others greatly extended, the fighting arm of the government equipped with the best weapons possible; in the absence of millions of laborers in the army and navy their

[1] It was reported that the factory system was being rapidly introduced in the cheese industry in New York state.

[2] *Statistical Abstract of the United States,* 1902; *Report of the Commissioner of Patents,* 1863, gives the records of the various states for 1857; the *Scientific American,* April 8, 1865, gives the report of the Commissioner of Patents of the Confederate States for 1864.

former tasks in the industrial world had to be carried on by labor-saving machinery as far as possible. Inventions for war purposes were very numerous, but they were far less numerous than those for the pursuits of peace and industry; inventors devoted themselves more to agricultural implements than to implements of war.[1]

Patents for purposes of war were the most prominent in the public eye, and of these the breech-loading, repeating rifle was the one most discussed. The end here sought was rapidity of loading and firing. The last great war, the Crimean, had decided the armies of the world in favor of the rifled muskets of the English against the old smooth bore in the hands of the Russians; but at once a new controversy arose. Should the new rifles be muzzle-loaders or breech-loaders? Three kinds of rifles appeared: first, the commonly accepted muzzle-loader; second, the single-shot breech-loader, which after every discharge had to be lowered from the shoulder for reloading, a numerous class, represented by the Burnside; third, the repeating breech-loader, or magazine gun, which could be raised to the shoulder and fired fifteen times, more or less, without reloading, a small class, with the Spencer and Henry as representatives.

In 1857 a board of officers, appointed by the Secretary of War, tested twenty different breech-loaders at West Point, and unanimously recommended the Burnside single-shot breech-loader; a second time, after another test of twelve makes, a report was made in favor of the same gun. The Secretary of War said, "I think it may be safely asserted now that the highest efficiency of a body of men with firearms can only be secured by putting into their hands the best breech-loading firearms."

The American war gave a practical turn to the question,

---

[1] In 1863 there were issued for war purposes 240 patents, but 490 for agricultural implements alone.

but, strange as it may seem, no definite decision in favor of breech-loaders was made down to the very end of hostilities. The war was fought and won by muzzle-loaders. Patents, however, for the new rifle increased in number very rapidly.[1] The strong argument in their favor was rapidity of action. Muzzle-loaders required sixty seconds to load and fire; the single-shot breech-loader could be fired fifteen times in sixty seconds, or four seconds to a shot; repeating breach-loaders thirty times in sixty seconds, or two seconds to a shot. Armed with breech-loaders, either single shooters or repeaters, a small body of men could put to flight a much larger body armed with muzzle-loaders; they could pour forth such a stream of shot and lead that to the enemy, as happened in certain actual cases, they seemed a veritable "Hell let loose." It needed no argument to prove that thirty shots or fifteen shots per minute were better than one. When troops were armed with the new rifles, an enemy could not draw their fire and then charge and rout them in the sixty seconds usually required for reloading. But breech-loaders were inaccurate, claimed the Ordnance Department; rapid firing heated the barrel too intensely; the barrel was not cleaned by the process of reloading, as was the case with the muzzle-loaders, and this prevented accurate firing; armed with them, men were tempted to fire too frequently, and thus to waste ammunition; the structure was too delicate and too complicated to be practicable in the hands of inexperienced volunteers. The department would not budge. In vain did the partisans of the breech-loaders point to the wonderful success of the breech-loading, repeating revolvers, Colt's revolvers; in vain they pointed out the decimating, dispiriting effects on the enemy of the rapid firers on the few occasions when they were allowed to be used, the enthusiasm and the courage

[1] Fifteen in 1860, 19 in 1861, 34 in 1862, 42 in 1863.

with which they inspired the army. Without a doubt the new guns were popular with the Northern soldiers; the Southerners did not have them.[1]

At last in 1865, when fighting was about to cease, the government was convinced and ordered seventy thousand Spencers. In the same year France, England, and Switzerland took decisive steps in the same direction, proceeding, it is fair to assume, on the basis of their observations of the success of the arm in the United States; and in the next year the Prussians, armed with the new rifle, fought and won the decisive seven weeks' war against the Austrians, who were armed with muzzle-loaders. The difference in arms undoubtedly contributed toward securing this immediate success, and it may be safely conjectured that the course of the American war would have been different if from the beginning one side or the other had been thus armed.[2]

Many old smooth bore cannons were changed into rifled cannons; many patents for breech-loading cannons were granted, but there was at that time little success in making such a cannon practicable. It proved difficult in this case to protect the mechanism of the breech from the force of the explosion.

Ironclads were another implement of war perfected during this period. The idea was not new. Suggested to Napoleon, patented in the United States during the naval war with Great Britain, suggested again later to the French govern-

---

[1] Sharpshooters at Fredericksburg, the Fifth and Seventh Michigan Cavalry at Gettysburg, certain Massachusetts regiments also in the Army of the Potomac, twenty-seven thousand men under General Rousseau in a raid from General Sherman's army in 1864, and other small bodies of troops tried the new gun with decided success.

[2] The *Scientific American*, January 26, 1860, March 9, May 18, July 20, August 17, and August 31, 1861, May 31 and December 20, 1862, March 7 and May 9, 1863, March 19, August 6, and October 29, 1864, January 9, April 29, and August 5, 1865; the *Philadelphia Inquirer*, April 27, 1864; the *Merchants' Magazine*, 1866, p. 336.

ment, in each case it failed to receive recognition; at the beginning of the Mexican War successful experiments with it were made under the auspices of the United States government, but again the question was strangely allowed to drop.[1] Shortly afterward, however, the French finally took up the idea, and French ironclads in the Crimean war successfully destroyed Russian forts at Kinburn, while English and French wooden vessels failed before the forts at Sebastopol. Immediately the English and French navies began to secure ironclads, and in other countries the same action was taken; before any important naval action in the United States the English Parliament voted millions for the new vessels. It is apparent therefore that at the outbreak of the American war European nations were far more advanced in the matter of ironclads than in the matter of breach-loading rifles; the Americans were the first to demonstrate the utility of the latter in actual war, although they armed no large body of troops with them, but they were behind in the matter of ironclads. The victory of the *Merrimac* over wooden vessels only reënforced a principle in which Europe had already expressed its faith to the extent of millions of dollars. In the success of the *Monitor* the practicability of an exclusively American invention, the revolving turret, was fully demonstrated. This invention the government had had the chance to adopt during the Mexican War, but had failed to do so.[2]

The Gatling gun was first successfully tested in 1862; it was "a regiment of men put into half a dozen gun barrels, and mounted on a light carriage." There were six chambers, revolved on a central barrel by a crank; the charges were poured into a hopper, while the gun itself was self loading,

[1] George Bancroft was Secretary of the Navy at this time.
[2] The *Atlantic Monthly*, August, 1861, p. 227, and January, 1863, p. 85; the *New York Journal of Commerce*, May 3, 1861; the *Commercial Bulletin*, Boston, June 29, 1861; the *Scientific American*, May 24 and 31, 1862, February 7, 1863.

and from seventy-five to one hundred balls a minute could be fired according to the speed with which the crank was turned. Many times after the first trial the murderous gun was tested and proved, but it was not used in actual conflict till late in the war, when under General Butler in Virginia and on canal boats in North Carolina it performed efficient service. But the "old fogies" in charge of the War Department were obdurate, and the weapon was not generally adopted up to the end.[1]

Patents for ordinary domestic and industrial purposes, although less discussed than those for war purposes, were sought in greater numbers. Inventors were working at many of the ideas that occupy the minds of inventors to-day and at many that have long since been realized.[2] The records of the Patent Office show an interesting array of articles patented during the period, while the papers were full of notices and advertisements of the new agricultural machinery, domestic devices and general conveniences.[3]

[1] The *Chicago Tribune*, August 15, 1862; the *Louisville Daily Journal*, March 17, 1864; the *Scientific American*, June 18 and December 10, 1864.

[2] Such as smoke-consuming devices, ice-making machines, adding machines, type-setting machines, steam carriages, steam plows, grain-binders, electric lights, gas engines, steam heat on railway passenger cars, dirigible balloons, submarine vessels, etc.

[3] Such as the McKay sewing machine, a process for condensing milk, the stereoscope, hotel passenger elevators, laughing gas, clothes wringers with rubber rollers, automatic steam fans for restaurants and public buildings, baby walkers, belt shifters, burnt-wood process, coal-oil lamps, clothes dryers, electric attachment for lighting gas, feed bags for horses, flying machines, fountain pens, hay presses, iron safes, knitting machines, milking machines, gold pens, paper-bag machines, paper collars, patent fly paper, patent washers, steam printing presses, portable bookcases in sections, refrigerators, apparatus for running pipe organs by water power, sewing machines, roller skates, ice skates, steam dredges, stereotyping apparatus, stone-crushing machines, machines for making toothpicks, washing machines, water filters, etc.

Information in regard to these various details has been gathered from various sources too numerous to mention, principally the *Scientific American* and *Reports of the Commissioner of Patents*.

CHAPTER V

COMMERCIAL LIFE

THE business houses of the cities passed through a panic at the announcement of secession, and then speedily recovered with the prosperity that was exhibited in the production, distribution, and manufacture of raw materials; banks, savings banks, and insurance companies flourished; government loans were readily subscribed to, taxes promptly paid. Boards of trade and chambers of commerce strove with redoubled vigor to advance their interests and took the lead in a widely extended discussion of business questions, touching not only the general development of the country's natural resources, but other phases of commercial activity as well, such as post-office reforms, bankruptcy and usury laws, reciprocity, and ship subsidies. It was distinctly a money-making age.

The frequency of mercantile failures may be taken as an index of general business conditions. During the financial crisis of the first year of the war 6000 Northern commercial houses failed for sums of $5000 and above, almost 2000 more failures than in the celebrated panic year of 1857, but fortunately with liabilities for $90,000,000 less. In the panic of the fifties the heavy liabilities were due to the fact that it was then the banking houses and the importing and commission merchants that were involved, while the increased number of failures and the diminished liabilities four years later may be accounted for by the fact that it was then the numerous jobbing houses that were the greatest losers, caught in the winter when their stocks were low and before spring orders had come in. In all, in 1861, probably 12,000

people failed, counting large and small suspensions. Although the greatest distress was felt in the spring, immediately after the actual hostilities of war began, the strain was
more or less severe in every month of the year, lasting even
into the early months of the next year. In January, February, and March, 1862, 1000 firms went under; in the next
month greenbacks appeared and the number of new insol-
vents suddenly diminished and was astonishingly small
throughout the remainder of the war, numbering only 495 in
1863, 520 in 1864, and 530 in 1865.[1]

The recovery of business was just as pronounced as was
the initial panic, and for both phenomena there were various
contributing causes. The recovery may be briefly dealt with.
In a general way the growing infrequency of mercantile
failures was the reflection of the prosperity that pervaded
every industry, but certain causes of the situation may be
mentioned in detail. First, short credits by merchants and
other business men to their customers, a tendency to resort
to which is usually characteristic of the period of recovery
after every panic, and was strong in 1857 and 1858 as well

[1] These are the figures of R. G. Dun and Company, which firm in its
reports regularly included only failures for sums of $5000 and above; the
failures for sums below $5000 were reckoned as equal in number to those
for sums above $5000, with liabilities amounting to one-third of those of
the latter. In the North in 1857 there were 4257 failures, with liabilities
for $265,000,000; in 1861, 5935 failures, with liabilities for $178,000,000.
In this reckoning the Border states of Delaware, Maryland, Kentucky,
and Missouri and the District of Columbia are not included as Northern
states; if they were included as Northern states, then the number of
failures for 1861 would be raised to 6520, with liabilities for $193,000,000.
In Boston, in 1861, 8 per cent of the business houses failed, 5 per cent in
New York, 4 per cent in Philadelphia, 4 per cent in Baltimore, 5 per cent
in Chicago, but a much smaller per cent in the West in general. The
record for 1862 was as follows: January, 374; February, 353; March, 263;
April, 179; May, 103; June, 84; July, 151; August, 118; September, 75;
October, 84; November, 57; December, 39; making 1652 in all for the
whole year. For the Dun reports, see the leading daily papers in the
first week of each year.

as in 1861–1865.[1] In flush times when all energy is devoted to building up trade, credits are invariably extended too far, and when the break comes, must be reduced.   Second, the enhanced value of goods on hand after the coming of greenbacks, and the consequent large profits, which for the typical year, 1864, were placed by R. G. Dun and Company at from twelve to fifteen per cent.   Third, easy collections, due to the plentiful supply of money.   Fourth, a universal spirit of caution. Fifth, participation in business by only the conservative, and comparatively strong, houses, for the weak houses were weeded out by the two panics, by the attractions of military service, and perhaps also by speculation and the civil service, until by 1864 there were in most cities far fewer places of business than at the beginning of the war; in Boston nine hundred firms disappeared, over thirteen hundred in Philadelphia and twenty thousand in the whole Union.

The causes of the panic itself, which accompanied the outbreak of war, must be considered at greater length; one of these arose from the intimate commercial relations existing between the South and the North.   There were 48,000 business establishments in the Confederacy and in the North four times as many, in the state of New York alone within 5000 as many as in the eleven Southern states, and in New York and Pennsylvania together 25,000 more than in the South.[2] Naturally the uncommercial South traded in the North, and naturally the Southern threats of secession in the presidential campaign of 1860, the Southerners' reception of the results of the election, their secession, and prompt repudiation of all debts due in the North tended to create a

[1] The shifting of money values was another cause of short credits, but the movement was in full swing in 1861 before paper money appeared.

[2] In New York City alone there were 19,000 places of business, in the seven cities of New York, Philadelphia, Boston, Baltimore, Cincinnati, St. Louis, and Louisville 42,000.

financial panic. Southern remittances to the North began to grow unsatisfactory some little time before the election, and after that event rapidly grew more and more unsatisfactory until they stopped entirely early in the next year. When the war opened there was due from the people of the South to the merchants of the North $300,000,000, and all this vast debt was practically a total loss; its payment was made a criminal offense. New York firms lost $160,000,000 in this way, and those in other cities smaller sums; the dry-goods merchants, the clothiers, the boot and shoe dealers, and the jewelers were the heaviest losers.

The state of war itself was another disturbing element. War was a portentous, unknown thing which might entail one knew not what changes; a spirit of economy seized all classes, and according to one estimate the average retrenchment in expense for the year amounted to over $100 for every family.[1] Sales in the retail stores fell off and manufacturers curtailed the scale of their operations. The *New York Tribune* observed: "Never before perhaps in the history of this country has such a feeling of uncertainty, of alternate hope and fear, prevailed in the business community. The elements of great commercial prosperity exist in such palpable form that the mere novice in business matters may place his finger on the points; and yet, with all this mine of wealth, to the man of trade plainly in sight, not one — not even the sagacious and enterprising — dares to take a step towards securing a share of it. The importer looking simply to the wants of the country, to the ordinary laws of supply and demand, sees a harvest of profits in the future, if those laws are allowed to rule, but hesitates when the cry of disunion and civil war threatens him with rude interference. The manufacturer, with the assurance of a home trade and a remunerative business, even under the

[1] *Report of R. G. Dun and Company*, 1861.

old tariff, if the country can be pacified, and a still better prospect under the new, feels inclined to put every loom in motion and to tax his every ingenuity in pattern and fabric, but halts and hesitates as the din of revolution meets his ears. Thus in every branch of business the story is the same, and the disposition is to move onward with the flow of the tide, but it is checked and chilled by vague apprehensions, which find no relief as yet. This state of suspense is perhaps the severest trial to which a business man can be subjected. He knows not whether to contract or to expand; to take credit or to give it; to buy or to sell; to continue manufacturing or to stop; to build ships, to cut lumber, or to mine. Enterprise, everywhere ready to leap into activity, halts at the verge of a chasm which seems to open before it. It would be a relief to know what is in store for us, that business men may shape their operations accordingly." [1]

The banks were responsible for the crisis in so far as they were maintaining too small cash reserves. Everywhere the reserves were far below the twenty-five per cent now demanded by conservative interests, [2] and this figure was finally the standard adopted by the New York banks to end the financial stringency that lasted for two weeks or more after Lincoln's election. While this stringency was at its worst, depositors wished to withdraw their deposits from the banks, holders of bank notes wanted the notes redeemed, and banks were forced to protect their cash by contracting their loans. The strain was severest on the day when the attitude of South Carolina toward the election of Lincoln was clearly known. Specie payments were not suspended in New

[1] The *New York Tribune*, March 23, 1861.

[2] In November, 1860, South Carolina banks had a cash reserve of 12 per cent of their liabilities; those in Philadelphia were liable for $18,000,000 and in cash reserve held only $4,000,000; the liabilities in the New York City banks were $95,000,000, the cash reserve $19,000,000; in the Massachusetts banks outside of Boston the reserve was 6.4 per cent of the liabilities.

York, and in general the banks of the North followed this example, but in Philadelphia, Baltimore, Washington, St. Louis, and in all the South outside of New Orleans suspension occurred, in the Border states to last only a short time, but in the South to continue to the end of the war. The New York institutions, in addition to agreeing to maintain the new cash reserve, issued clearing-house certificates; but it was quite generally believed that the only thing that prevented universal suspension was the heavy exportations to Europe, especially of grain, which turned the flow of gold away from that Continent toward the United States. If, in addition to the demands for cash by the panic-stricken depositors and note holders, there had been a demand for gold for exportation abroad, universal suspension of specie payment by the banks must certainly have resulted.[1]

Lastly, in this crisis great harm was wrought by the collapse of the wild-cat currency in the West, an event which was also due to the intimate relations between the North and the South. The paradise of these banks was in Illinois, but there were many of them in Indiana, Wisconsin, and Missouri. To form such a bank it was only necessary to deposit with the state treasurer a certain amount of state stocks as security for notes that were to be issued; neither a deposit nor a discount business was required nor yet a cash reserve. Such a bank might easily be without capital and without business in the place of its nominal location, a mere bank of issue, and in fact over one-half of the banks of Illinois were of this description. Thus easy was it to form a bank under the free banking laws of the West. More than twenty so-called wild-cat banks went into operation in a few months in the year 1860 in the state of Illinois alone, adding a million and a half to the circulating medium.

[1] The *Banker's Magazine*, January, 1861, p. 258; the *New York Independent*, January 14, 1861; *Report of the New York Chamber of Commerce*, 1860–1861, the reviews of the various trades.

The currency issued was a bond-secured currency of the worst sort, inasmuch as stocks of any description and of any state, no matter how depreciated, were available as security. It so happened that the cheap, trashy stocks of the time were those of Missouri, Tennessee, Virginia, and some other Southern states, and these formed almost entirely the security of the Western bank notes. Secession sent them on a wild career of decline; lower and lower, as one state after another seceded, the bonds fell in value and inevitably involved with themselves in their ruin the circulating notes. In the crisis people could not trust the financial honor of a seceding state; they believed that the Southern stocks and bonds were worthless, and that the bank notes based on them were worthless, and immediately great depreciation of the wild-cats set in. Almost every day some bank had its notes thrown out as worthless and was forced to close its doors. On a single day of November, 1860, soon after the presidential election, Chicago bankers and brokers threw out the notes of seven Illinois banks, and in the following April, the opening month of the war, thirty-seven Illinois banks failed. Out of a total of one hundred and ten banks in this state eighty-nine failed; Chicago lost practically all its banking capital. After the trouble had gone on for over a year only seventeen banks, with a circulation of $400,000, were left in the whole state, whereas the circulation before the crash reached over $12,-000,000. In Wisconsin thirty-nine banks were ruined, twenty-seven in Indiana and a number in Missouri.

Particularly discreditable was the manner in which the bankers threw their losses upon the people by refusing to redeem their notes when presented for redemption; rather they forced the officials to sell at auction for this purpose the security stocks deposited in the state treasury. Note holders could take what the auction sale would bring, although the auction was forced at a time when the price of the bonds was lowest. The loss to the public reached millions.

In Illinois the security of 38 banks was sold for only 60 cents on the dollar, that of 25 for from 61 to 70 cents, that of 11 for from 71 to 80 cents, that of 15 for from 81 to 100 cents; the security of only 4 sold at 100. In every section of the West there was in circulation paper money worth 100 cents on the dollar, 90 cents, 80 cents, 70 cents, 60 cents, and so on down to nothing, popularly classified according to its value as "money," "stump tail," " wild-cat," "yellow dog," "red dog," etc.; "yellow dog" might turn "red" over night or shorten his tail in an hour.[1] This shattering of the currency of the West was a blow to every section of the country in so far as there were trade relations with that section; many an Eastern business man was ruined because collections in the West were either impossible or very difficult.

Only the weakest Western banks came to grief, however, and state banks and state bank notes lived on through the war; in fact, despite the lessons of the crash, the latter were issued with greater recklessness and prodigality throughout the period than ever before. After the suspension of specie payments late in 1861 there was no longer the necessity of redeeming bank notes in coin; stimulated trade was everywhere calling for more money, and the bankers freely responded to the call by enlarging their circulation many times over, in whatever way they were permitted by the state laws. The Pittsburg banks may be taken as typical of a large class.[2] One with a capital of $500,000 in three years in-

---

[1] *Report of the Secretary of the Treasury on the Condition of the Banks of the United States*, 1860; *U. S. House Executive Documents*, 36 Congress, 2 Session, No. 77; *Report of the Chicago Board of Trade*, 1861, p. 63; the *Banker's Magazine*, December, 1860, p. 543, and August, 1861, p. 155; the *New York Independent*, April 18, 1861; the *Chicago Tribune*, May 13, 1861, and many other dates.

[2] In 1861, 900 banks in the United States were issuing notes without security; $170,000,000 of the $202,000,000 then in circulation had either no security or very bad security. See the *Banker's Magazine*, January, 1863, p. 551.

creased its circulation to $960,000, another on a capital of $500,000 reached a circulation of $950,000, and similarly the four other banks of the city.[1] There were numerous country banks in Pennsylvania whose circulation was two or three times the capital stock. Taking New York, New Jersey, and Pennsylvania together, the average increase in circulation in two years was almost fifty per cent.[2] The total amount of expansion during all the war by the banks, by individuals, and by the government must have reached many hundred millions of dollars, but there is no way to ascertain this figure definitely.[3]

The expansion was heydey for counterfeiters. It was estimated in the middle of the war that there were in the United States, excluding branches of state institutions, 1255 banks, in the Confederacy 140. Each issued for circulation separately engraved and printed notes, differing in form and figure, of the usual denominations of $1, $2, $3, $5, $10, $20, $50, $100, $500, and $1000, although in the West the denomination was seldom over $100. It is safe to say that each bank had at least six different forms of notes, which would make over 8000 designs in all. Then there were the issues of the fraudulent, broken, and worthless banks, 854 in number, which would possibly bring the total number of different kinds of notes up to 12,000. For any one banker or individual to remember the genuine form of so many notes was impossible, and the counterfeiter had a golden opportunity. The United States "beat the world" here, it was said; a special kind of literature arose, the *Counterfeit Detector* or *Reporter*, a necessary publication issued semi-weekly, weekly, and monthly in most cities, one in New York City attaining

[1] The *Chicago Tribune*, May 14, 1864.
[2] *The same.*
[3] One estimate was that by the end of 1862 the total inflation by the government, the banks, and by individuals was $400,000,000. See the *New York Tribune*, November 25, 1862.

a circulation of 100,000 copies.   Monstrous facts were thus disclosed.   The better the bank, the more the counterfeits on its issues; in Massachusetts there were 185 banks, and a certain *Detector* described counterfeits on the notes of 169 of these, while another noted counterfeits on 174; New York had 303 banks, the notes of only 45 of which were not counterfeited.   Similarity of titles of the banks helped counterfeiting along; for example, there were 27 union banks, and 7 of these were in New York State.   Furthermore, many banks used similar devices of engraving.   In all 6000 different counterfeits were in circulation, the number having doubled since 1856.[1]

The inconveniences of the system to the individual are obvious.   The purchaser in the store could seldom induce the tradesman to accept a note if the bank issuing it was situated at a great distance; New England and New York banks were an exception, their notes being recognized in all sections as good.   But if the tradesman consented to consider the proffered note, he must consult his *Detector* to see if there were any counterfeits on that particular note, and if there were, he would not accept it.   In this respect the notes of both good and bad banks were on a plane of equality. For the purchaser to present another note involved a repetition of the same operations.   Change would come in the same "stuff," and the purchaser hesitated to receive it; he might, if he accepted it, take it to the bank, only to find that it was bad.   This failure of notes to circulate far from home at their face value was a source, therefore, of much loss and inconvenience to unfortunate note holders.[2]

The same lack of uniformity hindered exchange between cities.   In one period it was impossible in Chicago to buy any exchange on the Eastern cities, inasmuch as the wild-cat

[1] The *Banker's Magazine*, May, 1863, pp. 843 and 847; *Proceedings of the American Geographical and Statistical Society*, October, 1863.

[2] The *Chicago Tribune*, May 13, 1864.

currency might depreciate in value in the short interval necessary for the communication of the transaction to the East, and in lieu thereof grain in some cases was secured and shipped to pay the debts. Exchange generally during the war was at a high premium.

The evils of the notes of the state banks were many; they were the possibilities of the system as exhibited in the West in 1861, namely, poor security, over issue, and loss to note holders, also the facility of counterfeiting, inconvenience for the ordinary purposes of retail trade, lack of uniformity in value, and the difficulty of exchange.

Many reforms were attempted. Almost every Western state revised its banking laws, and in some instances there was action by voluntary associations of bankers themselves. The Wisconsin Bankers' Association resolved that they would not receive the notes of any bank thereafter established in the state unless the bank was first sanctioned by the association; no bank could add to its circulation without the consent of the association; officers were directed to examine all the banks of the state, and if any were found unreliable, to wind them up; and the individual banks of the association would contribute toward winding up any bank by refusing to receive its notes.[1]

The greatest reform was that of the act establishing the national banks. Each of these new banks was to be managed by its own board of directors, just as were the state banks, but before it could circulate its notes it was required to deposit with the United States Treasury at Washington a certain amount of United States bonds as security; state bonds were no longer accepted. The notes were printed and furnished to the banks by the national government itself, so that instead of thousands of styles of engraving there was now a uniform system with but few variations, easily recog-

[1] The *Wisconsin State Journal*, February 5, 1863; these important resolutions are given in full on p. 152.

nized and difficult to counterfeit; every national bank note was of the same value in every state; retail transactions and commercial exchange were thus facilitated. One uniform law, administered by one set of officials, governed all. Every prominent evil of the old system seemed to be provided against, but the new law was permissive, and no state bank against its will could be forced to come under its provisions.[1]

The opposition to the new banks was to a large extent political, the opposition of the Democrats of the states' rights school, who could not accept the enlargement of the powers of the government at Washington. It was revolutionary, they declared, to supplant state authority by national authority over such an important power as that wielded by banks. Then there was the opposition of the pride and traditions of the state banks themselves, which was very pronounced in sections where these banks were strong and of good reputation, as in the East; an old state bank with well-known name and individuality was loath to give up its identity and suffer itself to be called simply a national bank.

The new banks made their way last in the East, first, as was natural, in the West, where the old institutions were weakest and in greatest disrepute. The Eastern bankers saw little that was of advantage in the change. Westerners, on the other hand, knew the evils which they wished to shun forever; they believed that unless the state notes were done away with once for all, they would again lead to disaster. This terrible day they would ward off, and thus they took a definite leadership in a movement to root out the evil; Cincinnati led the way, followed by Milwaukee, Cleveland, Toledo, and lastly by Chicago; the methods employed in

United States Statutes at Large, 37 Congress, Session III, Chapter LVIII, February 25, 1863, and 38 Congress, Session I, Chapter CVI, June 3, 1864.

each case were the same. By mutual agreement the Chicago merchants and bankers solemnly pledged themselves to refuse to accept the hated currency at par after an appointed day but rather to discount it, and to accept at par only greenbacks and national bank notes; notes of all state banks, even those of the East, were to be sent home for redemption. The discussion of this important step in Chicago was acute for a number of months. The true nature of wild-cats was well understood by all, but the country merchants for many miles around, in their trade with the city, continued to bring them into the city; should the merchants risk the loss of this trade by discounting these notes? On the other hand, there was the continued discrimination in the East against the notes of all the Western banks, hurting the pride of the Westerners and raising the rate of exchange; ought not something to be done to remedy this situation? The merchants took the lead in the discussion and in bringing about the decision, followed at last, though reluctantly, by the bankers.

The action of Chicago, the principal trade center of the West, practically committed the whole section. The West, according to the *Chicago Tribune,* supported $100,000,000 worth of state notes, every dollar of which it was sought to force from circulation. To Connecticut alone $4,000,000 was returned in a few months.

This voluntary action was the death blow to the old régime; formal national law only was needed to make the change permanent, and in the agitation leading up to this step the West again assumed the leadership. During the crash of the wild-cats in the early days of secession sentiment there crystallized in favor of taxing the state notes out of existence, and this step was finally taken by the imposition of an annual ten per cent tax on their circulation, a tax so high that few institutions could afford to pay it, and thus indirectly the old banks were forced to come under the new law.

The organization of national banks to supplant the old institutions now went on rapidly, so rapidly indeed that in a few months after the tax went into effect a thousand national banks were formed.[1] To have seen the culmination of the evils of state notes, their extinction, and the change to national currency was indeed a momentous experience, and the additional experience of greenbacks made the period one of the most important, if not the most important, in the financial and banking history of the country.

Greenbacks were another form of new national currency. In certain respects they were similar to wild-cats. A greenback was a promise to pay, printed on paper and issued by the government for circulation as money in every state, but with no security behind it; it bore no interest and was payable at no particular time. A wild-cat was likewise a promise to pay, issued by a private individual, a banker, but secured by stocks. Each was a poorly secured currency. In favor of greenbacks it was argued that the words "legal tender," stamped on each note, were credit, further that the tax laws and bond issues, by showing that the government could raise money, constituted credit, and lastly that the very name of the United States, a sovereign power, was credit, but on the eve of great battles, when the government was on the verge of ruin, this boasted credit did not materialize, and the notes of the United States depreciated just as did the wild-cats. In the reasons for their issue there was another parallel between the two forms of currency. The national government needed money greatly, its expenses were enormous, it was hard pressed by its creditors, the contractors, for payment, and it could not borrow on favorable terms; therefore it "made" money, that is, set up printing presses

[1] On the whole of the interesting movement against the state banks and in favor of the national banks, see a file of the *Chicago Tribune* for the first half of the year 1864. In the year ending June 30, 1863, there were 66 national banks; 1863–1864, 467; 1864–1865, 1294; 1865–1866, 1634.

and issued its notes without adequate security, just as the
speculating wild-cat banker, for the same reasons, issued his
worthless notes. Thus both the government and the
banker were enabled to satisfy their creditors with paper
promises and to continue these payments for the undertakings in hand. It was really a borrowing of money without the payment of interest; "mere suction pumps for the
borrowing of money from the community instead of lending
it" was the comment of the *New York Tribune* upon wild-
cats, and the greenbacks came under the same condemnation. The objections to the two systems were the same;
the issue was apt to be overdone, "run into the ground,"
and a general "smash up" was liable to follow. But although the government was for all practical purposes constituting itself a wild-cat banker, it persisted in its course in
spite of the Western experiences, and during the war it maintained in circulation as much as $400,000,000 in greenbacks.

The depreciation of the greenbacks may be measured by
the appreciation of gold. Not above 2 per cent in the
month when the government notes made their appearance,
April, 1862, this premium reached 20 per cent by July of
that year, when McClellan failed to take Richmond; the
later failures in the military operations of that summer
and fall and the battle of Fredericksburg took it up to 34 in
December; it then mounted and remained near 50, most
of the time above it, till Gettysburg and Vicksburg brought
it down to 24. Failures around Chattanooga soon took it
back again to the vicinity of 50, where it remained at the
end of 1863, notwithstanding Grant's successes around
the same city. In 1864 Grant failed to take Richmond,
and in July of that year the highest premium was reached,
185, on the famous 11th of July, when the fortunes of
the republic seemed to be at lowest ebb; Sherman at
Atlanta, Sheridan in the Shenandoah Valley, Farragut at
Mobile Bay, Sherman on the March to the Sea, and Grant

at Appomattox brought it down to as low as 28 in May, 1865. Thus battles, like secession, played havoc with paper promises circulating as money.

Under the influence of the greenbacks prices were deranged, the valuable metals, gold and silver, driven from circulation, speculation fostered by shifting values, and debts paid off in depreciated currency, just as had been the case in Illinois earlier. Debtors everywhere profited greatly. It was estimated that in a single year three times as much property as ever before in the same interval was freed from encumbrances; the records of deeds and mortgages showed this in many places. Insurance companies and other leading corporations found their funds, loaned out on mortgages, coming back to them in such amounts that they were puzzled to know how to dispose of them; hence the large investments of these companies in government bonds.[1] The records of civil suits before justices of peace and other magistrates, four-fifths of which were universally for the collection of debts, showed the same tendency to liquidate. In Ohio the number of these suits fell off one-half.[2]

The payment of the foreign-held debt presented a problem. Should foreigners for interest on stocks purchased in the fifties and previously be tendered greenbacks or gold? Two million one hundred thousand dollars of New York State bonds were held abroad, the annual interest on which, $125,000, was paid in gold for three years, while in 1864 paper was tendered, a saving to the state of $70,000, and a

---

[1] Recent Financial, Industrial, and Commercial Experiences of the United States, David A. Wells, London, 1872, p. 25; the New York Spectator, February 18, 1864; the Banker's Magazine, October, 1863, p. 286. This last is a famous pamphlet by Dr. William Elder, entitled Debt and Resources of the United States.

[2] Report of the Commissioner of Statistics of the State of Ohio, 1865, p. 40. There were in this state 25,147 of these suits in 1860, but 11,777 in 1865; in the same time the number of judgments fell from 19,938 to 8773.

robbery of its creditors of just so much. The New York Chamber of Commerce and the governor of the state in vain protested against the disgrace. Pennsylvania paid in paper and so did Indiana, the governor of the first-named state defending such action by citing the fact that Great Britain during the Napoleonic wars paid the interest on its national debt in depreciated paper. The Ohio debt, which was held chiefly in England and Germany, was similarly paid in paper, while the state sold its large reserve of gold at a premium and profited by the difference. The payment of paper to the native holders of these state bonds excited no comment.

Massachusetts was the only state and Boston the only city which maintained specie payments to all holders of their obligations contracted before 1861. This was done at great cost. The fortunate holders of these bonds received in paper from $2000 to $2750 on $1000 bonds. The same high standard was maintained by the United States, though this action was largely the result of selfish considerations, for payment in paper would have ruined the government's credit.[1]

In addition to state bank notes, national bank notes, and greenbacks there were shinplasters and postal notes, forming a part of the circulating medium. With the disappearance of gold and silver from circulation, the smaller ten-cent pieces, five-cent pieces, and even pennies also disappeared, and individuals in imitation of the government and the state banks began to issue their promises to pay in lieu of small change, with no security back of them, if it be deemed that a good name or perhaps a bad one was not security. This was necessary in order that there might be small change of some description. These individual promises to pay, shinplasters, were issued in colonial times, during the Revolutionary War and in the War of 1812, in every panic in the

[1] The *London Times*, May 10 and July 22, 1864; the *New York Spectator*, May 12, 1864.

country's history after these wars, and finally in the Civil War. Saloons, restaurants, barber shops, hotels, ferries, street railways, and small traders of all descriptions practically manufactured money, and some municipalities followed the example, including such important cities as Albany, Troy, Newark, and Jersey City. The city government of New York voted to issue $3,000,000 worth of them, but the comptroller of the city refused to execute the ordinance on the ground that the postal currency of the United States was already furnishing a sufficiency of small change, and that accordingly the city currency was unnecessary; he further charged that the ordinance was one of political corruption, designed to afford work for the printers. Sometimes the plasters were mere pieces of paper or cardboard, signed or unsigned, sometimes small coins of various alloy and description; postage stamps and private checks also circulated to some extent.

Abuses and frauds in this kind of small change were almost without number. Irresponsible persons issued their promises to pay, which circulated for a short time, but were never redeemed. Thousands of dollars must thus have been issued only to be lost, discredited, discarded, and forgotten in a short time; counterfeits were easy. An act of Congress attempted to prohibit all private issues for sums under one dollar, but met with little success, and at the end of the war the paper pieces were still in use. In the Confederacy the same plasters circulated, some of them to find their way into the booksellers' and stationers' shops of the North, and there to be sold as curiosities; a fifty-cent piece could be had for five cents.[1]

The refuge from shinplasters afforded by the government,

[1] In New Orleans the following humorous description appeared, and it is here reproduced as a typical account of shinplasters: "The new table of Southern currency. The old table of schoolboy days, 'Ten mills make one cent, ten cents one dime, ten dimes one dollar' is played out. A

the so-called postal currency, consisted of small paper notes of the denominations of one, three, five, ten, twelve, twenty-four, and ninety cents, each note legal tender to the United States for sums less than five dollars, but not legal tender between individuals for any amount. These notes had a wide circulation, but never succeeded in driving out the unlawful shinplasters.

In this régime of new money the banks flourished as never before. The deposits of the Associated Banks of the City of New York in five years jumped from $79,988,633 to $224,112,205, their liabilities from $193,897,638 to $352,333,551, and the annual exchanges of the clearing house of the city from $7,231,143,056 to $26,032,384,341. This represents an enormous increase in business, which is usual in times of speculation and inflation. Profits were correspondingly heavy and for the New York institutions, as set down in their regular quarterly statement, they rose in the period from $8,055,245 to $20,806,884. The yearly dividend of almost every bank in the city was 7 per cent or above, and of many it was 10 or 15 per cent, while that of the Chemical Bank was 24 per cent in each of the five war years. The same high rate of profit characterized the banks

dime or a dollar in hard spelter is a sight for diseased optics, and a five minutes' survey of ten dollars in specie would cure the most hopeless case of Asiatic cholera. But we have a new table of currency, and it is published here free of charge, for the benefit of those who choose to cut it out and paste it up for reference.

10 omnibus tickets make a half dollar.
5 Schelke's beer tickets make a man drunk if invested in lager.
10 Krost's beer tickets make one city shinplaster.
1 handful of shinplasters (with the pictures worn off) make a man cuss.
10 half dollars make a fool of a poor man.
25 beer tickets (Schelke's or Krost's) make half a cinq.
40 beer tickets, 10 omnibus tickets, 1 handful of shinplasters and nary half dollars make an honest man steal. If they don't, we should like to know what will." From the *Banker's Magazine*, February, 1862, p. 604.

in both Boston and Philadelphia.   The New York banks increased in number from 54 to 69.[1]

Savings banks, as financial institutions, although not as important as the ordinary banks, occupied a prominent place in the commercial world; they represented the "wealth of the million," encouraged in the wage-earning class habits of thrift and saving, and gathered their earnings and made them available for commercial purposes through the medium of loans and investments.   Throughout the war, from year to year after the panic, these institutions enjoyed unprecedented prosperity.   The business of the Bank for Savings in the City of New York, the largest savings bank in that city and probably the largest in the country, during the typical war year of 1864 proceeded on the following scale: accounts were opened by 13,000 new depositors, among whom were 1500 domestics, 800 laborers, 600 seamstresses, and 300 washerwomen, over 80 of the humbler trades in all being represented.   This was a striking increase over the record of any previous year.   Of the 52,000 depositors, new and old, 40,000 were credited with sums of $100 or less, 1200 for sums less than $5.[2]   In all the savings banks of the city 100,000

---

[1] *Report of the New York Chamber of Commerce*, 1865–1866, pp. 135, 138, and 139, contains the figures of the New York banks; for their dividends, see the *Merchants' Magazine*, January, 1866, p. 87; the dividends of the Boston banks are given in *Martin's Boston Stock Market*, p. 69; those for the banks of Philadelphia are given in the *Banker's Magazine*, June, 1864, p. 1004.

[2] One thousand accounts were opened in 1856, 5500 in 1861, 9000 in 1862, 11,000 in 1863, 13,000 in 1864, and 10,000 in 1865; 8000 accounts were closed in the panic year 1857, 10,000 in 1861, 6000 in 1862, 7000 in 1863, 9000 in 1864, and 11,000 in 1865.   Probably in 1857 and 1861 it was hard times that accounted for the closing of so many accounts; in 1863, 1864, and 1865 the same may be accounted for by the investments in the popular loans of the government.   See p. 130.   Of all the depositors in 1864, new and old, 3804 were for sums between $5 and $10, 8220 for sums between $10 and $20, 6483 for sums between $20 and $30, 4012 for sums between $30 and $40, 5684 for sums between $40 and $50, 10,000 for sums between $100 and $500, 750 for sums between $500 and $1000, 225 for sums between $900 and $1000.

new depositors came forward with their deposits during the period of the war, and 25,000 in Brooklyn, while in the whole state there were 200,000 new depositors and more than a score of new banks. Throughout the period the size of the average deposit also was on the increase. There was the same encouraging progress over all New England, rapid increase in the number of depositors, the size of deposits, and in the number of banks.[1]

Unquestionably these figures are a magnificent showing and clearly indicate habits of saving and the possession of much money on the part of the laboring classes. These classes were well employed and were saving money. Soldiers' bounties and soldiers' wages were another source of income to them. The provost marshal general estimated that the national government paid out as military bounties $300,000,000 and that the state and local authorities paid out for the same purpose $286,000,000; it is known that $800,000,000 was disbursed in regular wages to soldiers and sailors, which makes a total disbursement to volunteers of

[1] In New York City the number of banks increased, January 1, 1860, to January 1, 1866, from 18 to 25, the deposits from $43,410,083 to $76,989,493, the depositors from 196,979 to 299,538; in Brooklyn the number of institutions rose in the same interval from 4 to 10, the deposits from $5,624,050 to $14,429,734, the depositors from 30,112 to 62,844. In the state of New York in the same interval the number of banks increased from 64 to 86, the deposits from $58,178,160 to $131,769,074, the depositors from 273,697 to 488,501, the average deposit from $208.91 to $244.82. In Massachusetts the number of depositors increased from 230,088 to 291,488, in Connecticut from 84,614 to 121,682, in New Hampshire from 30,828 to 43,572, and in each of these states there was a corresponding increase in deposits. In the United States as a whole in this interval the number of depositors increased from 693,870 to 980,884, the deposits from $149,277,504 to $242,619,382. See *Annual Reports of the Bank Commissioners* of the various states; also *Savings and Savings Institutions*, J. H. Hamilton, New York, 1902, p. 190; a very valuable document is the *Annual Report of the Superintendent of the Banking Department, Relative to the Savings Banks*, New York, 1870; this contains a very valuable history of every savings bank in the state.

over $1,300,000,000. According to competent judges a part of these vast sums found its way to the savings banks. In the navy there was an allotment system whereby sailors allotted to friends or relatives a part of their salary, to be regularly distributed to them from Washington, and in the last two years of the war these allotments amounted to $3,000,000. Through the instrumentality of state agents who traveled among the soldiers under various titles millions more were secured for the home communities, in spite of the bitter opposition of sutlers, gamblers, and camp followers. In the first two years of the war over $5,000,000 was thus received in New York State, in one year $1,000,000 in Massachusetts, in two years over $2,000,000 in New Jersey.

Other sums were sent home directly by the express companies; from the rendezvous for recruits at New Haven in one month $57,000 was thus dispatched; from City Point, Virginia, $50,000 to $100,000 per day in the middle of the war; from Newbern, North Carolina, on a single day $430,000; from all points in five years millions must have been handled by the express companies. Much was sent in letters and in registered packages. Thousands of young men and boys as soldiers and sailors, with continuous employment winter and summer, seldom losing their positions, all expenses paid, under strict discipline, and with comparatively few chances for spending, securing $12 and later $16 per month clear money, with a bounty of a few hundred or perhaps of $1000 to their credit, undoubtedly saved more than they would have saved in peaceful pursuits at home. It was these savings that helped to swell the accounts of the savings banks. Of the many millions of dollars spent by the local communities in relief of the families of the soldiers and sailors at home probably only a part, if any, reached the savings banks; this money was distributed in small amounts as from time to time there was need, and little of it could be hoarded in the bank.[1]

An incentive to all, whether soldiers or sailors, to deposit savings in the savings banks was the high rate of interest paid by these institutions, free of taxes; this was six per cent in New York, seven per cent in Massachusetts. No other property was so lightly taxed; in New York there was no state tax on them at all, none in Connecticut, and only a slight one in Massachusetts, but the United States made a small levy on their dividends and another very small one on their deposits. Six per cent and but slight taxes was as good as some rich men realized in their ventures. The high rate was due further to the appreciation of gold; the banks invested heavily in the securities of the United States, interest on which was always paid in gold, and this gold, when received, was exchanged for paper at a high rate of exchange and dividends paid in the cheaper money.[2]

[1] For the estimate of the provost marshal general, see *Report of the Special Commissioner of the Revenue*, U. S. Senate Executive Documents, 39 Congress, 2 Session, No. 2, p. 28, note; the *Annual Reports of the Paymaster General* show the sums paid to the volunteers as salary. On the allotment system in the navy, see report of the *Fourth Auditor of the Treasury* in the Report of the Secretary of the Treasury, 1864. There is at present an allotment system in the navy participated in by at least ten thousand sailors, who have the privilege of allotting the whole or a part of their salary to their friends; payments by the department on these allotments are made monthly. For the system as it was carried out for the soldiers, see the *New Haven Palladium*, January 4 and 14, 1864; the *Whalemen's Shipping List*, April 29, 1862; *Harper's Weekly*, November 25, 1864; *Annual Reports of the Massachusetts Auditor; American Annual Cyclopedia*, 1864 and 1865, under the article on "New Jersey"; *Report to the President of the United States of the Commissioners of the State of New York, United States Allotment System;* the *Cincinnati Daily Commercial*, January 21, 1864. There was no allotment system for the soldiers in the Mexican War, but one is now in force, established March 2, 1899. On the deposit of the soldiers' money in the savings banks, see the *New York Independent*, February 25, 1864; the *Banker's Magazine*, May, 1864, p. 853; the *Christian Inquirer*, January 31, 1863.

[2] *Report of the Special Commissioner of the Revenue*, U. S House Execu-

Insurance companies amassed just as large sums and made just as large loans and investments as did the savings banks, and like them represented the thrift of the people and the possession by the masses of much ready money.   Life insurance made unexampled progress.   The stocks of all the leading companies were good, generally above par in all the war, with dividends ranging from six to twenty per cent. The two largest companies, the Mutual Life of New York and the Connecticut Mutual, doubled their business, 1861–1865, the one increasing the number of its policies in force from 12,000 to 24,000, the other from 10,000 to 29,000, while the amount of insurance in force in the one company rose from $38,000,000 to $84,000,000, and in the other from $26,000,000 to $82,000,000.   A steady advance was made by the Mutual Benefit, the New York Life, and the New England Mutual, the next largest companies, and in fact by the companies in general.   The companies operating in the state of New York wrote over 250,000 policies during the continuation of the war.[1]

This business had been built up in the preceding twenty-five years and was well established.   The sudden advance after 1861 was not due to "going to war," as this was expressly forbidden in the contract at the ordinary rate.   For all soldiers there was an extra war risk of five per cent a year on the amount insured, with an additional five per cent as climate risk for service south of thirty-four degrees north latitude, the insured having the option of paying this war extra or the right to the renewal of the policy on discharge from service upon evidence of good health; in case of death, the war extra not having been paid, the company would pay

tive Documents, 41 Congress, 2 Session, No. 27, p. XLIII and note; the *Banker's Magazine*, May, 1866, p. 861.

[1] The number of companies doing business in New York rose from 17 to 30, the number of their policies from 49,000 to 305,000, the amount of their policies from $141,000,000 to $865,000,000.   See the reports of the insurance commissioner.

the surrender value of the policy. Sixteen leading companies adopted this rule, but only a small proportion of the policies sold were war policies.[1] By secession, the companies held, the Southern policies were only in abeyance; the companies would not pay if the holder was killed in war, but like any lapsed policy the Southern policy could be renewed at the end of the war upon presentation of a certificate of good health and the payment of the back premiums. There was no war risk on these policies; when held by men of peaceful pursuits in the South, policies falling due while the war was still in progress were paid after peace had been declared.[2]

Accident insurance was new. The Travelers of Hartford, Connecticut, the first of such companies in the country, was formed in 1864 and in a year's time wrote twenty-seven thousand policies and was confronted by almost a score of rivals. Organizations for mutual relief had long existed in the Odd Fellows, Free Masons, Firemen's Benevolent Association, and other similar institutions, all of which continued to flourish.[3]

Fire insurance made progress. Premium rates on this form of insurance, like transportation rates for grain, went down rapidly in response to vigorous competition, despite paper money, and in five years the depreciation amounted to fifty per cent. Lowering rates, therefore, as well as the popular welfare, must be taken into account in explaining the surprising growth in the amount of the risks written, while increased valuations of property, expressed in paper money, are another element to be considered. The number of

---

[1] For the New York Life only about 7 per cent of the policies sold.

[2] *Annual New York Insurance Reports*, especially for 1868, pp. LXIV and LXXII; *Reports of the Insurance Commissioner of Massachusetts*, 1865; *Semi-centennial History of the New York Life Insurance Company*, James M. Hudnut, New York, 1895.

[3] *Insurance Blue Book*, 1876; the *United States Insurance Gazette and Magazine*, June, 1865, p. 77; the *American Railroad Journal*, April 1, 1865.

companies doing business, the premiums received, and the risks written all greatly increased.[1]

The few marine companies maintained their previous prosperity. The ordinary risks of ocean navigation were increasing as a result of the incursions of the Southern privateers, while the value of cargoes was rising as judged in paper money; the Atlantic Mutual of New York in one year declared a dividend of forty per cent.[2]

In this connection, as illustrating along with ordinary banks, savings banks, and insurance companies, what vast sums of money among the people were available for investment and general circulation, the popular loans to the government may be included; these certainly attained to the dignity of great financial institutions. For many years there had been substantially no national debt, and popular loans were all but unknown; but within a short time a great national debt was contracted, and the largest popular loans of the world's history floated. In twelve months practically all of the $500,000,000 loan of the five-twenties was subscribed for, bonds that could be paid off by the government in five years if it so desired, and must be paid in twenty years. In less than a year's time $830,000,000 of the seven-thirties were sold, treasury notes that bore seven and three-tenths per cent interest.[3]

General industrial conditions, the tide of battle, and the result of political contests, all seem to have affected the

[1] In New York State, 1860–1865, the number of fire insurance companies doing business increased from 96 to 109, the premiums received from $11,000,000 to $25,000,000, the risks written from $1,530,000,000 to $3,428,000,000. See *New York Insurance Reports*.

[2] The *Boston Shipping List*, June 15 and 30, 1864; the *Merchants' Magazine*, February, 1865, p. 166.

[3] As the amounts of the government bonds in the hands of the people increased there was a pronounced increase in bank robberies, which led to the adoption of the safety deposit vault; this appeared in Boston and New York in 1864, but had been in use in Europe since 1853.

progress of these subscriptions. In the fall months of the first year, when industries were in a backward condition and military success still lacking, less than $50,000,000 were subscribed to a national loan, although only $150,000,000 were asked for, although the most vigorous efforts were made to popularize the loan, and although the rate of interest was high, seven and three-tenths per cent. During the next year, which was characterized on the whole by both military and political reverses, when industries were not yet completely revived, no loan at all could be gotten from the people; the Secretary of the Treasury succeeded in selling but $25,000,000 of the five-twenties, and this he deemed a failure; in 1863, when industrial life was active once more and the results both on the field of battle and at the polls were favorable, the people readily parted with $500,000,000 to the government. It is noticeable that the sales this year were least in the summer and fall, while the results of the fall elections were still undecided. In the Presidential election year of 1864 there were comparatively few sales of the four-forties and seven-thirties till the fall when the victories of Sherman, Sheridan, and Farragut and the reëlection of Lincoln cleared the atmosphere; this year only $100,000,000 of the four-forties and $130,000,000 of the seven-thirties were sold;[1] in the summer, while the political and military contests remained undecided, the subscriptions were small. The final success of the Northern arms sent the sales of the seven-thirties up rapidly. During a single week of May, 1865, while the national enthusiasm over the success of the war was supreme in the public mind, the subscriptions

[1] It was complained that the interest rate on the four-forties was too low, only six per cent; some thought that with a higher rate the response to the appeal would have been more vigorous. The seven-thirties did not appear till toward the middle and end of the summer when the military and political contests were at their height and fully engaging the public mind.

amounted to $98,000,000.[1] The number of people subscribing to these loans was very large. Toward the close of the sales of the five-twenties it was estimated that 536,000 individuals had then sent in their names for these bonds; Senator Sherman thought that if the stock-holders of every bank that subscribed were included, 3,000,000 people were interested in the loan. In one week of the subscriptions for the seven-thirties over 28,000 persons subscribed for fifty and one hundred dollar notes alone; on a single day 12,000. "Martin's Boston Stock Market" is authority for the statement that in all the war the government sold $1,240,000,000 worth of coupon loans to the people and that of this amount there were 319,035 fifty-dollar pieces, 730,066 one-hundred-dollar pieces, 463,819 five-hundred-dollar pieces, and 927,665 one-thousand-dollar pieces. Over a million of these securities were of the denominations of fifty and one hundred dollars. This is significant, for it shows that the issue represented a very large number of people of small means, the rank and file of the nation, of all trades and professions; if to these are added the number of the rich men making subscriptions, all the stockholders of the banks, insurance companies, and other corporations subscribing, and the depositors of the savings banks who sustained a peculiar relation to all the investments of their banks, then the total number of those closely interested in the loans could be conservatively placed at 4,000,000 at least. It was reported that in central Ohio there was scarcely an independent farmer or mechanic who did not own more or less of the five-twenties.[2]

[1] For the week ending April 22, 1865, the sales reached $15,000,000, the next week $25,000,000, the first week of May $40,000,000, the second week of May $98,000,000. In July the loan was closed.

[2] At a night agency in New York in 1865 out of 150 applicants 27 were shopkeepers, 19 machinists, 17 soldiers and sailors, 12 clerks, 10 saloon keepers, 9 steamboat men, 5 bartenders, 4 hotel servants, 5 hatters, 4 saddlers, 4 car drivers, 2 cabmen, 2 farmers, 3 stall keepers, 5 shoemakers, 4 tailors, 5 bookbinders, 6 working women, 6 barbers, 4 cigar makers, 1 telegrapher, 1 actor, 1 journalist, and 1 peddler.

"Never in the history of nations," said the *New York Times*, "was such an enormous amount of money raised for the public use with such extraordinary rapidity and success as in the instance of the great seven-thirty loan which is now in the hands of the loyal people." The *Philadelphia Press* said : "The nation owes a debt of gratitude to Jay Cooke that it cannot discharge. Without his valuable aid the wheels of government might have been seriously entangled. Now that we have come out of the struggle successfully no one who appreciates the genius and patriotism that led us through the fiery ordeal will hesitate to place the financier of the war alongside its great generals."

In 1864, when subscriptions to the four-forties and the seven-thirties were coming in slowly, it was proposed to attempt the sale of the securities in Europe, but Secretary Fessenden set his face against this, and in the end it was a matter of rejoicing that all the popular loans were sold to the people at home.

The most amazing efforts were made to reach the people, especially with the five-twenties and the seven-thirties. To sell these securities Jay Cooke, a Philadelphia banker, was appointed loan agent and given entire charge of the undertaking; his methods, practically the same for both loans, were thorough. For the selling of the seven-thirties he appointed over four thousand subagents, bankers, brokers, and individuals, each of whom received a liberal commission, but against whom, however, the gravest charges of rebating were made; the records of these commissions and rebates read like the annals of modern railroading and insurance. There were paid traveling agents, who went constantly over the country, establishing new agencies, arousing interest, and in every possible way pushing the sales. Thousands of country newspapers were subsidized as never before in the history of the country; scarcely a one of them failed to print constantly column or half-column advertisements

of the different loans.   There was a press agent at a salary of
$5000 per year, whose duty it was to write editorials, news
items, accounts of the total daily and weekly sales and in
various ways to keep the public informed as to the progress
made.   Hand bills, circulars, and posters were distributed
by the millions; New York, it was reported, in the last year
of the war was literally plastered over with these from one
end to the other.   A poster was hung in every post-office,
and many postmasters put the loan circulars, unaddressed,
into the mail boxes; the trains and public places were
filled with the announcements.   Advertisements were distributed at conventions and in the country schoolhouses.
Night agencies in the large cities were opened for the sale of
the securities to the working classes, and army paymasters
in some cases paid the soldiers off in them; at every military headquarters, where soldiers were mustered out of the
service and paid off, there was a bond agency, with bonds
of all denominations on hand, ready to be delivered on
the spot.[1]

The progress and buoyancy of the commercial world thus
far portrayed, as well as the prosperity of the agricultural,
mining, transportation, and manufacturing interests, renders
it easy to understand the uncomplaining manner in which
heavy taxes were paid.   The generation of ante-bellum
days knew nothing of national internal taxes; for over forty

---

[1] Interest on the seven-thirties was 1 cent per day for every $50 note,
2 cents for a $100 note, 10 cents for a $500 note, 20 cents for a $1000 note,
$1 for a $5000 note.   These notes could not be taxed by states, counties,
and cities, while railroad and other bonds, stocks, and mortgages could
thus be taxed.   This meant a saving of from 2 to 5 per cent for investing
in the government securities.   This account of the popular loans is based
on many scattered newspaper references, and on the recent valuable
book, *Jay Cooke, Financier of the Civil War*, Ellis Paxson Oberholtzer,
Philadelphia, 1907, Volume I.   This book contains much original material
and many documents.   The quotations from the *New York Times* and
the *Philadelphia Press* are from p. 573 of this book, Volume I.

years the tax gatherer, and excise, stamp, income, and direct property taxes, had been unknown, and the entire reliance of the government for revenue had been on the tariff and the sale of public lands. But with the sudden oncoming of the war there was no more encouraging indication of popular conditions than the practically universal demand for heavy taxation; hardly anything was more unanimous than the cheerful patriotism with which exaction after exaction by Congress was met by all classes. Contemporary students observed this and believed that the spirit clearly proved the substantial well-being of the people. It is not necessary here to describe the various taxes, the tariff, the income tax, direct taxes, internal excise taxes, the special levies by towns, townships, counties, and states for soldiers' bounties and the relief of the soldiers' families. The extra assessments amounted to hundreds of millions of dollars, and a list of all the articles assessed would cover many pages. In view of the extraordinary situation in which the country found itself the editor of the *London Economist* printed the following "brilliant exaggeration," written by Sydney Smith when the United States was on the point of going to war on another occasion, in 1812; it is a description of the burden of internal taxation in England at that time, and may well serve as a description of the universality of taxes in the United States during the Civil War. "We can inform Brother Jonathan what are the inevitable consequences of being too fond of glory; taxes upon every article that enters the mouth, or covers the back, or is placed under foot, taxes upon everything which it is pleasant to see, hear, feel, smell, or taste, taxes upon warmth, light, and locomotion, taxes upon everything on earth, and the waters under the earth, on everything that comes from abroad, or is grown at home, taxes upon the raw material, taxes upon every fresh value that is added to it by the industry of man, taxes on the sauce that pampers man's appetite, and the drug that restores him to health, on the ermine which decorates the judge, and the rope which hangs the criminal, on the poor man's salt, and the rich man's spice, on the brass nails of the coffin, and the ribands of the bride, at bed or board, couchant or levant, we must pay.   The schoolboy whips his taxed top, the beardless youth manages his taxed horse, with a taxed bridle, on a taxed road; and the dying Englishman, pouring his medicine, which has paid seven per cent, into a spoon, that has paid fifteen per cent, flings himself on his chintz bed, which has paid twenty-two per cent, and expires in the arms of an apothecary, who has paid a license of a hundred pounds for the privilege of putting him to death.   His whole property is immediately taxed from two to ten per cent.   Besides the probate, large fees are demanded for burying him in the chancel; his virtues are handed down to posterity on taxed marble, and he is then gathered to his fathers to be taxed no more." [1]

There was indeed much grumbling over high prices, especially toward the end of the period, which must not be mistaken for direct dissatisfaction with government exactions. The spirit was most pronounced when the premium on gold was highest, in the summer of 1864, and when, consequently, the war was coming home to the people every day through high prices.   Every article of clothing or food, every article of necessity or luxury, took on added value, until at last croaking and grumbling became common.   But protests against the spirit were just as common.   The editor of the *Providence Journal* wrote: "Many of us are compelled by high prices to deny ourselves certain luxuries to which we have been accustomed.   It is not pleasant to dispense with them. Perhaps at times some of us complain and murmur at the burden the war thus lays upon us.   But at such moments let

[1] The *London Economist*, March 29, 1862; for soldiers' bounties, and amounts paid to soldiers' families, see p. 289.

us think for an instant how utterly insufficient and worthless are our sacrifices compared with those which the soldiers are making for us day after day and month after month, and let us be shamed into silence that we count our petty trials as anything, while our brothers and friends, living on hardtack, sleeping on the ground, fighting with unsurpassed desperation and vigor, are facing death every hour, and many of them daily laying down their lives, and all in the behalf of us who are grumbling for the lack of some delicacy to tickle the palate, some superfluous luxury which perhaps we are all the better for dispensing with." [1]

The post-office, although in the hands of the government, was an important commercial institution. The report of the Postmaster-General, which in the previous decade disclosed an annual deficit ranging from $1,000,000 to $7,000,-000 annually, gradually became more and more favorable as the war advanced, until in the last year of the struggle it showed an actual surplus; this was the most favorable report made by the department in many years. The unusual result is to be explained by several considerations. First, the mail to and from the soldiers was very heavy; on one day the Army of the Potomac sent to the Washington post-office over 800,000 letters, quickly accumulated in the army in a time of stress and fighting. Soldiers and their friends at home were frequent letter-writers, and although many of their letters were franked for them by obliging congressmen, their mail was a heavy addition to the business of the post-office. From a business point of view the withdrawal of the Southern routes from the jurisdiction of the Washington authorities was highly advantageous. The North before the war usually sent three times as many letters as the South, at an average cost, in the one case, of two cents and three mills per letter, and in the other of

---

[1] The *Providence Journal*, June 23, 1864.

five cents and three mills; in Arkansas to carry a letter cost the government eighteen cents and three mills, in Massachusetts only one cent and five mills.[1]

The condition of postal facilities inherited from the past was as follows: general postage was three cents for three thousand miles, prepayment compulsory; beyond three thousand miles ten cents — the rate to California. There was no free delivery, although in the large cities there were carriers for whose services extra charges were made. All extra payments, and there were many of them, were made to the postman personally, and in every city there were mail boxes on the lamp posts. In the post-office there were yet few key boxes, as a rule only call boxes, and to get his mail the individual was compelled to stand in line in front of the delivery window, waiting his turn. All mail was made up in the offices, and there was no railway post-office and no fast mail trains.

In improvement of these methods and partially as the result of the favorable financial balances of the department, a remarkable series of reforms was instituted. One of the most important was free delivery, copied from Europe. It took too long to go to the central office and there wait for mail; to send a messenger was to run the risk of theft or loss of letters. Moreover, it consumed too much time and energy for the employees at the office to distribute the mail into the separate boxes. These delays were now saved; in forty-nine cities the new system was set up in 1863. Postage to California was reduced to the common rate of three cents. The post-office money-order system, originated in England twenty-five years before and soon in universal

[1] In Florida the cost to the government per letter was 11 cents and 5 mills, in Texas 8 cents, in Mississippi 7 cents and 3 mills, in Alabama 6 cents and 5 mills, in South Carolina 6 cents and 4 mills, but in New York 1 cent and 6 mills, in Rhode Island 1 cent and 4 mills, and in Pennsylvania 1 cent and 9 mills.

use on the Continent, was introduced a few weeks before the presidential election of 1864. Business men distrusted registered letters, the only special way outside of a common letter provided by the government for the transmission of money; $100,000,000 was carried in this way annually, and one thousand crimes annually reported in connection with the service. The new plan was simply that already employed by the banks and express companies, and still in use by these institutions, a draft or money-order, which required no actual transmission of money. Immediately before the same presidential election the railway post-office was started in imitation of European methods, the first cars running from Washington to New York. Mails were now to be sorted and made up *in transitu*, before arriving at the post-office, thus allowing distribution to the public much more quickly than formerly, when all the sorting was done in the office. Fixed salaries were granted to the postmasters in place of fees. It is doubtful if so many valuable reforms in the postal service have ever been achieved in any other administration in the whole history of the nation.

Many other postal changes were discussed, though not adopted. There was a wide demand for two-cent postage, based on the success of the low rate in England, where in proportion to population four times as many letters were written as in the United States; the number of English letters had marvelously increased with the introduction of penny postage, advancing from seventy-six million in 1839, the first year of the new rate, to three hundred forty-seven million in 1850 and six hundred forty-two million in 1863. The experience of other countries proved the same, namely, that a reduction of the rate tended to a large increase in business; and here in this country, it was argued, a reduction would produce the same effect. It became known that the Adams Express Company was willing to assume the entire work of the post-office for a net return of two cents per letter, paying to the government one cent per letter for the privilege. Could not the government afford to perform the service at the same net rate?[1] Furthermore, certain private letter-carrying companies in the cities were already carrying millions of local letters for two cents. This local service was a most profitable field, which the government should cultivate; in London in proportion to population the people sent almost twenty times as many letters as in New York.[2] In spite of everything, however, the lower rate did not come for a score of years, although free delivery and the grant of a two-cent rate for local letters were important steps forward. Post-office savings banks were urged, as well as the abolition of the franking privilege, a cheapening of the dead-letter system, and uniform postage for all services.[3]

Every city had an active board of trade or chamber of commerce, and in some instances new boards were instituted or new buildings erected, especially in the Western cities. All these events were occasions of large gatherings of business men and many excursions. The National Board of Trade was organized in 1868.[4]

Trade excursions were common. Members of the Philadelphia Board of Trade, at the invitation of the Pennsylvania

[1] There were many comments in the public prints in favor of thus giving up this work to private parties.

[2] In London, in 1860, 63,221,000 letters were handled, 202,600 per day, 25 for each person per year; in New York in the same year there were only 500,000 local letters, 4800 per day, 1½ for each person per year.

[3] *Annual Reports of the Postmaster-General; U. S. Senate Miscellaneous Documents*, 37 Congress, 2 Session, No. 50; the *Merchants' Magazine*, May, 1862, p. 443, and June, 1862, p. 527. Other material on the reforms may be found in the newspapers, especially in the year 1864, for as the Presidential election loomed in the distance the Republicans paraded these reforms in every possible way.

[4] A new board of trade was organized in Louisville, new board of trade buildings were erected in Detroit, Chicago, Buffalo, and Milwaukee.

Railroad, in 1860 made a three weeks' tour of various Western cities, Cleveland, Chicago, Milwaukee, St. Louis, Louisville, and Cincinnati, and in a few months one hundred twenty-five merchants of Chicago and Milwaukee on free railroad passes returned the visit to Philadelphia. In the opening year of the war Cincinnati merchants visited Chicago. The following year, on free passes, one hundred twenty-five business men from Baltimore, Pittsburg, and Allegheny visited the same city. Most important of all, perhaps, was the visit of two hundred thirty business men of the West to Portland, Maine, in 1863, where they were elaborately entertained, much to the chagrin of the merchants of Boston, who did not know of the event before it was well under way and were therefore unprepared to offer to the Westerners, passing through their city on the return trip West, anything beyond a formal greeting. But the seeming neglect was later atoned for, when representatives from all the West were entertained in Boston on a large scale. Finally the delegates attending the Chicago Canal Convention and the Detroit Reciprocity Convention were entertained in many different cities in the interests of trade.

The discussions of business questions by these commercial bodies touched every important phase of business life, covering as wide a range as the whole field of investment. The leading questions considered, aside from those already mentioned, were bankruptcy, usury, reciprocity, and ship subsidies.

Although the progress of the war added so few new bankrupts, there were still thousands of this unfortunate class left over from the past; from thirty-five to forty thousand would be a conservative estimate of their number. Accordingly, the agitation for a national bankruptcy law rested upon a foundation of actual conditions that called for a remedy. Newspapers and commercial bodies took up the subject. A bankruptcy law had been passed on two previous occasions in the country's history, only to be repealed within a short time after enactment, and in the absence of the national law the courts had decided that the separate states were privileged to pass state insolvency laws. These state laws were now in effect, some good, some bad, all uncertain, unequal, and conflicting. A bankrupt, relieved of his debts in one state, and thus set on his feet, was still liable to apprehension by the sheriffs of another state, if he entered that other state and owed debts there; and in many states a failed debtor could not make a cent without having the sheriff on his heels. Debtors were really in bondage and could not easily get set up again in business on account of the persistence of creditors. The laws allowed preferred creditors;. a man on failing could indicate a preference among his creditors and assign his property to some before the others could get anything. To such an extent had this abuse gone that in three years after the panic of 1857 $286,000,000 were paid to preferred creditors. A national law on the whole subject was now demanded that would be uniform in all the states, and that would at once relieve an honest debtor of his debts and at the same time prevent preferred creditors. All other nations of the civilized world had such a law; it seemed to be recognized everywhere that a man, failing in business, should not be forced to pass the remainder of his life in misery. In New York City, it was pointed out, many men, once prominent, had sunk into obscurity because there had been no such national law, and were forced to become a class of perpetual debtors.

To all these arguments it was objected that it was not fair to allow rogues to escape; to set such men free of their debts would in effect amount to encouraging them in overtrading, in speculation, and in fraud. Especially the rogues of the South should not be allowed to escape, for if the law was then passed, the Southerners might derive benefit from it. Shortly after the war closed, after much discussion in

Congress, in the newspapers, and before commercial bodies, the desired national bill was enacted into law.[1]

Usury laws existed in most of the states, notably in New England, where the legal rate of interest was six per cent, in New York, where it was seven per cent, and in certain states in the West. Some states prohibited any rate higher than the one stipulated in the contract, others allowed a high rate in the absence of a written contract. To work the repeal of all these laws there had been unavailing efforts as far back as the two panic years of 1837 and 1857, with the commercial classes in favor of their abolition and the country classes in favor of their retention. Changes came with the war. Sovereign states now found themselves forced to pay higher than the legal rate to raise the necessary loans, while the United States paid many different rates, sometimes as high as seven and three-tenths per cent. This was the working of the ordinary laws of supply and demand, and to this phenomenon, the common disregard of the laws on the subject both by individuals and states, was due the gradual development of moral sentiment that was to lead to changes in all the laws of interest.[2]

Reciprocity was a topic of general interest, because a treaty providing for reciprocal trade relations with Canada, made in 1854 to continue for a period of ten years, was about to expire unless renewed. The question of its renewal was insistent. On the following articles all duties between the two countries were abolished: grain, flour, and breadstuffs of all

[1] The *New York World*, June 21, 1862; the *American Railroad Journal*, July 19, 1862; *Reports of the Philadelphia Board of Trade; Report of the Boston Board of Trade*, 1860; *Hallet's Circular*, December 20, 1863; the *New York Independent*, June 13, 1861, April 3 and July 24, 1862, February 19 and December 24, 1863, April 7, 1864, and January 12, 1865.

[2] Massachusetts changed her laws in 1867; there was no usury law in California. See the *Reports of the New York Chamber of Commerce* and the *Philadelphia* and *Boston Boards of Trade*. The *Banker's Magazine*, March, 1861, has a digest of the laws of all the states on the subject.

kinds; animals of all kinds; fresh, smoked, and salted meats; cotton wool, seeds, and vegetables; undried fruits, dried fruits; fish of all kinds; products of fish and of all other creatures living in the water; poultry, eggs; hides, furs, skins, or tails, undressed; stone or marble in its crude or unwrought state; slate; butter, cheese, tallow; lard, horns, and manure; ores of metals of all kinds; coal; pitch, tar, turpentine; ashes; timber and lumber of all kinds, round, hewn, and sawed, unmanufactured in whole or in part; firewood; plants; shrubs and trees; pelts, wool; fish oil; rice, broom corn, and bark; gypsum, ground or unground; hewn, or wrought, or unwrought burr or grindstones; dyestuffs; flax, hemp, tow, unmanufactured; unmanufactured tobacco; rags.

Many things combined to procure the abrogation of this arrangement by the United States. Its term of life fortunately or unfortunately came to an end at a time when high protection ruled in the councils of the nation, whereas reciprocity was an offspring of the free-trade sentiment of the Southern statesmen who ruled the Pierce administration. Naturally 1864 was no year for free trade. The war was continually directing attention to protection as a means of raising much needed revenue; seldom has protection seemed a more natural system. All but six of the articles included in the treaty were agricultural products of which Canada produced a surplus, but which were also largely produced here; protectionists could see no advantage in a right to export free of duty to Canada articles that that country was not likely to buy because she herself had them to sell. The six articles that Canada did not produce were cotton, rice, tobacco, pitch, tar, and turpentine, articles which she must import or do without, but articles the exportation of which would almost exclusively benefit the agriculture of the states that were then in rebellion. To put it mildly, Northern protectionists, who were also at that time ardent patriots, saw nothing in this feature of the treaty. Manufacturers opposed further tariff favors to Canada for a variety of reasons. Their products were not only not on the Canadian free list, but were in fact more highly taxed than when the treaty had been made, a decidedly unfair situation.[1] As government contracts appeared more and more lucrative, manufacturers increasingly desired to retain those contracts for themselves and to shut out foreigners from competition, and hence they attacked reciprocity as being a dangerous break in the tariff wall. Then there was the internal taxation, which the Americans paid in high rates, but from which the Canadians were entirely free. The latter, therefore, could produce more cheaply than the former and undersell them in the markets of the United States. What was wanted was not continued free trade but an increase of the tariff to make up for the inequality. The large flouring interests of the country, and those of coal mining and lumbering, urged this with great force. Undoubtedly it was a strong argument; the *Montreal Gazette* even went so far as to declare that it was the only argument for abrogation by the United States that appealed to reasonable people.

Transportation lines were solid against the Canadians. Under reciprocity these interests saw Western grain admitted free of duty into Canada on its way to Europe; they saw numerous Western vessels, despite the well-known difficulties of the route, making their way free down the St. Lawrence from the Lakes to the Ocean; they saw Canadians, who were desirous of increasing this use of their waterways as an outlet for the states, contemplating vast improvements, and doing this partly at the solicitation of the Western farmers of the United States. This was a blow aimed directly at the canals and railroads of New York and other states;

[1] Whereas in 1859 American manufactured goods exported to Canada were worth $4,000,000, they were worth in 1863 only $1,500,000; the Canadians had raised the rate for purposes of revenue.

it was an attempt to take business from them and to foster competition over foreign routes in order to keep down domestic rates; and against all these attacks the attitude of the transportation lines was simply one of self-defense. In opposing Canadian reciprocity they were seeking to protect themselves from competition, and when reciprocity was at an end, they considered that a great stroke in their interests had been accomplished.

Political hatred was an important factor in the discussion. Canada was one with Great Britain, it was felt, in assuming an attitude of active sympathy with the Confederacy and hostility to the Union. Were not rebel emissaries present at Niagara Falls in the year 1864 plotting against the North? Did not hostile Confederate expeditions appear out of Canada to harass the cities of the Union on the northern border, to burn them and to free prisoners? Among the masses of the people whose minds were imbued with an ardent war spirit, this conduct constituted an unanswerable argument against further reciprocity; they would have no community of interests with their enemies. A curious statement, somewhat inconsistent with the preceding argument, but seriously advanced in the Detroit Reciprocity Convention and in Congress, was that complete abrogation of the treaty would be beneficial in that it would lead Canada to seek admission into the Union; she was dependent on the trade of this country and rather than lose it would come into the Union. Comparatively little attention in all the discussion was given to the free fisheries rights guaranteed to the American fishermen by the treaty. The loss of this right and the consequent revival of the old disputes with Great Britain over the fisheries were not feared. It was protection, and protection only, that was in the air.[1]

[1] *Review of the Proceedings of the Detroit Convention; Report upon the Treaty of Reciprocity*, U. S. House Executive Documents, 39 Congress, 1 Session, No. 128; the *New York Herald*, December 26, 1864; the *Mer-*

The most terrible blow struck by the war upon any interest was that upon the merchant marine. In the first part of the century the commerce of the Atlantic had been almost entirely in the hands of Americans and had been very profitable, but foreign ships began to appear after the Napoleonic régime, and by 1860 almost one-half of the tonnage entering American ports was foreign. Then in the short space of five years of war the change to the foreign ships proceeded so rapidly that 5000 American vessels disappeared, which was a gain to the foreigners of almost as many ships. The total value of the foreign trade of the United States in American vessels in 1860 was $507,000,000, and in 1864 only $184,000,000, while that in foreign vessels in the one year was $255,000,000, and in the other $485,000,000; the preponderance in favor of the foreign vessels during the latter year was $300,000,000.[1] No merchant shipped in an American vessel if there was a foreign vessel at hand; many ships under the American flag did not have full cargoes, while those flying foreign flags were always filled, and the valuable cargoes without exception were secured by foreigners. In the harbor of New York, where it had once floated proudly

chants' Magazine, May, 1864, p. 376, and January, 1865, p. 75; the London Economist, September 6, 1862; U. S. Senate Miscellaneous Documents, 37 Congress, 2 Session, No. 26; the New York Sun, January 21, 1865; U. S. House Reports, 38 Congress, 1 Session, No. 39; the Railroad Record, September 10, 1863; the United States Economist, February 6, 1864; the New York Journal of Commerce, December 26, 1864; the New York Herald, December 26, 1864, has remarks and extracts of speeches made at the Detroit Reciprocity Convention. This convention was held after Congress had decided to abrogate the treaty; four hundred delegates of boards of trade and chambers of commerce were present and passed strong resolutions in favor of the renewal of the treaty but without any effect; and from that day to this protection sentiment has been stronger than reciprocity.

[1] Report of the Special Commissioner of the Revenue, U. S. House Executive Documents, 41 Congress, 2 Session, No. 27, p. XXX. In 1860, 12,682 American vessels cleared American ports, and in 1864, 7967; in 1860, 10,912 foreign vessels, and in 1864, 15,039.

in the ascendency, the American flag seemed almost to disappear.[1] At this humiliating record Northerners were filled with the deepest indignation and concern, and annually the feeling ran higher as the statistics for each new year were published.

Several causes contributed toward bringing about this situation. First, the captures made by the *Alabama* and kindred Confederate ships. Twenty-five Southern privateers preyed upon the commerce of the Union, and, as reported by the secretary of the American Shipmasters' Association, succeeded in capturing 284 vessels, representing a tonnage of 132,307 tons; the value of vessels and cargo was placed at $25,000,000. A large part of this ruin was the work of the *Alabama*, which in two years captured over 64 vessels, burning most of them; hardly any vessel of war had ever done so much damage. When the news was received of her destruction off the coast of France by the *Kearsarge*, Captain Winslow, the country was filled with genuine exultation and relief; merchants especially rejoiced. The Philadelphia Board of Trade later tendered to Captain Winslow an elaborate banquet, with a complimentary address, the Boston merchants banqueted and praised captain, officers, and crew at Faneuil Hall, while the New York Chamber of Commerce in expressing their appreciation sent hearty thanks and $25,000 for captain, officers, and crew.

Hundreds of other vessels, not captured by privateers but fearful of such a fate, only escaped by transfer to foreign flags, especially to that of the British. In times of peace an average number of such transfers to the British alone was forty per year, but in the first three years of the war it reached

[1] November 14, 1863, out of 176 entries at the port of New York 93 vessels flew the British flag, 20 that of Bremen, 10 the French, 6 the Danish, 6 the Hanoverian, 6 that of Hamburg, 4 the Prussian, 3 the Belgian, 3 the Norwegian, 3 the Austrian, 2 the Dutch, 1 the Swedish, and only 19 the American.

six hundred, and for the entire period one thousand.[1] Another cause of the revolution was the transfer of some ships to the government for transport service.

Finally there was the failure of American capital to be attracted to ocean transportation, a phenomenon which was noted from the very beginning of transatlantic steamers. Millions were lavished in securing the mastery of the seas for American sailing vessels, and millions on the conquest of a new continent by steam railroads and river steamers, but steam on the ocean was neglected. There were, to be sure, eight American ocean steamship lines, all confined to coastwise service, in which by law foreign vessels could not engage; none crossed the Atlantic to Europe. On the other hand, in the port of New York alone there arrived from over the ocean the boats of eleven foreign steamship lines, mostly British.[2]

Almost as soon as the pioneer steamers, the *Sirius* and the *Great Western*, had proved the possibilities of steam for ocean service, her Majesty's government interfered in favor of the vessels of its subjects by a grant of liberal subsidies for the carrying of the mails, and in the fifties these subsidies amounted to sixty cents per mile more than those of the United States.[3] The latter country did not begin its subsidies until 1847, after the British ships were well established. In a short time iron steamers were perfected, and here Great Britain not only anticipated the United States but easily surpassed her in the cheapness with which she could furnish the iron, coal, and labor necessary for the building of such ships. Thus was the foundation for British supremacy on the sea established and the tide

[1] The average number of these transfers in 1858, 1859, and 1860 was 40; in 1861 it was 126; in 1862, 134; in 1863, 348.

[2] In 1863 the Cunard line made 71 voyages to America, the Inman 76, the Allan 64, the Galway 9, the Anchor 11.

[3] Great Britain was paying her principal lines $2.39 per mile, the United States $1.80.

turned away from the ships of the United States. It was
a process that would undoubtedly have continued had the
Confederacy never existed; the war merely quickened it and
turned public attention to it.

Naturally with the eclipse of American shipping the old
demand for liberal ship subsidies reappeared with increased
vigor. The Collins Line, the leading American line, in its
tragic struggle in the fifties with the Cunard and other
English ships had doubtless been the victim of bad luck, and
it had surely suffered from great initial cost of construction,
as well as from extravagance and recklessness; but plainly
its subsidies from the government had been too low to enable
it to prolong the competition. So it was urged that the
policy of subsidies be now taken up again, and that the
grant be made more liberal. The New York Chamber of
Commerce and other bodies petitioned Congress in favor of
the measure, and there was a wide discussion of it in the
newspapers and elsewhere, but Congress would not be moved.
It was no time for such an extravagant step when the expenses of the war were so heavy; high protection, that is,
government assistance to private capital, was indeed the
ruling sentiment in the nation, but it was a protection actu-
ated primarily by a desire to obtain revenue and only
secondarily by a desire to assist individuals. The close of
the war brought no change, and from that time down to the
present foreigners have successfully maintained their pre-
dominance in American shipping, and American shipowners
are still without the government stimulus which they crave.[1]

[1] *Sixth Annual Report of the New York Chamber of Commerce*, 1863–
1864; the *New York Journal of Commerce*, July 28, 1864; the *Merchants'
Magazine*, March, 1864, p. 193; the *North American Review*, October,
1864; the *Commercial and Financial Chronicle*, July 22, 1865; *Report
of the Commissioner of Navigation to the Secretary of the Treasury*, 1884,
p. 160; the *Boston Shipping List*, July 9, 1864; the *Merchants' Magazine*,
December, 1865, p. 445; the *Whalemen's Shipping List*, November 29,
1864; *Report of the Special Commissioner of the Revenue*, U. S. House
Executive Documents, 41 Congress, 2 Session, No. 27, p. XXX.

This account of commercial enterprise, of its manifestations and actual conditions, clearly shows that the spirit of
commerce proved to be consistent with the spirit of war.
Great transactions, and more of them than ever before,
characterized the world of business; there were few backward
steps but rather a general forward movement. Public discussion of business questions was acute. In the following words
the *New York Sun,* in an editorial entitled "New York as
Affected by the War," described the situation in that city in
the last few months of the war, and the same words may
fitly be ascribed to most of the cities of the time: "It was a
favorite theory of the rebel leaders, at the beginning of the
rebellion, that the withdrawal of the Southern trade from
the North would cause a complete prostration of business,
and 'make grass grow in the streets of New York.' Could
these prophets have been here yesterday and witnessed the
grand 'opening' of the spring fashions, the throng of elegantly
attired ladies in search of the 'latest styles,' together with the
bustle and activity of business among the wholesale merchants throughout the city, they would have concluded that
their augury in this respect, like most of their predictions in
regard to the war, were 'baseless as the fabric of a dream.'
New York has not suffered, in a business point of view, in
consequence of the rebellion. It is true that the city lost a
large and lucrative trade by the secession of the Southern
states, but it is also true that this loss has been made good by
the vast increase of Northern and military trade since the
commencement of the war. There never was a time in the
history of New York when business prosperity was more
general, when the demand for goods was greater, and payments more prompt, than within the last two or three years.
Manufacturers have been crowded with orders, dealers have
had an abundance of customers, and every branch of legitimate trade has flourished. There have been virtually no
suspensions of business houses, and there has been no cause

for them.   Rates of interest have been very low, and there
has been no trouble in obtaining money to meet obligations.
Improvements of real estate, too, have suffered little or no
abatement.   Business structures and residences have been
constantly in course of construction, and some of the finest
buildings in the city have been erected since the beginning of
the war.   In short, New York has shown no evidences of
business prostration.   Everything has indicated a remarkable degree of prosperity, and there is, as yet, no sign of the
'grass' in the streets, as was gravely predicted by the rebels.
All this shows the firmness of the foundation upon which
the commercial metropolis of the country stands.   The
hundred and fifty thousand men whom it has sent to the
army, the hundreds of thousands of dollars it has poured into
the national treasury, the loss of the rich Southern trade, have
not shaken its stability, and to-day it stands more prosperous in every way than at the outbreak of the rebellion." [1]

ADDITIONAL NOTE

RESOLUTIONS OF THE WISCONSIN BANKERS' ASSOCIATION

(These resolutions are inserted here for the light they throw
on the banking methods of the West at this time.)

"*Whereas*, all classes of citizens of Wisconsin, and especially
its responsible bankers, have suffered severely in the past from the
issue of bank notes by irresponsible parties, and whereas, the suspension of specie payments, and the stimulus given to all forms of
business and trade by the immense expenditures of the national
government, and the large amounts of legal tender notes it has been
necessary to issue, furnish at the present time an inducement to those
engaged in banking, to issue a larger circulation than their actual
capital would justify, while an opportunity is also offered to parties
of little or no responsibility or capital to organize banks with
scarcely any other object in view than to set afloat a currency,
which, however well it may keep up for a time, may, on the decline

[1] The *New York Sun*, March 24, 1865.

of the value of its security, or the resumption of specie payments, eventually become depreciated, thereby causing a recurrence of all those troubles and losses which the business interests of our state so recently experienced; and whereas, the present time is unusually favorable for the issue of bank notes by persons of doubtful responsibility, we believe such a currency must now be discouraged in every legitimate way, and that it behooves every responsible banker in the state to coöperate with and strengthen the wholesome restraints imposed by law to check the evil, and ward off its deplorable results: we therefore feel impelled by our duty to the business community and citizens generally, as well as our regard for the character and safety of the banking institutions of our state, to adopt the following resolutions: —

"Resolved, That we, the members of the Bankers' Association of Wisconsin, will not receive the notes of any banking institution which may be hereafter established in this state unless said bank shall first have been sanctioned by a majority of the directors of the Association.

"Resolved, That no banking institution now in existence in this state shall add to its circulation without having received the written consent of a majority of the directors of this Association, and in case any bank shall do without such consent, we agree not to pay its notes out, but to proceed to wind it up by protest.

"Resolved, That when a majority of the directors of this Association decide to sustain the establishment of a new bank, or an increase in the circulation of an old one, they shall publish a notice to that effect over their own signatures for two weeks in two of the daily papers of Milwaukee, and a new bank or the new circulation of an old one shall not be considered to have received the approval of a majority of the directors of the Association until such notice has been given.

"Resolved, That the directors of this Association be instructed, and are hereby instructed, to carefully and impartially scrutinize the character and condition of the existing banks of this state, and if any of them are found in their judgment to be in a condition so unstable and unreliable as to render their continuance incompatible with the public good, and as likely in time of financial trouble to bring loss on the community and injury to the more stable banks of the state, they shall proceed to wind up all such banks without delay, inasmuch as they can now do so without loss to the public; and their attention is more especially called to those banks which have no office, and are not engaged in the transaction of a regular local business, but are exclusively banks of circulation.

"*Resolved*, That whenever the directors of this Association shall deem it advisable to wind up any bank, as contemplated in the foregoing resolutions, they shall notify the several banks of this Association, and upon the receipt of such notice we hereby severally agree to assent and to send to our correspondents in Milwaukee the circulation of such bank." — The *Wisconsin State Journal*, February 5, 1863.

CHAPTER VI

CAPITAL

A S soon as expansion set in, it was evident that the existing industrial machinery was inadequate to the tasks
imposed upon it. Industrial enterprises in the past under a
system of free competition had been very numerous, and each
had been conducted on a small scale; there was no unity of
effort in allied lines and over large areas of territory, while
in some cases unwise laws had created inequalities. This
lack of unity needed to be corrected, more harmony
among common interests introduced, and unequal privileges
swept away, if business was to be transacted on an increased
scale. This was the fundamental reason for the sudden and
pronounced tendency towards consolidation that characterized the world of capital as soon as the war began, although
other factors doubtless contributed to the same end, such as
internal taxes, large fortunes, the progress of inventions,
peculiar transportation conditions, the tariff, high prices,
and the assaults of the laboring classes.

A typical example illustrating the growth of capital was the
progress of the Western Union Telegraph Company. Originally telegraph lines were built in small sections, each by a
small company, and processes of consolidation set in early.
There were over fifty companies in the United States in
1851, when the Western Union was formed to control a line
running from Buffalo to Louisville, and in the next five
years this line acquired eleven small companies in the one
state of Ohio. Its first genuine title to greatness, however,
was the institution of telegraphic communications between

the Atlantic and the Pacific by the building of the overland line to California. No other company had the courage to undertake the work, but the Western Union took it up, and in spite of the prevailing excitement brought it to a successful conclusion shortly after the opening of the war; the event was almost unnoticed by the press. At this time the company did not own its connection in the Eastern states with the Atlantic.

The Morse patents on the telegraph were just expiring,[1] and there sprang up at once a fierce free-for-all competition between rival companies for supremacy; many new lines were built, many new companies formed, and many consolidations consummated, and from it all the Western Union emerged triumphant. It succeeded in the middle of the war, by two important consolidations, in extending its wires to New York and Philadelphia, and thus acquired a completed single line from ocean to ocean. In the East it now controlled practically all the country west of New York and north of the Ohio, and was continually absorbing new lines. The remainder of the country was given over to its rival, the American Telegraph Company, which by similar methods of absorption of smaller companies acquired control of New England, the South, and the Southwest. In opposition to these two growing lines numerous new companies were immediately formed, particularly three strong ones which shortly consolidated into the United States Telegraph Company; these new interests built lines from Portland through Boston, New York, Philadelphia, and Baltimore to Washington; from New York to Albany, Buffalo, Cleveland, Chicago, and Milwaukee; and from Philadelphia to Pittsburg, Cincinnati, Louisville, and St. Louis. Before their union the three new companies in three years erected

---

[1] These patents were finally renewed in 1861 by the Commissioner of Patents for seven years.

ten thousand miles of wires, and in the succeeding year three thousand miles more, which, added to the construction of other new lines, brought the total telegraph construction during the war, exclusive of the line to the Pacific, up to at least fifteen thousand miles. In the words of the *Springfield Republican* there was a "telegraph fever"; in every direction, in every section, the work went on. Probably more was now accomplished for the telegraph than at any other period of equal duration in the history of the country.

The profits of the business abundantly account for this activity. It was stated in Congress, during the struggle over the extension of the Morse patents, that the line from New York to Boston paid for itself in profits every three months; the stock was watered for large amounts more than the line cost, and on these artificially inflated sums annual dividends of twenty per cent were declared. The stock of the Western Union began to rise in 1863, and in that year was watered one hundred per cent; again in the same year it was watered one-third more; the quotations continued to go up until one-hundred-dollar shares sold for two hundred thirty dollars, when the stock was again doubled by watering. It is doubtful if any fuller records of the business of the company are available, but this certainly is enough to justify the belief that the business was extremely profitable.

The third step in the development of the dominant company was its bold initiative in the struggle with the United States Telegraph Company and the Atlantic Cable Company to establish telegraphic communications with Europe. Two years before the initial success of the Atlantic Cable the United States commercial agent and consul at St. Petersburg was at work on a scheme to connect Russia and America by a line of telegraph through Siberia and Alaska; this came to be regarded as a natural extension of the existing line to the Pacific, and accordingly the Western Union took up the project as its own and pushed it vigorously. It was designed to build a line up the shores of the Pacific through the United States and British Columbia to Behring Straits, whence a cable was to lead to Asiatic Russia, and an overland telegraph to the Amoor River, to which point Russia was already engaged in building a line. Rights of way across government land, with liberal grants of privileges, were secured from the United States, Great Britain, and Russia. Preliminary work began, and in one year seven hundred miles of wire, including a cable across Puget Sound, were extended into the Northwest, and when the company gave up after the final successful working of the Atlantic Cable, it had extended its wires many hundreds of miles farther. Thus to be thwarted in a great undertaking after so much had been accomplished was discouraging, but there was nothing but universal praise for the daring of the company that passed so rapidly from one great achievement to another.

There was much to justify the expectations of those who believed in the Atlantic Cable. Whereas up to 1858, the, date of the first working of the wires under the Atlantic, there was no ocean cable that would reach more than a third of the distance from Newfoundland to Ireland, while all the cables of the world together reached less than a thousand miles, six years from that date, on the eve of the final success of the Atlantic enterprise, there was six times that amount of successful cable, one stretching from Malta to Alexandria in the Mediterranean and measuring only one hundred miles less than the distance from America to Europe.[1] Only persistence seemed to be necessary to make the Atlantic Cable a success, and this quality was supplied by Cyrus Field, who kept up public interest and secured the necessary subscriptions from capitalists; success was achieved in 1866.

The fourth step in advance, and the one which permanently established the supremacy of the Western Union, was its absorption of the American Telegraph Company and the

[1] It is 1640 miles from Newfoundland to Ireland.

United States Telegraph Company, its only important rivals.[1]
In the short space of fifteen years the company had either
built or acquired fifty thousand miles of line, and this final
consolidation added twenty-five thousand miles more. A
monopoly, which was gladly welcomed by all classes, was
in reality created. The business world rejoiced in uniform
service and praised the company that had achieved it. It
was a notable development in which the names of S. F. B.
Morse, Ezra Cornell, Hiram Sibley, and J. H. Wade were
prominent. From forty to fifty small companies still remained.[2]

The railroads, which, like the telegraph companies, were
built in small sections, each by a different company, also made
progress in consolidation; indeed, so strong was the movement here that it constituted one of the striking characteristics of the existing industrial world.[3] Two small roads in
Maine joined to form the Maine Central; seven roads from
Boston to Ogdensburg, New York, combined; the Erie,
by gaining possession of several small roads, changed its
Western terminus from Dunkirk to Buffalo; the Pennsylvania
took possession of the Philadelphia and Erie, the Oil Creek
Railroad, and the Pittsburg, Fort Wayne, and Chicago;

[1] This was in 1866.
[2] This account of the telegraph companies has been gathered in small
bits from many different sources. There is *A Retrospect of the Western
Union Telegraph Company*, by A. R. Brewer, New York, 1901, which gives
the story of the one company. Most of the material is to be found in the
ordinary news items in the daily press; see the *Eclectic Magazine*, August,
1864; *American Annual Cyclopedia*, 1861–1865, under "Telegraph";
the *Springfield Republican*, April 14, 1864; the *National Intelligencer*,
June 11, 1864; the *New York Tribune*, October 26, 1861; the *New York
Spectator*, August 29, 1864; the *New York Times*, August 27, 1864; the
American Railroad Journal, July 1, 1865; and a very large number of
other references too numerous to mention.
[3] The movement was not entirely new. The New York Central was
the result of the union of ten small roads in 1853; three more were soon
added. The Michigan Southern was made up of five small roads, united
in 1855. It was the same with most of the large roads of the time.

the Atlantic and Great Western took over the Cleveland and Mahoning, to enter Cleveland; the Cincinnati, Hamilton, and Dayton by a lease extended its lines from Dayton to Toledo; four roads leading from Quincy, Illinois, to Toledo were brought under one management; the Galena and Chicago Union united with two small Iowa roads and was then absorbed by the Chicago and Northwestern, which also gained control of the Peninsular Line just completed across the northern part of Michigan to the iron and copper mines there. These new roads represented such comparatively long distances as from Lake Superior, *via* Chicago, to Omaha, from Toledo to Quincy, Illinois, from Cincinnati to Dayton, and from Philadelpia to Chicago. Consolidations of lesser importance were numerous.[1]

Most desirable combinations in some instances failed to be realized; for example, the five lines between Buffalo and Chicago along the shores of Lake Erie could not reach a common agreement; the New York Central was balked in reaching out for the Harlem, the Hudson River, and the Lake Shore lines; the Boston and Worcester and the Western, between Boston and Albany, could not be joined. These four combinations were constantly and vigorously discussed by the papers and by commercial bodies; the business interests of whole cities seemed to be at stake. But success came shortly.[2] Where complete consolidations could not be consummated there was commonly a resort to temporary consolidations of earnings.[3]

---

[1] The Lehigh Valley, the Pennsylvania, and the Cleveland, Columbus, and Cincinnati absorbed many small lines.

[2] The present Lake Shore and the Boston and Albany were formed in 1867, the New York Central and Hudson River in 1869.

[3] An interesting case of a railroad consolidation was the formation of the Chicago Stock Yards; previously each road had maintained its own stock yard. This was inconvenient, especially with the great advance of the live-stock business, and in 1865 the roads united and formed the common stock yards, to be used by all the roads.

One end to be accomplished by this process was better railroad service; plainly with rapidly increasing traffic better service could be rendered by more harmonious action. It was desirable, further, to cut down the expenses of management which were advancing with the common advance of prices. The strongest motive for combination, however, was the desire to do away with "cut-throat," "ruinous" competition. Even more powerful than the effects of the inflated currency, which kept general prices soaring, was too free competition, for under its influence some rates, for example, those for grain, actually went down, while most rates made but a slight advance. Average freight rates per ton on the New York Central were less in 1864 than they were nine years earlier, and generally on all roads the advance during the war barely restored the former rates.[1] It was competition that had caused low rates after the panic of 1857 and that prevented them from going higher after that event. This ruinous situation the roads sought to eliminate; they felt that they were not getting their share in the general prosperity.

Railroad consolidation was bitterly opposed by the public. The people wished to keep rates down. It was impossible to get through the New York Legislature any increase of the New York Central passenger rate of two cents a mile; this was but one symptom of the opposition. There was a very definite fear of large corporations, which appeared especially in Massachusetts, where the country members in the Legislature stood solidly against the commercial interests of the city of Boston in opposing the merging of the Boston and Worcester and the Western; the proposed capital of the new road, $15,000,000, was "monstrous," "unheard-of," and would corrupt the politics of the state. The same jealousy

[1] See *Aldrich Report*, U. S. Senate Reports, 52 Congress, 2 Session, No. 1394, Volume I, p. 615.

was arrayed against the other combinations.   The combined capital of the New York Central, the Erie, the Pennsylvania, and the Baltimore and Ohio equaled $120,000,000.   Such vast aggregations of wealth were a menace in the eyes of the public, which had not even dreamed of the developments of the near future, and they were hated, feared, and opposed with the spirit which is now displayed against a billion-dollar corporation.[1]

In the telegraph and transportation business centralization was more pronounced than in other lines.   The movement was unnoticeable in agriculture and just beginning in mining, manufacturing, and commercial life.   It was a matter of congratulation that the farming lands of the

[1] The *American Railway Times*, December 14, 1861, March 12, 1864, February 18, 1865; the *New York Nation*, September 14, 1865.   The displacement of numerous ferries by great bridges, the extension of double tracks, the building of grain elevators, and the attempts to obviate the evils of a non-uniform gauge represent movements of the railroads towards offering a more uniform service.   Then there were the private car lines, fast freight lines, sleeping-car companies and express companies, subsidiary companies, all of them, seeking further to advance the interests of a more uniform and long-distance service.   This was not consolidation, but it was an approach to it, an attempt to achieve the uniformity of service which was one of the fruits of consolidation.   The subsidiary companies had had an existence before 1860, and in the interval 1861–1865 they flourished, especially the express companies, whose business was very heavy.   There was the carrying of dead bodies, and of packages to and from soldiers; furthermore, the needs of ordinary business life were large. The American Express Company in 1864 on a capital of $2,000,000 paid dividends of 38 per cent in cash and 50 per cent in paid-up stock; on the capital thus increased to $3,000,000 it declared in the first half of 1865 cash dividends of 25 per cent and 20 per cent in stock, with every prospect of 25 per cent more in the remaining months of the year.   The *United States Revenue Commission* reported that the rates of profit in all express companies far exceeded the rates of profit in almost any legitimate business.   In 1865 they paid an internal revenue tax of $529,276, or 3 per cent on gross receipts; their total gross receipts, therefore, were over $17,000,000.   The owners of the express companies were largely owners of the trunk line railroads, and thus the former received favorable treatment at the hands of the latter.

country were in the hands of small landholders, but there was more cause for this congratulation in the North than in the South, for in the Confederacy large landholders predominated and in the Union small holders; four-fifths of the twenty-five thousand farms of the United States containing over five hundred acres were in the Southern states, also a very large percentage of those above a thousand acres. In Illinois there were 194 farms of over 1000 acres in extent, 112 in Ohio, 74 in Indiana, 11 in Wisconsin, and 10 in Iowa, but 641 in Virginia, 482 in South Carolina, 311 in North Carolina, 902 in Georgia, 696 in Alabama, 481 in Mississippi, and 371 in Louisiana. A farm in the South averaged four hundred acres, but one hundred in the North. Moreover, while in the South the average size of farms was on the increase in four states, there was not only no such tendency in the North, but a very pronounced tendency in the opposite direction; in the one section, therefore, lands were falling into the hands of the few, and in the other into the hands of the many. From this point of view the war was a struggle between a landholding aristocracy with its dependents and a nation of small, independent landowners.[1]

The ownership of mines showed but little combination. There were many independent operators of coal mines in eastern Pennsylvania,[2] and many companies owned producing copper mines in Michigan;[3] hundreds, and perhaps thousands, of different owners drilled oil wells; the Comstock Lode in Nevada was owned by a hundred different companies. In general, mineral resources of all kinds, as well as those of lumber, were being developed by a multiplicity of companies, but towards the close of the war it was reported that the capitalists were rapidly buying up the lumber lands and that the owners of coal mines were uniting.

In the manufacturing world a very large number of differ-

---

[1] *United States Census*, 1860, volume on " Agriculture," pp. 221–222.
[2] Two hundred forty.   [3] Sixty-five.

ent firms were making mowers and reapers;[1] over fifty were making salt in the Saginaw Valley; two hundred were engaged in refining oil. These are typical instances to show the absence of centralization in manufacturing; there was little unity of action, and the market was liable to be glutted by overproduction. Only one prominent combination seems to have received the attacks of popular wrath; namely, the National Paper Manufacturers' Association, which according to the statement freely made by the association itself "recommended prices," which were not binding but were considered as an expression of the views of the meeting that the prices specified would only fairly remunerate the manufacturers. And yet the advance was always uniform. This was what the newspapers and the general public noticed, and the storm over the "outrage" was general. It is significant that the method recommended for curbing the hated combination was to reduce the tariff on paper, which Congress did.[2]

Soon there was imitation. Representatives of the Michigan salt works before the war closed visited Syracuse, New York, to study the methods of the successful combination of the salt works there, and in a short time three-fourths of the Michigan works were associated in two companies. At the same time, according to the testimony of John D. Rockefeller, the first combination of oil refineries, a union of five firms, was consummated. "The cause leading to its formation was the desire to unite our skill and capital in order to carry on a business of some magnitude and importance in place of the small business that each separately had theretofore carried on."[3]

When once started concentration of manufacturing went

---

[1] Two hundred; seventy-five in New York State.

[2] The *New York Sun*, February 4, 1863; the *National Intelligencer*, April 30, 1863; the *Springfield Republican*, January 9, 1863.

[3] *Report of the United States Industrial Commission*, Volume I, p. 95.

on swiftly. Soon after the war was over the special commissioner of the revenue noted a rapid concentration of the business of manufacturing into single vast establishments and an utter annihilation of thousands of little separate industries, the existence of which was formerly a characteristic of the older sections of the country.

The spirit of closer union was strong in the commercial world. Said the editor of the *Commercial and Financial Chronicle* less than a year after the close of the war: "There is an increasing tendency in our capital to move in larger masses than formerly. Small business firms compete at more disadvantage with richer houses, and are gradually being absorbed into them. Thus we have more men worth one hundred thousand dollars in some of our large commercial cities than were reputed five years ago to be worth fifty thousand dollars. No doubt much of this reputed capital is fictitious. But the power accumulating in the moneyed classes from the concentration of capital in large masses is attracting the attention of close observers of the money market. It is one of the signs of the time and will probably exert no small influence over the future growth of our industrial and commercial enterprise." [1]

The explanation of the growth of consolidation in various lines is not difficult to find; it was the same with investors and business interests in general as with the telegraph and railroads. There was the need of uniformity for the transaction of business on a large scale, the necessity of lowering the expenses of management during a period of rising prices, and the desirability of dispensing with the diminished incomes resulting from free competition.

Another element entering into the situation was the peculiar effects of internal taxes. There was a tax on the sales

[1] The *Commercial and Financial Chronicle*, January 13, 1866. An example of a large business that had failed as yet to consolidate was fire insurance; it suffered greatly; see p. 129.

of most industrial products, placed finally at six per cent ad valorem, which bore heavily on manufacturers, inasmuch as most products represented more than one process of manufacture.[1]   To sell raw cotton meant a tax of two cents per pound; the manufacturer whose business it was to spin this into yarn, upon selling his finished product, paid a tax of six cents per pound; the weaver, selling his product, paid six per cent; the dyer another six per cent, a course of procedure that naturally proved burdensome.   It was the same in the manufacture of steam engines and locomotives.   The manufacturer with little capital, who could afford only a small establishment, was discriminated against in favor of the rich man; if the cotton manufacturer could afford not only to spin but also to weave, he escaped one tax; if he could have his own dyeworks, he escaped another tax.   Such a man, after enlarging his plant, could undersell his poor neighbor. Concentration in manufacturing, therefore, came to be the rule, for the more nearly complete and comprehensive the plant, the less was the tax.[2]

A further incentive to change has been hinted at, the growing prevalence of large fortunes.   Big industrial and commercial undertakings necessitated capital and as this came to exist in large quantities with the wave of prosperity, a natural inducement to consolidation was at hand.   The *New York Independent* asserted in the middle of the war that there were then in that city alone several hundred men worth $1,000,000, and some worth $20,000,000, while twenty years

[1] Some articles, like bread, were exempt from this tax.

[2] An interesting case was that of the manufacture of umbrellas and parasols.   Here there were involved sticks, handles, brass runners, tips, bands, rubbers, silk tassels, buttons, and covers, each representing a distinct process of manufacture, and each a separate tax.   After all these parts were gotten together and made up, the total tax on the finished product amounted to from twelve to fifteen per cent.   The tax on a book amounted to the same figure; here there were paper, cloth, boards, glue, thread, gold leaf, leather, type, ink, etc., each bearing a separate tax.

back there had not been five men in the whole United States worth as much as $5,000,000, and not twenty worth over $1,000,000.[1]

A practical invention hastened the consolidation of the shoe industry, peculiar transportation conditions that of meat packing. Undoubtedly, too, in that early day of high tariffs it was realized that the barring out of foreigners from competition with natives in the home market created an opportunity for Americans to unite; by union the latter could better take advantage of their immunity from outside interference.

Apart from the formal merging of one company into another, represented by complete consolidations, there were other unions of a more temporary nature, large combinations of many firms acting together for various purposes. One impelling cause of this was the advance in prices. Whenever prices went up in any particular industry, the movement was bound to be more or less concerted, covering a greater or less extent of territory; agreements to fix prices, now so unpopular, were numbered literally by the hundreds and seem seldom to have aroused opposition. Only when the number of firms entering into the agreement was large enough to constitute a monopoly was there an outcry, as, for instance, in the combination of the paper industry; but this was seldom. It was universally recognized that it was just that prices should advance. By common agreement in large public meetings the saloon keepers in New York raised their prices uniformly, as did the milk dealers, the music publishers, and the twine manufacturers of that city, the Illinois plow makers, the Chicago ice companies, and the country newspapers of New York, etc.

[1] A. T. Stewart, dry-goods merchant in New York, who was then reputed to be the richest man in the United States, in 1863 paid an income tax on a declared yearly income of $1,843,637; Cornelius Vanderbilt and W. B. Astor paid almost as much.

To object to internal taxes and to suggest changes in the rates brought many firms temporarily together. The petroleum refiners met to consider a proposition to change the tax of ten cents a gallon from crude to refined petroleum; the tobacco growers in Connecticut and Kentucky were continually meeting to resist the proposition made by the tobacco manufacturers in many meetings to shift the tobacco tax from the manufacturers to the growers. The brewers, with numerous local associations, finally formed a national association to object to their tax; the California Wine Growers' Association and the Cap and Hat Manufacturers' Association in New York objected to their tax; there were local associations of manufacturers to oppose taxation, and finally the National Manufacturers' Association was formed.

Plainly the National Association of Wool Manufacturers, the National Woolgrowers' Association, the New England Cotton Manufacturers' Association, and the American Iron and Steel Association, all of which were formed at this time, owed their existence largely to a desire to influence Congress in regard to the tariff. A national convention of newspaper publishers met for the purpose of securing a reduction in the tariff on paper, and similar purposes brought together many different associations.

Finally the action of the laboring classes in forming labor unions for the purpose of increasing wages was met by a counter action of employers for the consideration of the same subject, and this led to many unions of employers of more or less strength.

Never in the history of the country up to that time had there been such a strong tendency toward united and harmonious action on the part of the employing classes, whether this resulted in a complete merging of one company into another or looser and more temporary organizations to consider the subject of prices, internal taxes, the tariff, or wages; never had there been such an incentive to consolidation and union. Combination in every line was the tendency of the hour. A determination was growing to merge small, isolated units, often hostile to each other, into larger and more harmonious groups; big corporations supplanted smaller ones; things were done on a more extensive scale than had ever before been attempted. Although the new spirit appeared suddenly, it did its work thoroughly, and while it was not carried as far as at the present time, it must still be recognized that its advent created a new epoch in industrial and commercial life, the foundation for all that has come later. There was a definite turning away from the independent self-reliant localism and small units of the past, a decided right-about toward centralization.

The hated monopolies of the time were only in small part the result of the prevailing trend toward consolidation; they were rather the result of unwise legislation passed during the régime of states' rights, and small local groups, when business was carried on within narrow boundaries, and the opposition to these old monopolies came from those who desired to overthrow the multitude of boundaries and make every section free to all.

Of the monopolies the most scathingly denounced was the Camden and Amboy Railroad in New Jersey, running between New York and Philadelphia. In the days of the early thirties, when it was a hazardous enterprise to build a railroad over such a long distance as from New York to Philadelphia, the Legislature of the state of New Jersey, in order to attract capital to the project, in its charter guaranteed to the Camden and Amboy Railroad "that it shall not be lawful at any time during the continuance of the charter to construct any other railroad, without the consent of the companies, which shall be intended or used for the transportation of passengers or merchandise between the cities of New York and Philadelphia, or to compete in business with the Camden and Amboy Railroad." This was a legalized monopoly of all transportation across the state between the two points mentioned. For this protection the company was obliged to pay to the state in return ten cents for every passenger carried between the two cities, and fifteen cents for every ton of freight. Later this tax was commuted, and the state was presented with one thousand shares of stock in the company, which as a result of stock dividends soon amounted to two thousand six hundred sixty-six shares, the annual cash dividend on which, $200,000, was sufficient before the war came on to pay the debt of the state, the ordinary annual expenses of the state government, and to create a surplus.

Two features of the enterprise were open to question: first, the erection of a transportation monopoly by a state between two points on a route of interstate commerce; second, the imposition of a tonnage tax on the business of such a company. The situation in itself was not unusual. Massachusetts had granted a similar monopoly to the Boston and Lowell Railroad, and through its courts protected the grant by preventing the Boston and Maine from entering Lowell; the same state created two different steamboat monopolies of traffic on the Merrimac River; a similar river monopoly was granted in Georgia. Moreover, in every state there were monopolistic toll gates over roads, monopolistic toll bridges and monopolistic ferries, all existing by the express permission of the Supreme Court.[1] The state of New York at one time exacted a tax for every bushel of wheat carried by the New York Central Railroad. Pennsylvania up to 1861 collected a tonnage tax of two cents on every bushel of wheat and seven and one-half cents on every bushel of flour carried by the Pennsylvania Railroad through that state.

---

[1] The case of Gibbons vs. Ogden only destroyed state monopolies of coasting navigation and had no effect on state monopolies of interstate transportation by land or water when not coastwise. See the *Federal Power over Carriers and Corporations*, E. Parmelee Prentice, New York, 1907, pp. 88 and 91.

Maryland received one-fifth of the passenger fares collected by the Baltimore and Ohio Railroad between Baltimore and Washington. New Jersey subjected the Erie to a transit duty of three cents on every passenger and two cents on every ton of freight carried by the road in that state, excepting only the passengers and freight transported exclusively within the state. Such monopolies and taxes were common and no question was ever seriously raised as to their legality. Their expediency was another question.

The war at once put the Camden and Amboy into a very threatening position. New Jersey, contrary to its solemn stipulation in that road's charter, had allowed a series of small roads to be built which after consolidation amounted to an effective rival to the Camden and Amboy for the New York and Philadelphia traffic, known as the Delaware and Raritan. This new road was finished after the war began and was at once put into operation for war purposes by the Secretary of War, who passed over it at his own express direction soldiers, horses, and freight.[1] The step was necessary, for the old road was unable to perform all the services required of it; traffic was too heavy, and the emergency pressing; but the monopoly took offense. It demanded at once of the Secretary of War and of Congress that the money to be paid by the government for the services on the illegal road be paid to it, the only legal road over the territory in question, and on the refusal of its demands it carried the case to the state courts, which by injunction soon closed up the intruding road and ordered it to pay its revenue over to the monopoly. Throughout the remainder of the war the Delaware and Raritan remained inoperative.

The outcry in the rest of the nation, especially in the East, was almost frantic. It was entirely a cry of expediency. On the highway between the nation's commercial and political

---

[1] Seventeen thousand two hundred forty-eight soldiers, 649 horses, and 806,000 tons of freight.

capitals a selfish and unpatriotic state, for a profitable consideration, in a time of crisis, when the very life of the nation was at stake, was maintaining and profiting by an odious monopoly; the rates charged by the monopoly were very high, and even higher for through than for local traffic; and the service was "notoriously inconvenient and inadequate," as was declared by resolutions of the state Legislature of New York and of Congress. The far-off state of Maine joined in the cry of denunciation. It was insufferable that one state by creating and taxing a monopoly should seek to pay its expenses out of the commerce of other states, but this was in substance New Jersey's position. The right to tax involved the right to destroy and to prohibit, and for one state to assume such an attitude toward the commerce of sister states was the very destruction of national unity.

It was "the discord of intolerable state pretensions," declared Senator Sumner, of Massachusetts, in what was probably the most important speech on the subject. "If New Jersey," said he, "can play successfully this game of taxation, and compel tribute from the domestic commerce of the Union as it traverses her territory on the way from state to state, then may every other state do likewise. New York with her central position may build up an overshadowing monopoly and a boundless revenue, while all the products and population of the West traversing her territory on their way to the sea, and all the products and population of the East, with the contributions of foreign commerce traversing her territory on their way to the West, are compelled to pay tribute. Pennsylvania, holding one of the highways of the Union, Maryland, constituting an essential link in the chain of communication with the national capital; Ohio . . .; Indiana . . .; Illinois . . .; Kentucky . . .; and finally any one of the states on the long line of the Pacific Railroad may enter upon a similar career of unscrupulous exaction until anarchy sits supreme, and there are as many different tributes as there are states. If the Union should continue to exist, it would be only a name. The national unity would be destroyed."

It was proposed in Congress to open up the condemned Delaware and Raritan through the congressional powers to regulate commerce between the states, to build post roads, and to raise and support armies. The debate was most spirited. Before it was plain what form the action of Congress would take, New Jersey's governor sent a special message of protest to the state Legislature. There were two points to be considered, he said: "First, would the proposed action of Congress, if consummated, affect the pecuniary interests of the state? Second, and chiefly, would such action infringe on the sovereignty of the state?" The pecuniary interest of the state was of little importance compared with the principle involved. New Jersey was a sovereign state, and it was its duty, by every lawful means, to protect and defend that sovereignty and to transmit, unimpaired, to posterity all her rights as they were received from the fathers. "In the exercise of her lawful powers she may build, maintain, and manage lines of public travel within her territory; or she may grant to others the right to construct such works, under such regulations and upon such conditions as she may see fit to impose. When the states entered into the national compact, they yielded to the general government the right to establish post roads for the conveyance of the mails, and the power to construct military roads in the time of war for the transportation of troops; but even these roads must be operated by the government, and not through the agency or for the benefit of private corporations. A law of Congress, proposing to exceed the powers granted by the states, infringes upon their reserved rights and detracts from the state Legislatures a portion of their rightful authority. The roads which Congress proposes to invest with such extraordinary powers are already post roads;

and the President has been authorized by law to use every railroad in the country for military purposes. Therefore no additional legislation is needed to make the roads post or military routes; nor has any been asked for by the President, the Secretary of War, or by the Postmaster General. The third section of the bill declares the real object of its originators, which is to empower the companies named, not merely to carry the mail or convey troops and munitions of war, but to transport goods, wares, and merchandise between New York and Philadelphia, notwithstanding any law of this state to the contrary. If such a law be valid, the Legislature of the state is a powerless body and our citizens must hereafter beg Congress for the privilege of constructing works of public improvement on our own soil. The passage of such an act (although of no binding force because unconstitutional) would be an insult to the people of New Jersey. It would take the creatures of our law, now under the ban of judicial injunction for violation of our statutes, and in direct opposition to the decision of our courts, attempt to make them independent of and superior to the power that created them. Such action deserves, and should receive, the strongest legislative remonstrance. Let it be distinctly understood by those who would inflict this wrong and indignity upon our state that while New Jersey will comply with every legal obligation and will respect and protect the rights of all, she will not permit any infringement of her rights without resorting to every legal means to prevent it."

In compliance with this mild but dignified expression of states' rights the Legislature passed strongly worded resolutions, condemning any special legislation by Congress aimed at New Jersey alone as a "wanton insult to the dignity of the state." Legally the state's attitude was unassailable, but the moral doctrine of the general good prevailed, and finally by act of Congress a general law on the subject was passed which applied to all states,[1] asserting that it was lawful for any continuous railroad to carry goods and passengers from state to state and to charge for the same. Immediately the state gave up, and the monopoly, true to its character, celebrated the surrender by absorbing the now legalized competitor! As a general principle, therefore, while the action of Congress represented an advance in the development of the doctrine of congressional control of interstate commerce, in this particular case it accomplished little practical good.

This disposed of but one-half of the question, the maintenance of the monopoly; there was yet the subject of the transit duties. Such a moral blow, however, had already been dealt them in the course of the spectacular and stubborn struggle over the constitutional question, that it was a matter of but a short time when they, too, ceased to exist. New York and Pennsylvania for reasons of commercial expediency had already abolished their transit duties, and after much discussion, at the termination of the Camden and Amboy charter in 1869, New Jersey abolished them, and in their stead resorted to ordinary taxation of railroad property.[2]

[1] United States Statutes at Large, 39 Congress, 1 Session, Chap. CXXIV, June 15, 1866.

[2] New Jersey still derives large revenue from corporations. In 1907 the state incorporated 1828 companies, the fees for which amounted to $141,075; in 1906 the fees amounted to $223,181. The revenue in 1907 was the smallest from this source since 1897, and was far below that of the banner year, 1899, when fees to the extent of $771,845 were taken in. In 1895 the fees were $63,482. In thirteen years the total amount received was $3,579,284. See the *New York Times*, January 5, 1908. For Senator Sumner's speech, see *Congressional Record*, 38 Congress, 2 Session, p. 790. The question was extensively discussed in the newspapers, particularly in New York and Philadelphia. The *Federal Power over Carriers and Corporations*, E. P. Prentice, New York, 1907, p. 95, contains some material on the subject, but the best reference is the congressional speeches. See *U. S. House Reports*, 38 Congress, 1 Session, No. 31, for the exercise by Congress of the power to establish post roads. The various instances were, (1) the Wheeling bridge case, (2) Steubenville bridge case, (3) act of January 31, 1863, giving the President power over railroads for military and post road purposes.

In a neighboring state was another "odious and unjustifiable" transportation monopoly, that of the five leading coal-
carrying roads of Pennsylvania, the Lehigh, the New
Jersey Central, the Reading, the Delaware and Hudson,
and the Delaware, Lackawanna, and Western. These were
monopolies for two reasons. With their lateral branches
they were the only roads to accommodate the whole coal
region of eastern Pennsylvania where two hundred forty
master colliers were dependent upon them, and this was
deemed limited service, since each road in general was confined to a particular region with no serious competition
from the others. Rates on these roads after the war began
went up as they would have gone up in all the country if the
lack of competition had prevailed in all the states as in the
coal regions; they were practically trebled.[1] Only the small
independent operators, however, paid the high rates, while the
largest operators shipped at the bare cost of transportation,
for the large operators and the transportation companies
were one and the same. This was the second count in the
charge against the roads as monopolies; four of them at
least, through an unfortunate grant in their charters, were
allowed to own mines, and while they oppressed ordinary
shippers with high rates, they themselves paid the very
lowest rate; and if desirable, when the lines were busy
with their own coal, the roads were in a position to refuse
entirely to carry coal for others, and thus the small operators
found themselves effectually shut off from the market.
It would be difficult to find more successful monopolies.
The public suffered with the small mine owners. Prices of
coal were exorbitant. In three years Lehigh, beginning at
$3.29 at tidewater, on the 1st of January, 1862, reached
$9.76, while Schuylkill went even higher; this was an ad-

---

[1] From the Lehigh mines to tide water, January 1, 1862, coal transportation cost $1.44 per ton, at the end of the season of 1864 $4.26; from
the Schuylkill mines the rate advanced from $1.73 to $5.12.

vance of nearly two hundred per cent. In the same time flour, in which there was no monopoly, barely doubled in price.

Governor Curtin, of Pennsylvania, thoroughly understood the problem. With ringing messages he vetoed two bills passed by the state Legislature, one creating a new coal-carrying and mine-owning company, with the privilege of holding five thousand acres of coal lands and of transporting coal to market, the other increasing from three thousand to fifteen thousand acres the amount of coal lands to be owned by a certain road. In the latter message he said: "To give the control of the work by which the mineral products of a district are to be transported to market, to a company themselves engaged in mining, transporting, and trading in such products, is evidently to give them an unfair and unjust advantage over the other producers in the district. In part it enables the company to monopolize the whole trade of the district, and either prevent individual holders of mineral lands from working their mines at all or compel them to dispose of the products thereof in such manner and at such prices as the company may dictate. Useful enterprise, freedom of trade, even the legitimate enjoyment and use of private property, are thus checked or destroyed. The deleterious effects of such a state of affairs are strongly exemplified at this moment in one of the most important coal fields in this state, and they are so great and manifest that I am determined to approve no bill creating a new monopoly of any kind, or giving to one already existing the right of holding a larger quantity of land than they are now already authorized to acquire." A vast increase in the quantity of land to be held by the company in question, from three thousand to fifteen thousand acres, "would permanently diminish the chances that individual operators would be permitted to transport the products of their mineral lands on the Lykens railroad, which the law designed to be a public highway, open to the use of all citizens." [1]

The local transportation lines of the cities, the horse-car lines, were in the position occupied by the Camden and Amboy and the coal-bearing roads thirty years previously; they were in the beginning of their career, when the public was willing, through unwise and hasty legislation, to grant them easy terms of franchise if only they would establish themselves. In almost every city valuable privileges were being bestowed on the street-car lines without any pecuniary remuneration to the public being demanded, and almost without any conditions whatever; the public welfare was being sacrificed, and the foundation of great monopolies was being laid. Public sentiment seemed to be only slightly alive to the real situation; the newspapers raised some faint voices of protest, and in some cases there was opposition in the Legislatures, which, however, was easily overcome. The *New York Journal of Commerce,* referring to the chartering of lines in that city, declared: "A premium was offered for the attendance on the Legislature, every session, of a host of speculators and contractors, corrupting members by their venal propositions, and embarrassing legitimate business

---

[1] *Journal of the Pennsylvania House of Representatives,* January 7, 1864; see the *Merchants' Magazine,* May, 1865, for an elaborate article on coal. It has already been pointed out that the canal agitation of the first part of the war arose out of a cry of monopoly against the railroads centering in Chicago and leading thence eastward. The fault lay not so much with the roads as in the fact of discontinued river traffic and increase of crops; the high rates that followed were simply a check on traffic that was too heavy to be handled. The outcry was a general one; no one road was involved, no one road had a monopoly; and by the final play of competition the roads soon got the situation in hand and rates went down. Thus the suddenly created monopoly just as suddenly disappeared; it had been created not by unwise legislation, as was the case with the Camden and Amboy and the coal-bearing roads, but by the fortunes arising out of the war and the voluntary action of the roads themselves destroyed it.

coming before that body." There was the same complaint over the chartering of the lines in the city of Philadelphia.

At least one lively manifestation of public sentiment must be set over against the prevailing apathy; the people of at least one city rightly appreciated the value of a street-car franchise. The Illinois State Legislature enacted a law extending to a term of ninety-nine years the street-car franchises of the city of Chicago, whereupon the *Chicago Tribune* called a mass meeting of protest. "The people of Chicago, desirous of protesting against the great railroad swindle, will meet at Metropolitan Hall this Saturday evening, at 7 and $\frac{1}{2}$ o'clock. All honest citizens who want to defeat the swindle, come. All who would keep the fares down to five cents, come. All who believe that the people should control their monopolies instead of being controlled by them, come and prevent the property of the city and of the people from being taken from them without compensation." At the appointed time the hall was filled with twenty-six hundred citizens of all classes, who received with deafening cheers the announcement that "the gallant, noble 'hero of Shiloh,' whom the people love as Dick Oglesby and honor as the governor of Illinois," had vetoed the infamous bill. But the veto was of no avail, for the Legislature passed the bill over the head of the governor, whereupon another mass meeting passed resolutions, a part of which follows. "Resolved, that in view of the unparalleled outrage that has been imposed upon the city and the public of Chicago by the General Assembly of the state of Illinois, by the mere force of numbers, without and against all reason, all justice and right, by which they have been deprived of franchises valued at millions of dollars, and against the solemn written protest of nine thousand of her citizens and the most emphatic expression of her will in mass meeting assembled, contrary to the votes of a majority of her own delegates, and over the veto of the Chief Magistrate of the state, and in violation of the constitution itself, our city has been delivered for over three-quarters of a century, bound and shackled to the tender mercies of a mammoth monopoly, vested by this legislation with exclusive control of all her streets, an event unprecedented in the legislation of the state, and utterly without excuse or justification, and with no other result than to enrich a few private individuals at the expense of the whole community, that we feel that where there is any power strong enough to consummate such an outrage upon popular rights, and such a gigantic scheme of corporate monopoly as this, that the rights and liberties of the people are in danger, and we are called upon to act at once; and that all good and true men should unite to arrest the tide of fraud and corruption which is sweeping over our state and municipal affairs, before it is too late." [1]

Two other monopolies attracted wide attention, one of which was United States patents. At this time patents were granted for fourteen years, subject to renewal at the hands of the commissioner of patents or by Congress, and the expiration of every valuable patent was attended by a vast agitation for and against the continuation of the same, carried on not only before the commissioner and in the halls of Congress but in the daily press. The patents on the McCormick reaper, those of Morse on the telegraph, of Goodyear on rubber goods, of Fairbanks on scales, of Fitzgerald on fireproof safes, of Woodworth on planing machines, and of Sherwood on Janus-faced clocks expired at various dates during the period, and in most cases their renewal was successfully opposed, but only after vigorous and bitter lobbying and speeches in Congress, many resolutions in the state Legislatures, and a persistent campaign in the daily press. The patentees were denounced as monopolists

[1] The *Chicago Tribune*, February 4, 6, and 10, 1865; the issue of the last date contains the resolutions quoted, while the governor's veto is in that of February 6.

of the worst sort and received no more popular sympathy than the railroad monopolies.[1]

The peculiar monopoly granted to local merchants was particularly obnoxious. In Philadelphia up to the time of the war resident merchants enjoyed a practical monopoly of the trade of the city; drummers from the outside, offering goods for sale within the city limits, were subject to arrest and fine and imprisonment, and the law was rigidly enforced. Agents of Boston jobbing houses were arrested in Maine and "treated with greater rigor than sharpers or swindlers." Boston itself enforced such a law, and so did Louisville and Pittsburg. St. Louis passed an ordinance requiring a heavy license from all drummers doing business in that city, who themselves were not residents of the state. These laws were common in every state, but they were seldom enforced; they were incompatible with the transaction of business on a large scale. Like tolls on bridges, ferries, and roads, and tonnage taxes on railroads, they stood for the spirit of local monopoly, and were doomed to disappear entirely before the growing spirit of freedom and nationalism.[2]

It must be recognized that while all the great monopolies of the time, the Camden and Amboy Railroad, the coal

[1] Up to March 2, 1861, a patent was granted for fourteen years, subject to renewals of seven years each; under a new law of the above date the period was extended to seventeen years with no extensions, but patents granted under the old law were still granted extensions. Inventors of all nations were placed upon an equal footing, except those of the nations that discriminated against the patents of the United States. Canada, for instance, would give no patents to foreigners, and Canadians, therefore, received a patent in the United States only after a fee of $500 had been paid; formerly Englishmen had paid $500 and Frenchmen $300, because those nations discriminated against the United States, but under the new law they paid the same fee as the Americans, namely, $15. Under the old law the fee for Americans was $30.

[2] The *Commercial and Financial Chronicle*, July 29, 1865; the *American Druggist's Circular and Chemical Gazette*, February, 1864.

roads, the street railways, the rights of patentees, and rights of local merchants, were fairly the products of statutes and protected by them, the opposition came from a new nationalism, which stood for freedom in every line. There was a growing national spirit that sought to strike off every shackle from business and to give complete liberty to all the interests of every state in every other state. Business men saw advantages in doing things on a larger scale than ever before and with less competition, and the new spirit dictated that they should be allowed to follow their inclination; it was upon this principle that the old monopolies were attacked, but almost unawares the new spirit itself was laying the foundations of other monopolies which would be in every respect as odious as those of the former days.[1]

[1] Examples of the new monopolies were that of the paper industry, that of the grain elevators in Buffalo, and of the Syracuse salt works. Whatever the size of the corporations of 1865, large or small, the largest of them were small when compared with those of the present day; but they had many of the characteristics of the present-day corporations. There was the same undying existence, the same limited liability with its possibilities of abuse by unscrupulous directors. Stock dividends abounded; on twenty leading railroads, from 1867 to 1869, these stock dividends amounted to $113,648,000; $32,000,000 on the Erie alone, $25,000,000 on the New York Central. The Waltham Watch Company watered its stock in 1865 one hundred fifty per cent. References are the *Merchants' Magazine*, May, 1869, p. 377; also a note in *Martin's Boston Stock Market* on the Waltham Watch Company. The writer in the *Merchants' Magazine* urged four reasons for the tendency noted among the railroads: (1) needs of increased construction; (2) the increasing values of the land grants to the roads demanded to be represented by more stock; (3) increasing cost of the roads; (4) there were earnings enough to pay the dividends.

CHAPTER VII

LABOR

NOWHERE in the world, avowed the correspondent of the *London Times*, was the laboring man so prosperous as in the United States before the war. American labor at that time was scarce, precious, independent, and fastidious; whoever condescended to work was sure not only of his daily bread but also of a certain amount of decent comfort; the very hedger and ditcher had it in his power to raise himself. He knew how to strike the best bargain, how to stand on his rights and interests, and how to put by a penny for a rainy day. "If ever there was a country in which labor was in clover, in which it was looked up to, petted, and humored, it certainly was this North American community." [1]

Suddenly with the introduction of paper money this was changed. Peace in the industrial world gave way to discontent; labor indeed remained scarce, even more scarce than before, but the laborer was no longer sure of his daily bread and of decent comfort; the ability to lay by for a rainy day was threatened, and instead of being petted and humored labor came to regard itself as aggrieved; it assumed an attitude of hostility toward employers and took concerted measures in self-defense.

While there were many causes for this revolution, there was one of far more influence than any other, one in fact that created the atmosphere through which all other possible grievances quickly loomed large. This was stationary wages in the face of rising prices of commodities.

---

[1] The *London Times*, December 1, 1863.

183

Employers were wont to appropriate to themselves all or nearly all of the profits accruing from the higher prices, without being willing to grant to the employees a fair share of these profits through the medium of higher wages. The situation in New York City at the end of the year 1863, after prices had been rising almost two years, is typical of the period in this respect. Eggs had then reached $.25 per dozen from $.15 in 1861, cheese $.18 from $.08 per pound, potatoes $2.25 from $1.50 per bushel, and for all the necessities of life there was an advance ranging from 60 to 75 and in some cases even 100 per cent. Wages, on the other hand, lagged behind; the blacksmith's increase was only from $1.75 to $2 per day, that of common laborers from $1 to $1.25, that of bricklayers from $1.25 to $2, and the average increase in all the trades was about 25 per cent, or less than one-half the increase of prices. The winter of 1863–1864 and the ensuing months were accordingly a time of unusual industrial unrest, which increased in severity as the discrepancy between wages and prices continued. A dollar was slowly but surely diminishing in value, and labor engaged in a determined struggle to force wages up, capital to keep them down. The advantage lay with the employing classes, but labor in 1864 recovered much of the ground that had been lost in the two previous years, and the war closed with wages much nearer prices than a year earlier; it was generally agreed at the time that prices during the entire war period advanced approximately 100 per cent and wages from 50 to 60 per cent.[1]

[1] These figures are only averages. For the daily prices and wages in New York, see the daily press, especially in December, 1863, and January, 1864; for more general estimates on prices, see *Money and Banking*, Horace White, Boston, 1908, pp. 123 and 124. Averages are difficult to determine. A leading cotton manufacturer in Providence, Rhode Island, reported in May, 1865, that the increase of wages up to that time in that city was 50 per cent; see the *Scientific American*, May 5, 1865. For iron molders in general the increase was 56 per cent; see the *New York Trib-*

Other things, however, supplemented low wages, and the severity of the situation so long as the war lasted must not be exaggerated; the labor world received not only industrial wages but also military wages, soldiers' bounties, and charitable support to soldiers' families, and the actual condition of labor may be studied in the allotment system whereby soldiers were induced to send money home from the army, in the accounts of the savings banks, insurance companies, and popular loans, in the records of the administration of charity by the charitable societies of the cities, and in the prosperity of popular amusements, as well as in wage schedules. On the whole, the habitual working classes were probably as well off in the height of the war as in normal times, possibly better off. After the war the condition of labor was undoubtedly worse than in 1860, for the reason that the extraordinary payments then ceased.[1]

But however bounteous, the indirect aid was no justification for low industrial wages; under any conditions the employer ought to have paid the men directly under him a fair wage for the service rendered, a wage proportionately increased as prices increased, and until this was done the men were bound to fight. They were struggling with capital for what they deemed their rights, quite apart from the extraordinary circumstances arising out of the war.

une, January 9, 1866 (report of the molders' convention). The increase for common laborers was somewhat more than the average, ranging from 60 to 75 per cent, as appears from a comparison of the advertisements for this class of labor in the people's penny paper, the _New York Sun_. A mass of interesting statistics has been collected by the author on this point from these advertisements. The special commissioner of the revenue, from much data in his possession, put the average advance of wages at 60 per cent, and this in the opinion of the author is plainly substantiated from the hundreds of notices of increase, resulting from strikes, appearing from day to day in the newspapers.

[1] Consider the allotment system, the savings banks, insurance companies, and popular loans as described in Chapter V; for the work of the charitable societies, see p. 301; for amusements, Chapter X.

The low wages of women were a special grievance. When it was known in the winter of 1863–1864 that these had practically made no advance, general sympathy was aroused; and when, a year later, it appeared that only a paltry advance of twenty-five per cent had been achieved, less than half that for men, the sympathy was increased.[1] In some lines of women's work no advance at all was made by the latter date, but on the contrary an actual decline. This seems scarcely credible, and yet the evidence is overwhelming. The most pitiable case was that of the seamstresses, thousands of whom were employed in making army clothing, some hired directly by the government, some by contractors under a vicious system of contracting and sub-contracting. In the Philadelphia Armory in 1861 women were paid by the government seventeen and one-half cents for making a shirt, three years later, at the very time when prices themselves were highest, only fifteen cents, and at this latter date the contractors were paying only eight cents. A small advance by the government toward the close of the war was of little real benefit, since most of the work was then being given over to the contractors whose prices grew lower and lower. Protests in public meetings, the most harrowing tales in the newspapers, and petitions to the Secretary of War and to the President appeared useless, and the poor victims were left to their fate, undoubtedly the greatest sufferers of any class from the war; they suffered even more than clerks in mercantile pursuits and college teachers.[2] Aside from

[1] These figures are reliable, coming from the secretary of the Women's Protective Union of New York; the *New York Tribune*, December 14,1864.

[2] There is an abundance of material on this subject. See the *New York Sun*, June 12, and September 21, 1864.   An average week's wage paid by the contractors in 1865 was $1.54.   In the middle of 1864 a woman in New York, using the sewing machine and furnishing her own thread, and working fourteen hours per day, made four pairs of cotton drawers at four and one-sixth cents each, or sixteen and three-fourth cents per day; another woman got five and one-half cents for making a pair of canton flannel drawers, and succeeded in making two per day.

the greed of the contractors and the apathy of the government, other explanations of the low wage were the well-known competition of women with one another and their immoderate pride. Nine-tenths of the sewing women were Americans who preferred to stick to the needle and starve rather than engage in domestic service, which was more remunerative, and thus put themselves on a plane of equality with the negroes and the Irish.[1]

In resisting increase of wages capital naturally called to its aid every possible form of cheap labor; more employment was given to women, to young boys as apprentices, to unskilled labor, negroes, and immigrants, and more use was made of labor-saving machinery; toward these cheap rivals the unchanging attitude of the labor world was that of extreme hostility.

To a surprising degree women were already the rivals of men in the industrial world when the war opened. Such important industries as those of the cotton, woolen, and paper mills, and the manufacture of shoes and rubbers, were very largely dependent on women, while many others employed them to a less extent; in all, according to one estimate, they performed one-quarter of the manufacturing of the country.[2]

[1] The *London Times*, April 14, 1864. Another example of the working of this principle of pride in industrial affairs was brought to light in the cotton mills of Lawrence, Massachusetts, in 1865. There, owing to the scarcity of labor, almost any one presenting himself or herself for a position was accepted; this was necessary in order to fill up the ranks of the operatives. But the quality of the operatives declined, mill work became for the time less respectable, and many women whose place was naturally in the mills refused longer to remain there, but went rather into dressmaking and similar vocations.

[2] This is the estimate of the director of the census of 1860. See a valuable book, *The Employment of Women, A Cyclopedia of Women's Work*, Virginia Penny, Boston, 1863. Women were largely employed in the manufacture of jewelry, gold pens, watches, ready-made clothing, matches, perfumery, fireworks, flavoring extracts, hats, bonnets, etc.; in all industries, in other words, where the work was light. The author has collected a mass of statistics as to the proportion of men and women

In itself this was not objectionable; the grievance lay rather in the opening of new places to women. Striking printers were frequently superseded by women, as were also dissatisfied clerks in commercial offices, in dry goods stores, shoe stores, and other mercantile houses, and in the great department offices of the government at Washington; their work in all kinds of light manufacturing, on the farms, and in the country schoolhouses increased in extent. Thus to many men, whose positions they usurped, the low wages of women were far from being a matter of commiseration.

The employer's attitude toward the apprenticeship system was a standing grievance. Sometimes running his shop with few hands, he would accede to the demands of his men for more wages and then fill up the shop with young boys to learn the trade, who received very low wages or none at all. Formerly the unions had assumed to dictate, according to the number of journeymen employed, how many apprentices should be accommodated in each factory, but now when capital was especially aggressive, they found themselves helpless. The molders lost a number of strikes on the question, notably a long strike in Philadelphia, while the molders' union officially declared that the "boy question" was one of their leading grievances. "The true secret of this move of the employers," said *Fincher's Trades' Review*, "is to glut the market with journeymen." It meant less pay, no work, and finally no occupation. "With no check upon them to prevent this inundation of apprentices, are we to expect that the employers will magnanimously refrain from using this unpaid labor?" It was a mere subterfuge, whereby the employers hoped to escape from their obligation to grant honest wages.[1]

employed in the various industries. The census of 1860 declared that there were then employed in manufacturing pursuits 1,100,000 persons, of whom 285,000 were women.

[1] *Fincher's Trades' Review*, June 6, 1863.

Just as noticeable was the tendency to hire more unskilled labor to do the work which really belonged to skilled men. This was done as a matter of necessity in some instances because labor was scarce, in others as a matter of choice because the inferior labor was cheap. Especially deteriorated was the quality of the operatives in the cotton mills of Massachusetts when these resumed operations in 1864; all applicants, even the most ignorant, were given places and no questions asked. The same tendency was noted in other lines.[1]

The competition offered by negroes was small, but in many places it called forth opposition which frequently passed beyond mere protest into bloodshed and murder. Longshoremen especially took offense at this invasion. These laborers were Irish, who at that time in the industrial world seldom got beyond the pick and the shovel, and therefore felt the threatened competition keenly; furthermore, the two opposing classes felt a violent racial antipathy toward each other. Along the docks of Chicago, Detroit, Cleveland, Buffalo, Albany, New York, Brooklyn, Boston, and other places, the introduction of negro strike breakers was often a signal for fierce riots, in which the striking Irishmen sought by stones and brickbats to prevent the new hands from taking their places. In the spring of 1863, in the months immediately preceding the draft riots in New York, the two races on a number of occasions clashed in this way on the water front of the city, and murders were frequent. In June, the month before the riots, three thousand longshoremen began a strike for higher wages, which for most of them ended in failure, and in this, their supreme effort, the sons of Erin saw their black rivals, under police protection, taking their places. It was the heaping of insult upon injury, the

[1] *Report of the Special Commissioner of the Revenue*, U. S. Senate Executive Documents, 39 Congress, 2 Session, No. 2, p. 21.

culmination of months of bad blood and ugly feeling. In
another month's time came the drafts, which in the minds

of a large part of the industrial classes, already deeply stirred,
was another name for forced military service in behalf of the
hated negro rivals, and at the head of the rioting mobs were
the angry and defeated longshoremen.   Industrial discontent was a fundamental cause of the riots.

Immigrants as a class of cheap labor greatly surpassed in
numbers and importance any of the classes yet considered.
A foreigner, usually mild and docile in new industrial relations, was generally sure of a position, his services were
openly advertised for in many instances as preferable to
those of native labor, and extraordinary efforts were made
to attract him to the country.   Employers of labor, ward
politicians desiring to swell the number of newly made voters,
and recruiting officers for the army stretched forth arms of
welcome abroad; on almost every side there was genuine
welcome.   Only labor stood apart and took offense at every
manifestation of the country's attitude toward the oncoming
tide.

It was exasperating to the labor leaders to see the many
persistent attempts of employers to encourage immigration.
Oftentimes shops, against which a strike was declared, sent
private agents to Europe to secure help; mines and railroads
suffering from the want of labor did the same; fifteen thousand foreigners were imported to build the Atlantic and
Great Western Railroad.   State governments lent their assistance, especially the state of New York.   By the income
from a head tax on every immigrant she was safeguarding the
interests of the newcomers at Castle Garden, just as she had
been doing since the late forties.   Officials were at hand to
board incoming vessels for the purpose of checking baggage
and preventing irresponsible outsiders from tampering with
the passengers; there was a medical inspection, man by man,
and certain classes were excluded, such as women with young

children and no husbands and incapable of earning their
own living, young unmarried girls about to give birth, and the
aged and infirm of both sexes unable to earn their living and
without friends.[1] On being admitted to the premises the
strangers were addressed in a company, letters were distributed, advice given not to listen to strangers, where to procure railroad tickets, where to apply for work, and where to
find baggage wagons; there were registration and information bureaus, ticket offices, and registries of boarding houses.[2]
Some states, less favorably situated for immigration than
New York, maintained permanent agents at Castle Garden to
induce settlement in their respective borders, while other
states, such as Ohio, West Virginia, and Missouri, dispatched
their agents abroad.

Finally the United States was induced to create the office
of Commissioner of Emigration, with offices and assistants in
New York, and by way of further national encouragement
Congress made legal in this country contracts signed in
Europe by prospective emigrants, whereby the latter guaranteed to repay out of future wages all money advanced for
their transportation; and, further, Congress took pains formally to declare that no man, claiming citizenship in a
foreign country, would be forced against his will into the
military service of the United States. To take advantage
of these laws the American Emigrant Company was formed,
with a capital of $1,000,000,[3] with the avowed purpose of

---

[1] Ship captains bringing such were liable to a fine, but any of the classes
were allowed to land if they could give a bond of $1000 that they would
not become a charge on the institution, that is, Castle Garden, in five
years.

[2] See a very valuable document, *Report on the Labor Market, etc., in
New York*, by T. D. Shipman, in Canada Agricultural Reports, 1865–
1866 ; this is a complete description of the administration of Castle
Garden. Castle Garden was supported by a head tax of $2 on each immi-
grant.

[3] $500,000 of this was paid up.

NB

importing labor to order through the medium of agents scattered in all the principal cities of Europe; an employer, desiring workers, needed only to make his wants known at one of the many offices of the company scattered in the cities of this country, and the men would be imported as ordered.[1]

The welcome of the naturalization laws, the same in war as in peace, was a strong inducement to immigration and in the crisis seemed to work against the interests of labor. In the city of New York, which boasted of more naturalized than native voters, sixty thousand foreigners had been admitted to citizenship in the previous decade; in the beginning and middle of the war the number admitted was small, for men with their first papers refrained from taking out their final papers in the hope that thereby they might escape conscription and other military responsibilities, although this was legally impossible.[2] But in 1864, in the two or three months before the war election of a President of the United States, twenty-five thousand foreign residents of the city came forward and were naturalized; the figure was of "prodigious and unheard-of dimensions," declared a leading paper. The occasion was extraordinary, the supreme test of strength between political parties in time of civil war on the fundamental questions of the war, and hence the incentive for the politician to roll up big lists of new voters was very strong. In Brooklyn, Boston, San Francisco, and other places, as well as in New York,

---

[1] The company charged a fee of $1 on application for workers, and on the delivery of the same $10 each for skilled workers, $6 each for agricultural workers, $5 each for house servants, and $5 each for boys learning a trade.

[2] By an express law it was sought to make foreigners with their first papers liable to the draft like full citizens; this caused a storm of wrath and was one of the things that helped to make the draft riots in New York. At the approach of a draft the foreign consulates were crowded with the first-paper men, claiming the protection of their country.

the naturalization courts before the election were equally
crowded.[1]

In this last year of the war foreigners widely accepted the
generous welcome to citizenship. Few phenomena of the
period fill the present generation with more amazement.
The new voters in the one city of New York might have
determined the fate of the most important election ever
held in the history of the country, and yet the privilege
of casting a ballot in the crisis was freely bestowed on
strangers, who understood little of the issues at stake in the
struggle. Certain elements in the labor world, especially
the newly formed unions, bitterly opposed this eagerness to
make new voters, because it constituted an invitation to
men of the old world to come to these shores.[2]

To the question how far the government sought to attract
foreigners hither for military reasons it is impossible to give
a definite answer; unquestionably, however, considerable
effort of this nature was expended. A conscious step in this
direction was the homestead law and other laws for the
liberal disposition of Western public lands and the building
up of that section, another the law granting to foreign
soldiers, honorably discharged from the service, full rights of
citizenship without the necessity of first papers; then there
was the establishment of the office of the Commissioner of

[1] In Brooklyn in 1864, up to October 27, 1200 had been admitted to
citizenship, "750 of whom were granted on the ticket of the chairman
of the regular Democratic committee of King's County." In Boston
3200 were naturalized in the three leading courts in 1860, 600 in 1861,
300 in 1862, 180 in 1863, 2500 in 1864, and 450 in 1865. In San Francisco 980 were naturalized in 1864; in the Probate Courts and the Courts
of Common Pleas in the state of Ohio, 1861–1865, 24,000 new citizens
were made, and the records of the city and the United States courts would
increase this figure. See *Reports of the Commissioner of Statistics of the
State of Ohio.*

[2] There is an important book, *Naturalization, Embracing the Past History of the Subject and the Present State of the Law,* Charles P. Daly, New
York, 1860; this is in the Lenox Library, New York City.

Emigration, which the mayor of New York, in an acrimonious public correspondence with the commissioner of emigration, stigmatized as a "bait under fraudulent pretenses to enlist foreigners." [1]   Moreover, there was a strange lack of interest on the part of the government in regard to the common charges that immigrants were fraudulently enlisted and that they were led over to these shores in some instances by fair promises, and then through whisky, bluff, and threats, just before landing, led to join the army. After all, it was only necessary to get the foreigners landed; when this was accomplished, bounties could be relied upon to complete the work.   The correspondent of the *London Times* threw light on the subject when he pointed out that within twenty yards of Castle Garden there were two large recruiting tents with their flaming banners offering high bounties for recruits, and a half-dozen other such offices nearby.   If the immigrant had no purpose, no friends, and no money, as often happened, it was hard for him to resist the proffered temptation; the bounties offered generally were of sums larger than any he had ever handled or even seen, and the agents in the recruiting tents were of European nationalities, who well knew how to play on the weaknesses of their countrymen. [2]

Inasmuch as army service would tend to remove the newcomers from the field of active competition in the labor world, it might be supposed that labor would not object to the government's attitude and practices.   If the removal to the army had been permanent, this almost certainly would have been labor's position; but military service was temporary, and some of the foreign soldiers were sure to return to industrial pursuits.

[1] The *New York Times*, September 15 and 19, 1864.   For the laws in regard to the liberal disposition of the public lands there were many reasons existing before the special military consideration arose.

[2] The *London Times*, June 4, 1863.

Other influences favorable to the movement of European peoples westward over the Atlantic were to be found in that continent itself.   There were among other factors the depression of the English cotton industry, poor crops in Ireland, military conscription in Germany attending the Schleswig-Holstein War, and most cogent of all very low wages in comparison with the wages in this country.   This last must have had considerable influence over ignorant peasants, who little understood the mysteries of American paper money; to them $1.50 or $1.75 per day must have seemed a large sum.   A responsible official of Massachusetts at this time reported that an agricultural laborer in England, boarding himself, received thirty-seven cents per day, and in Germany smaller sums were paid for such labor.[1]

It is plain that practically all classes in the United States save native labor were a unit in favor of immigration; national officials, state officials, private corporations, the press and public in general supported the movement.   The opposition, based on the fear of cheap labor, called a few public meetings in the large cities, and representations on the subject were sent to various European labor papers, but the efforts could go no farther.[2]   A united national sentiment placed the laborites in a small minority.   In a brief period a remarkable change had taken place.   Ten years previously the whole country had been on fire with hatred of foreigners in the Know-Nothing movement; the war came on, and the country gave the foreigners a welcome that was as ardent as was the former hatred.   Few instances of such a rapid and complete transformation in public sentiment can be cited in the whole history of the country.   Only stern necessity

[1] See a reference in the *New York Spectator*, December 1, 1864, to a report of the Secretary of the Massachusetts Board of Agriculture on this subject.   This official had just visited Europe.

[2] The *Coöperator*, London, May, 1864, p. 182.   This publication may be found in the Boston Public Library.

could have brought it about, and labor stands convicted of class selfishness in insisting on its supposed interests in the face of the general welfare.[1]

Statistics show that more immigrants arrived in each of the last three years of the war than in either of the two preceding years; the arrivals in 1861 and 1862 respectively were naturally few in number, amounting to only about 89,000 people, but thenceforth to the end of the period they reached 200,000 per year. The total in the five war years was 800,000. In the newspapers of the time, along with column after column of the names of the drafted, the wounded, and the dead, long descriptions of battles, and various accounts of the manifestations of popular excitement, there is noted briefly the arrival in Castle Garden now of 1000, of 2000, or of 3000 immigrants on a single day, 10,000 or more in a week. To the present generation this phenomenon in time of war is as strange as that of the naturalization courts.[2]

Still another expedient of capital for withstanding increase of wages, in addition to the cheap labor of women, apprentices, unskilled laborers, negroes, and immigrants, was the use of labor-saving machinery. So far as possible employers sought to dispense with the necessity of relying on manual labor and to place more reliance on machinery, and

[1] Revulsion from Know-Nothingism had begun before the war.

[2] Slightly more than half of each year's arrivals were males, and this percentage did not materially increase during the war, as it must surely have done if any considerable number of foreigners came for the express purpose of being soldiers. Fifty per cent ranged from the age of fifteen to thirty, only ten per cent were above forty years, eight per cent below five years. Each immigrant brought into the country on the average $80. It was estimated in 1865 that up to that time immigrants had brought into the country $400,000,000. The British Commissioners of Emigration in their report for 1864 expressed the opinion that during the war there had been sent to the United Kingdom by late immigrants to the United States over $8,000,000. Between 1850 and 1860 no less than $50,000,000 was sent to Europe in this way by the banks and commercial houses. Much must also have been sent in packages and letters.

this tendency constituted one of the chief causes of the remarkable increase in the period of the number of patents issued by the national government. All that the laborers could do in opposition was to declare a strike, which in these instances usually proved a losing strike. The master coopers of New York endeavored to increase the use of machine-made hoops and staves; machine-made horseshoes became more popular; various patents were introduced for cleaning the streets by machinery; in the oil business pipe lines, tank cars, and tank steamers came into use. Each new device, as it proved successful, supplanted many men. The adoption of floating grain elevators in the harbor of New York, to lift the grain from the lighters and canal boats to the steamers, was attended with interesting results. The first one was erected in 1861, five in the next year, and many in the succeeding years, each doing its work in one-tenth the time required to do it by hand, and by the middle of the war all together succeeded in depriving thousands of laborers of their positions. In 1862 two thousand Irish laborers struck against their use, but after the men had stayed out for a long time, they lost their strike miserably. The next year the same scenes were enacted in Brooklyn, and while their countrymen across the river in New York were killing negroes and destroying property in the draft riots, the Irish shovelers in Brooklyn burned to the ground two large land elevators, which is another piece of evidence to show that industrial discontent was closely connected with the military crisis. Perhaps the greatest advance in the use of labor-saving machinery was made on the farms, where each new device was heartily welcomed, for farm labor was more scarce than labor in the cities and more contented.

The question arises, to what extent the industrial world was affected by the scarcity of labor. The army and the Western farms and mines were drawing thousands away from their accustomed positions. Did the increased employment of cheap substitutes and the use of labor-saving machinery succeed in filling the vacant places? In viewing this matter it must be remembered that it was literally as "Boys in Blue" that most of the Northern patriots took up arms; two million were twenty-one years of age or under, one million eighteen or under, eight hundred thousand seventeen or under, two hundred thousand sixteen or under.[1] Plainly thousands upon thousands of these soldiers left no vacancies behind them in the industrial world, inasmuch as they enlisted in the service before they had taken such a position for themselves. Some came from the well-to-do classes and had never worked with their hands. Moreover, the industrial world then, in proportion to population, contained fewer places than at present; industrial organization was in its infancy. Many more men than at present were outside the organization, on the farms, busy in the small home industries, or occupied in other ways, and they constituted an army of reserves which the expanding industries had yet to call upon. Therefore the formation of armies crippled industry much less than would be the case now. A suggestion of the movement of these reserves into new spheres is to be seen in the tendency of population, much commented upon at the time, to move into the city from the country, especially in the East, where the cities were rapidly gaining in population and the country districts losing. Other reserves were from the cities themselves. It was as members of this growing industrial army that more women pushed forward in industrial pursuits, and more apprentices, unskilled laborers, negroes, and immigrants found employment. The advantage of labor-saving machinery lay in the same direction. The result was a total output of manufactured product that exceeded anything of the kind that the country had ever seen. War-

[1] Estimates of the adjutant general of Iowa.

time scarcity of labor has surely been exaggerated. It is not intended here to deny that the war contemporaries saw and complained of labor scarcity; it cannot be denied that the railroads, which inserted in a people's penny paper like the *New York Sun* standing advertisements calling for thousands of laborers, were in great need; it is known that the Atlantic and Great Western Railroad, after importing its laborers from Europe, had almost infinite difficulty in holding them to their tasks, that the incorporators of the Union Pacific Railroad wished some power given them, whereby they might hold their laborers to their tasks, and that the mines and factories in many instances would have taken more men than actually presented themselves. All these facts are admitted. But actual manufacturing accomplishment was manifestly large, and on this fact is based the claim that the labor scarcity of the time has been exaggerated by succeeding generations. Industrial positions were readily vacated, but in a very large number of cases readily filled; comparatively few remained permanently unfilled.

In the light of these things the failure of wages to advance as much as prices is partially explained. The quality of labor deteriorated. If a man took a position higher than that for which he was fitted, his employer was justified in refusing to him the increase of wages which would have been the due of the skilled man. Thousands of unskilled men in this way stepped into improved positions; their lot in life was bettered; and in view of the quality of the work done the wages were probably not very low. To these men, who took higher positions and whose number is unknown, the war was a blessing.

In addition to the forced competition of cheap rivals labor had other grievances. One was the order system. In cotton, iron, and glass factories, in the mines of Pennsylvania, in printing establishments quite generally, and in some other concerns the men were paid in whole or in part in orders on

stores. Sometimes the men had no use for the articles called
for in the order; they could not pick their store; and they
were forced to pay the prices asked. In some cases the
stores were owned by the company employing the men,
and were situated in secluded places where there was no
possibility of competition and prices were high. In the annual strike in the Pennsylvania coal mines the practice was
always presented as a grievance until it was finally abolished
by the Legislature in 1863. In the glass and iron districts
of New Jersey, and in certain industries in New York,
there was also great abuse of the system, and by the end of
the war in the last-named state a bill was pending in the
Legislature for its abolishment.[1]

"Eight hours for work, eight hours for rest, and eight
hours for social and moral recreation" was another rallying
cry. Long hours, said the resolutions of a large meeting in
Philadelphia, called to advance the eight-hour movement,
caused physical demoralization, mental non-development,
premature old age, compulsory idleness, and overproduction. A day's work on the street railroads was sixteen hours,
twelve and twelve and one-half hours in woolen mills with
time out for breakfast and dinner, twelve in the paper mills,
and eleven in the cotton mills; but these were exceptions.
The average day was ten hours. This represented a decided
reduction from the common twelve and fifteen hours of 1850,
brought about in the short space of fifteen years not so
much by legal enactment as by the force of public opinion.
Now the law's aid was sought to secure a further reduction to
eight hours. Many mass meetings demanded the change,
and in a number of states the question became of political importance; it was easily the most widely discussed reform
in the whole labor program after the question of wages, and

---

[1] The *New York Herald*, May 9, 1862; the *New York Coach Makers'*
Magazine, November, 1863; the *Printer*, January, 1863; *Fincher's*
Trades' Review, June 27, 1863.

acquired special prominence when with the close of the war
the latter question lost much of its prominence. The agitation continued to increase until in 1869 the movement
received an impetus by the passage of a national law requiring eight hours for all laborers and mechanics employed
by or in behalf of the United States.[1]

Akin to this movement was the early closing movement,
an attempt on the part of the clerks in mercantile pursuits
to force their employers to close the stores at seven in the
evening and on Saturday afternoons. Little was accomplished. Clerks were afraid to organize after the manner
of laborers, for in any one establishment they were fewer
in number than the latter and constantly under the eye of
the employer; moreover, their station in life was higher
than that of the men in the shops and their places consequently were easily filled. Not even on the question of wages
did they make strong united demands, so that in general there
was no advance in their wages until near the end of the war.[2]
As a class clerks probably suffered from high prices more than
most other classes living on a fixed income, although probably
not as much as college professors and sewing women; ministers of the gospel had the substantial benefit of being "tided
over" by donation parties, of which social institution there
were hundreds of instances in all parts of the country.

The employers' treatment of the unions was naturally
a cause for complaint. Capital was moving in larger masses
than ever before; allied interests were constantly drawing

[1] The *New York Tribune*, July 7, 1865, contains an abstract of a report
on the subject by a committee of the Massachusetts Legislature. See
also the *Aldrich Report*, U. S. Senate Reports, 52 Congress, 2 Session,
No. 1394, Volume I, p. 179. The newspapers and labor papers are filled
with material on the subject. The national law of 1869 was not enforced.

[2] This late increase ranged from fifty to seventy-five per cent. No
advance was given earlier because the clerks were generally working on a
yearly contract, which did not expire till the close of the year; this was
an arrangement that was not so flexible as that of the shop workers.

together in closer and closer relations, while to the laboring classes the same right to organize was only grudgingly conceded. There were the employers' lockouts. The Piano Manufacturers' Association of New York, by rigidly locking their doors and refusing to take back any employee who would not leave the union and sign his name as a guarantee, threw twelve hundred men out of work. Many of the much-heralded victories of labor were won only when the men consented to treat with the bosses man for man and not as a union. Letters of recommendation, a certificate from the man's last employer to the effect that the former had been regularly and honorably discharged, were often insisted upon before giving a position to a man, while only immigrants were freely taken without such letters. This was galling. One letter issued in Massachusetts assumed to give to the bearer "liberty to work elsewhere." On resolving to fight the custom the Machinists' and Blacksmiths' Union officially declared to its members: "This will be a struggle that will call forth all that is noble in our organization to carry it to a successful termination." The use of the judicial injunction in labor disputes, prominent at the present time, was almost unknown.[1]

There were two hardships suffered at the hands of civil governments. One was the practice of the state penitentiaries, which not only sold prison-made goods in the open market at low prices, but even hired out the prisoners to work for contractors outside the prison walls at low rates. Rhode Island let her men for forty cents a day, New Jersey for from twenty to thirty cents, Massachusetts for one dollar and sixteen cents. The evil is obvious.[2]

[1] On the letters of recommendation, see *Fincher's Trades' Review*, February 20, 1864. Injunctions were frequently used in other lines; for example, in the constant disputes that arose in the progress of the railroads.

[2] For a report on this subject, see *Report of the Board of Inspectors of the Rhode Island State Prison*, 1866.

Then there was the strong military arm of the government, which on occasions was harsh to labor as well as to every other class in society. In St. Louis and Louisville the military commanders in charge, by stern proclamations, forbade strikes and enforced the order by military arrest; four leaders in a strike in a government gun factory near West Point, New York, were arrested and sent to Fort Lafayette; General Thomas in Tennessee arrested two hundred striking mechanics and sent them north of the Ohio River, while the Reading Railroad in Pennsylvania, tied up by striking engineers, was seized and run by the military power of the United States; the striking longshoremen in New York stood by idle while the government transports were loaded by deserters under a strong guard of soldiers.

Certainly labor's grievances were many and by no means trivial; and yet, although the wages question, the employment of cheap substitutes, the order system, long hours, capital's uncompromising attitude toward the unions, the unfavorable practices of the state, all were fundamental grievances and the claims advanced against them just, still because of the popular interest in the war and in politics it was exceedingly difficult to secure an adequate hearing for them before the public, and for everything that labor gained there was a hard struggle.

The behavior of the laboring men in the struggle and the methods which they employed in waging it may be anticipated. Some, moved by patriotism, put aside their troubles and joined the army; some, faint-hearted or perhaps discouraged by long disappointment, withdrew to the farms of the Middle West or to the mines of the far West; others roved about from city to city in search of work and satisfaction; while a stanch band in every labor center remained at their posts, and of these a still smaller fraction organized labor unions. It was this small fraction that accomplished the most for the cause. They saw that individual complaints and demands were too often spurned by the employer, and that redress could better be gained by united action. Unions of capital were forming fast, and unions of labor seemed the logical defense for the working men.

Labor unions were not new. They had existed in large numbers in the flush times before the panic of 1837, when industrial conditions, although on a smaller scale, and the grievances of labor, were much the same as thirty years later. From 1837 to 1861 their number gradually diminished, and at the end of the period only a few local unions existed, together with a few national unions, such as the National Typographical Society, the International Union of Machinists and Blacksmiths, the Iron Molders' International Union, the Ship Carpenters' and Calkers' Union, and possibly one or two more. In general labor was contented when the war came, and little need of united action was felt.[1]

With rising prices the period of contentment ended and organization reappeared, much more active and extensive than earlier, commensurate in its extent with the increased wealth and size of the country. The formation of the new unions continued to 1865 and after that date, more vigorous in the beginning and middle of the war than in the last year of fighting, and more pronounced in the winter months when industry naturally somewhat languished than in the summer when all trades were apt to be busy. In the big industrial cities like New York and Philadelphia, in the middle of the period, there was scarcely a week when some new union was not formed, and in some weeks of November and December,

[1] Ely, in his *Labor Movement*, p. 60, says that the statement was made that in 1860 there were twenty-six trades with national unions; this is probably an exaggeration. After an investigation covering a period of over six years and including much newspaper and other material, the present writer has found certain evidence of only the four national unions mentioned in the text as existing before 1861. Of these that of the printers was formed in 1852, of the machinists and blacksmiths and of the molders in 1859, and of the ship carpenters in 1861.

1863, scarcely a night passed without new societies; on some days the papers chronicled the formation of two, three, and even a half-dozen. Everywhere the labor leaders were urging the men to organize; this was the watchword. At one mass meeting in New York over fifty different unions, most of which were new, were represented, and by a conservative estimate the total number of new unions in the city may be placed at three hundred.

At first many of the new societies embraced only a single shop, while few originally went beyond the confines of a single city. But gradually new national organizations were effected, eleven at least by 1865.[1] These larger groups sought to unite all the local societies of a single trade; to establish a system of intelligence whereby employers and employees might be better enabled to get and fill positions, without the necessity of travel over the country in search of one another; to make known the state of the trade in different parts of the country; to afford assistance to members while traveling; to guard against unprincipled journeymen and employers; and to provide benefit in case of sickness and death.[2]

The unions, both national and local, were small. That of the iron molders was perhaps the largest, having 157 local unions and from 7000 to 8000 members;[3] the machinists and blacksmiths had 140 local unions, the railroad engineers 57, while other national unions were much smaller. Membership in the local unions was small; 500 out of 7000 to 8000 machinists in New York belonged to the union; the pianomakers' union of the same city mustered 600 out of a possible

[1] This number is probably incomplete; it includes the organization of the coach painters, railroad engineers, and the telegraphers in 1863; the miners, the plasterers, and the cigar makers in 1864; the hat makers, carpenters, coach makers, bricklayers and masons, and the journeymen tailors in 1865.

[2] The *New York Tribune*, January 16, 1865.

[3] The *New York Tribune*, January 9, 1866.

1500.[1] These significant figures plainly caution the present generation against exaggerating the importance of the wartime unions; they were numerous and bold in leadership, but they were small in membership and embraced only a small part of the labor world; the unions and the labor world were not synonymous terms. While the societies remained new and strange many men were loath to join them just because of their newness; another deterrent influence was the fear of the bosses, as was also the fact that in a large number of cases the pinch of low wages was not acutely felt as long as the extra contributions arising out of the war were coming in.

The unions had elaborate banners, badges, and cards of membership; there was usually an initiation fee of one dollar, and penalties for infractions of the rules, such as fines or occasionally expulsion for working for wages less than the sum demanded by the union. Meetings were regularly held monthly, weekly, and often during a strike daily. Week after week in the exciting summers of 1863 and 1864, when the claims of the war and of politics were so urgent, in a city like New York a hundred or more small meetings of the workingmen convened, earnestly planning for increase in their membership and for their class interests. It was one of the most significant characteristics of the social and industrial conditions of the times, unrecorded generally in the newspapers, unnoticed by citizens in general, yet important. Equally unnoticed but significant was the constant traveling about of the walking delegates, stirring up interest, forming new unions, settling difficulties, and stimulating local unions. The tyrannical nature of their sway was recognized, but the real need of their

---

[1] The national convention of the telegraphers in 1863 was attended by 9 delegates, that of the printers by 40; in 1864 the molders' convention consisted of 50 delegates, that of the ship carpenters of 20, that of the cigar makers of 23.

services acutely felt; young organizations could not dispense with them.[1]

The activities of the unions reached out in many different directions. In many cities one or more small labor papers were established, three at least in New York, and two in Philadelphia.[2] Because of high prices numerous coöperative stores were organized; there were over thirty of these, according to one estimate. Interest in this movement and in the contemporary undertaking of a similar nature in England was large; all the labor papers discussed the Rochdale experiments and the possibility of repeating them in this country.[3] In the large cities the small local unions of the different trades often united themselves for mutual benefit into trades' associations, and in Louisville, Kentucky, in the last year of the war these held a small national convention.[4] The unions, as a rule, did not go into politics, but for

[1] There is an interesting and rare book, *The Life, Speeches, Labors, and Essays of William H. Sylvis*, by James G. Sylvis, Philadelphia. Sylvis was president of the Iron Molders' Union, and as such was really a walking delegate; so also was J. C. Fincher, secretary of the Union of the Machinists and Blacksmiths, and editor of *Fincher's Trades' Review*. The letters and addresses of these two men frequently appeared in *Fincher's Trades' Review*.

[2] These included the *Daily Evening Voice* in Boston; the *Workingmen's Advocate*, the *Telegrapher*, and the *Monthly Advocate* in New York; *Fincher's Trades' Review* and the *Woman's Journal* in Philadelphia; the *Sentinel* in Buffalo; the *Iron Molders' International Journal* in Cincinnati; the *Mechanics and Workingmen's Advocate*, and the *Detroit Daily Union* in Detroit; the *Workingmen's Advocate* in Chicago; the *St. Louis Daily Press* in St. Louis; the *Miner's Weekly* in Belleville, Illinois; there was also the *Blacksmiths' Journal* and the *Printer*. Only one or two of these papers existed before 1860; their combined circulation did not equal twenty thousand copies weekly, whereas the largest labor paper in England, *Reynolds's Weekly*, had a circulation of three hundred thousand copies weekly.

[3] The *London Economist*, May 3, 1862; the *Coöperator*, London, gives full historical information of the movement in England. This may be found in the Boston Public Library.

[4] For an account of this convention, see *Fincher's Trades' Review*, October 15, 1864; this also contains a copy of the constitution adopted.

mayor of Boston one year a labor candidate received 613 votes;[1] this was an isolated instance and was universally deplored. In New York the workingmen themselves quickly foiled an attempt of the politicians to gain the control of the executive committee of the trades' association of that city and Brooklyn and even refused to allow laboring men, who were also politicians, to belong to the organization.[2]

The most important work of the unions was to formulate the complaints and demands of the men and to wage the strike that almost invariably followed upon the presentation of these to the bosses; this was the union's chief function, although there were many strikes waged without a union and many grievances redressed without any strike. Strikes were numbered literally by the hundreds, and like the formation of the unions, were far more numerous in the winter and spring than in the summer; although the strikes were usually peacefully settled and of short duration, seldom lasting more than a few days, there were some long and bitter struggles, lasting from two to six weeks and even longer. In Philadelphia two hundred machinists remained out for over a year, the machinists of New York for over two months; the grain shovelers and longshoremen of New York and the molders of Philadelphia and Troy also had long strikes. Acts of violence were few; there were some assassinations in the annual Pennsylvania coal strikes, there was the wreaking of vengeance on negro strike breakers and some violence in the molders' strikes in Troy, but beyond these instances obedience to law characterized the movement in almost every case.

A strike, then, differed from one of the present day in that

---

[1] This was in 1863; the total vote was 8966.

[2] The *New York Sun*, June 7, 8, and 11, 1863. In New York the trades' association held meetings in favor of municipal reform in 1864, but did not put up a labor ticket. The *Workingmen's Advocate* in Chicago came out openly for McClellan for President in 1864, but its action caused a storm of wrath.

it was less comprehensive; sometimes only a single shop was affected, and when all the shops of a certain trade were concerned, the men resumed work shop by shop as shop by shop gave in to their demands. A whole trade rarely stayed out till every employer capitulated, and sympathetic strikes, engaged in by a number of trades because of the troubles of one trade, were practically unknown. Finally strikes did not extend from one city to another, and no trade ever adopted as its own the grievances of the same trade in the next city. Oftentimes, in fact, far from assuming an attitude of mutual sympathy, kindred trades of different cities worked against one another's interests. Thus, the striking machinists in New York felt compelled to advertise in the papers of quite different cities, in those of Philadelphia, Baltimore, Washington, Boston, Providence, and Albany, requesting machinists in those cities not to come to New York, and the striking cigar makers of Chicago advertised even in the far-off papers of New York, asking the cigar makers in that city not to go to Chicago. This was a common custom, showing that labor was as yet but loosely organized.

The methods of the strike itself are familiar. After the newly formed union had voted the step, in many cases there followed a street parade, with its bands of music and flying banners; as many as fifteen hundred bakers paraded in New York, at another time twenty-five hundred coopers. The shop that resisted the union's dictation was "foul"; non-union men who worked there were "scabs," "rats," "blacklegs," and "black sheep." Union men who deserted the cause and went back to work contrary to the orders of the leaders were "blacklisted," that is, their names were posted in a "blacklist." In conspicuous places also were posted the names of all firms refusing to yield and the names of those complying. "Pickets" were stationed outside the store or shop against which a strike was declared, to incite others to strike and to interfere with and to persuade the strike breakers.[1] "Intimidation" of laborers was bitterly defended as labor's right, and a bill introduced in the New York Legislature to forbid it aroused the most passionate remonstrances of fifteen thousand workingmen assembled in mass meeting in New York.[2] Without the existence of the word itself there was yet the principle of the "boycott," as may be seen in the request of the New York coach drivers that all people refuse to deal with certain livery stables of that city, or in the efforts of defeated printers in different parts of the country to influence the public to withdraw patronage from certain newspapers. Arbitration as a method of ending strikes was not approved either by the men or by their employers, and was not in vogue.

Funds in aid of strikers came from many sources, from the particular trade itself, from the other trades of the city, and occasionally from distant cities. This was the nearest approach to sympathetic action that appeared. For a part of the time the striking machinists of New York received from all sources as much as $5 per day for each man. Agents were sent over the country to collect this, and more than $5000 was obtained, Philadelphia sending $2000. New York morocco dressers sent nearly $1000 to their striking brethren in Lynn, Massachusetts. A well-organized union like that of the molders regularly assessed its members for strike purposes, so that from this source molders, when on a strike, were sure to receive from $7 to $10 weekly; the national union in this way sent $5000 to the striking molders of Philadelphia.

Up to the autumn of 1864 strikes were generally successful, although to this statement there are important exceptions. The long-drawn-out contests were almost always victories for capital; almost without exception year after year the

[1] A New York judge dismissed a man arrested for this offense; the *New York Sun*, April 10 and 13, 1863, and November 10, 1864.

[2] The *New York Sun*, March 10 and April 8, 1864.

printers lost their strikes against the big newspapers;[1] the Brotherhood of the Footboard, the union of the railroad engineers, failed in a number of its efforts;[2] every strike against labor-saving machinery was lost. After the military victories of Sherman, Sheridan, and Farragut, and the reëlection of Lincoln in 1864, when gold began to go down and it seemed that prices might follow it in downward tendency, almost every strike failed. Capital was then obliged to be cautious and to retrench in every possible way and would make no concessions; there was even a possibility that the wages would have to be reduced if prices continued to go down.[3] The Workingmen's Union in New York at this time complained of the failures of strikes, and the newspapers affirmed the same, recording many instances of lost strikes. It was noticed that the men were then tending to leave the unions.[4]

In further proof that strikes were not altogether successful it need only be pointed out that wages never got as high as prices, and that all grievances were not swept away; labor did not get all it asked. Perhaps in any particular strike it put its demands high, expecting a compromise; but whatever the reason, it was not a complete success to demand a twenty-

---

[1] Horace Greeley of the *New York Tribune* was the first to suggest the union of the printers on a national scale, and he was the national union's first president, and after his presidency an honorary member of the society; but when the testing time of a strike on the *Tribune* came, he would not suffer dictation as to how to manage his paper.

[2] For example, with the Galena and Chicago Union, the Pittsburg, Fort Wayne, and Chicago, and the Reading; the first two roads were tied up for two or three days, the Reading for over two weeks.

[3] In 1865 reduction of wages caused a number of strikes.

[4] One reason given by the employers for not acceding to the demands of the men for more wages was that the work which they had in hand at any particular time was contract work, the agreement for which had been signed when prices were at a certain point; accordingly no advance in wages could be given till work came in on new contracts and higher prices.

five per cent increase of wages and then to accept one of ten, fifteen, or twenty per cent, yet this is what often happened.

The war closed with labor still regarding itself as aggrieved and persecuted, still arrayed against capital, still on the defensive and probably, from the standpoint of labor alone, entirely apart from all outside sources of aid, worse off than in 1860. But from the time when labor finally rose up in self-defense there had been improvement. Industrial wages had advanced from the low figure of 1863, the laborer was more sure of his daily bread from this source and of decent comfort than at the middle period of the war; his ability to lay by a part of the wage for a rainy day was improved, but he was still far from the good times of the previous decade. The crisis had been an extraordinary one. It was neither a time of industrial peace nor yet of profound strife; rather a time of peaceful agitation. With paper currency and rising prices, scarcity of labor, and extreme industrial activity, an unusual set of new conditions arose, to which it behooved labor as well as capital to seek adjustment. It was a time of changing relations on every hand. Capital and labor alike organized and pushed out along new lines; each sought to augment its share in the extraordinary profits of industry, and naturally the advantage lay with the richer and better organized class; but labor was perfecting its organization and laying foundations for the future.

CHAPTER VIII

PUBLIC IMPROVEMENTS

FROM industrial prosperity some degree of progress in public improvements may be inferred. Cities were the centers of transportation, manufacturing, and commercial life, and the profits of these operations were largely drawn thither, so that in spite of heavy taxation there must have been money for municipal betterment. Definite knowledge confirms this inference. In every city, in spite of the war, new buildings of every kind were being erected, dwellings, business houses, schools, and churches; the streets were blocked as in normal times by these operations, by the digging of water, gas, and sewerage systems, the construction of fire-alarm telegraphs, by paving and sidewalk construction, and by the laying of street-car tracks. Fire departments were progressing, and new parks were being opened.

Of Chicago in the middle of the war the *Chicago Tribune* said: "On every street and avenue one sees new buildings going up, immense stone, brick, and iron business blocks, marble palaces and new residences everywhere; the grading of streets, the building of sewers, and laying of water and gas pipes, are all in progress at the same time. The unmistakable signs of active, thriving trade are everywhere manifest, not at any particular point, but everywhere throughout the city, where the enterprise of man can gain a foothold." [1] The following year, 1864, more buildings were erected

---

[1] The *Chicago Tribune*, October 8, 1863.

than in any previous year; every street was blocked by mortar, bricks, and lumber.[1]

The city, originally built on the dead prairie level of the lake, without the possibility of cellars and adequate drainage, with a contaminated water supply and almost perpetual epidemics of disease, but fired now by an ambition for improvement, was literally torn up in every direction; in the words of the *London Times* correspondent, it was being "rebuilt all over." Every street was in process of being raised seven or eight feet, buildings, great and small, were being raised, moved, and repaired, cellars built under them, and drainage introduced.[2]   To reach a supply of pure water, a great tunnel running two miles out under Lake Michigan was begun, and after the war rapidly brought to completion. The statistics for street improvement are imposing. Twenty-one miles of sewers, 50 miles of water mains,[3] and 29 miles of gas mains were constructed, while the consumption of both water and gas increased 50 per cent, that of water rising from 1,700,000,000 gallons in 1860 to 2,500,000,000 gallons in 1864, and that of gas from 125,000,000 cubic feet in the one year to 170,000,000 cubic feet in the other.[4]   Twenty-two miles of streets were macadamized or graveled, and many miles paved; in one year over 20 miles of sidewalks were constructed.   Street-car mileage was increased, 125 miles of fire alarm telegraph installed, the pier into the lake extended and a tunnel under the river voted.

Counting buildings of all kinds and sizes, and probably also repairs and additions, 7000 structures were erected in the

[1] The *Chicago Tribune*, January 1, 1865.

[2] The change to the new level began in 1856.   On the health of the city, see p. 80.

[3] *Report of the Chicago Board of Public Works*, 1862–1865; this reviews both the water and the sewerage construction.

[4] These gas figures are for one company alone; there was a second company after 1862.   See *Report of the Chicago Gas Light and Coke Company*, 1864 (Yale Library).

city in 1863, and 8000 in 1864,[1] estimates, the approximate
accuracy of which is substantiated by the enormous consumption of lumber.[2] Population mounted from 109,000 to

[1] The *Chicago Tribune*, January 1, 1864, and January 1, 1865; the
Chicago Tribune, January 1, 1863, gives estimates for the buildings erected
in 1860, 1861, and 1862, but in values only, based on an inspection of archi-
tects' books. The values of the new buildings for the different years were
put as follows: 1860, $1,118,300; 1861, $797,800; 1862, $525,000; 1863,
$2,500,000; 1864, $4,700,000. The city building department, later organized, put the annual figures for later years much lower than the *Tribune's*
estimates for 1863 and 1864, but undoubtedly the department did not
count small buildings, while these were included in the paper's estimates;
furthermore, perhaps the *Tribune* included in its count all alterations of
buildings, which at that time were large in number because of the raising
of the level of the city.

[2] CHICAGO LUMBER TRADE

Receipts

	LUMBER	SHINGLES	LATH
	(feet)	(number)	(number)
1847	32,000,000	12,000,000	5,000,000
1852	147,000,000	77,000,000	19,000,000
1857	459,000,000	131,000,000	80,000 000
1860	262,000,000	127,000,000	36,000,000
1861	249,000,000	79,000,000	32,000,000
1862	365,000,000	131,000,000	23,000,000
1863	413,000,000	172,000,000	41,000,000
1864–5	501,000,000	190,000,000	65,000,000
1865–6	647,000,000	310,000,000	66,000,000

Shipments

1860	225,000,000	168,000,000	32,000,000
1861	189,000,000	94,000,000	31,000,000
1862	189,000,000	55,000,000	16,000,000
1863	221,000,000	102,000,000	30,000,000
1864–5	269,000,000	138,000,000	36,000,000
1865–6	385,000,000	258,000,000	61,000,000

— Reports of Chicago Board of Trade.

178,000, and the total enrollment in the schools from 16,000
to 29,000.   Such a record is indeed astounding for a period
of civil war, but it accords with the city's activity as a
meat-packing and grain center and with its progress in
manufactures and in the consumption of coal already set
forth.   The only possible explanation is the wave of prosperity that swept over the nation, particularly over the
agricultural West.

Philadelphia was almost as progressive.   In this healthful
manufacturing city the number of gas consumers increased
by 6000, the consumption of gas 33⅓ per cent, that of water
50 per cent, while 45 miles of water mains and 92 miles of gas
mains were laid, 1000 new street lamps set up,[1] and 45 miles
of street railways constructed.[2]   For three years over 2400
building permits were granted annually,[3] and in view of the
rapid extension of the water and gas systems it is impossible
to believe that any large number of these permits were not
used; moreover, there is contemporary evidence that in any
particular section of the city the extension of the public
services and building operations went along together.[4]

In some respects the growth of improvements in these
two cities was paralleled throughout the North, but not
without exception.   There was quite general advance in
municipal water systems where these were already established before the war opened, as in New York, Brooklyn,
Cleveland, Detroit, Hartford, Jersey City, and Louisville;
in Cincinnati there was but a slight advance, and in Boston

[1] Water pumped in 1860 amounted to 7,465,000,000 gallons, in 1865 to
11,050,000,000 gallons; gas manufactured in 1860 was 639,578,000 cubic
feet; in 1865, 844,516,000 cubic feet.   See the *Annual Reports of the Chief
Engineer of the Water Department* in Philadelphia City Documents, and
Annual Reports of the Trustees of the Philadelphia Gas Works.

[2] *Reports of the Several Railway Companies of Pennsylvania,* etc., Pennsylvania State Documents.

[3] *Reports of the Philadelphia Building Inspectors,* 1863, 1864, 1865, in
the city documents.

[4] The *Philadelphia North American,* March 9, 1864.

a falling off.[1] A few cities, such as Charlestown, New
Bedford, and North Adams in Massachusetts, New Haven,
Connecticut, Elmira and Auburn in New York, completed
their works and celebrated the event with great public rejoicing, but the active period for the development of waterworks did not set in till the next decade.[2] In all the Union,
when the war began, there were sixty-eight public water
systems, of which fifty-nine were in the North and nine in
the Confederacy;[3] at the same time the number of private
water systems was eighty.

With the expansion of the water systems there was constant improvement in the methods of fighting fires, as in
Springfield (Massachusetts), New Haven, Albany, Utica,

[1] In New York the consumption of water was 42,000,000 gallons daily
in 1860, 54,000,000 gallons in 1865; the Croton Reservoir in Central Park
was finished here in 1862, and over 25 miles of mains were laid. Brooklyn
laid 40 miles of mains and raised her consumption from 3,292,000
gallons daily in 1860 to 7,900,000 gallons in 1864; Cleveland consumed
260,000,000 gallons per year in 1860, 476,000,000 gallons in 1864;
Detroit 870,000,000 gallons per year in 1860, 1,000,000,000 gallons in
1864; Hartford 897,000 gallons daily in 1860, 1,500,000 gallons in 1863;
Jersey City 97,000,000 cubic feet daily in 1860, 148,000,000 cubic feet in
1864; Louisville 233,000,000 gallons per year in 1861, 453,000,000 gallons in 1864; Cincinnati 1,763,000,000 gallons per year in 1860,
1,980,000,000 gallons in 1864; Boston 18,000,000 gallons daily in 1861,
16,000,000 gallons in 1864, and 12,000,000 gallons in 1865. These figures are in every case taken from the city documents.

[2] Throughout the war such important cities as Providence, Milwaukee,
and Portland, and the smaller manufacturing centers in New England in
general were without waterworks. A typical celebration of the introduction of water was that in Charlestown, Massachusetts; see the *Boston
Daily Advertiser*, November 30, 1864. Business was generally suspended
and a vacation was granted in the public schools; there was a street
parade and public exercises. In 1800 there were 16 towns with waterworks, 12 of which were built, 1790–1800; 15 of the 16 were private
works. In 1825 the total number was 32, 44 in 1830, 64 in 1840, 83 in
1850, 136 in 1860, 243 in 1870, 3196 in 1896.

[3] One in Alabama, Georgia, Louisiana, North Carolina, and Tennessee
respectively, and 4 in Virginia; see the *American Gas Light Journal*,
November 1, 1861.

Washington, Augusta, Concord, Salem, Lynn, etc., where steamers were introduced to supplant the old hand engines; or in New York, Chicago, Cincinnati, Cleveland, Washington, Louisville, and San Francisco, where the fire alarm telegraph took the place of the watch towers and bell ringers. New York, the largest city, finally organized its paid fire department, while the next largest city, Philadelphia, did not take this step until six years later.

The consumption of gas, too, made quite general advance not only in Chicago and Philadelphia but in New York, San Francisco, Portland, Louisville, Providence, and many smaller cities.[1] Gas companies were everywhere prosperous. Of the 381 cities and towns supplied with gas at the beginning of the war, 337 were in the North, 44 in the South.[2]

In 27 cities, notwithstanding the war, the streets were dug up and street cars started for the first time, in Portland, Lowell, Lynn, Salem, Beverly, Somerville, Worcester, Providence, Hartford, New Haven, Norwalk, Albany, Troy, Rochester, Utica, Trenton, Paterson, Hoboken, Wilmington, Washington, Harrisburg, Detroit, Toledo, Columbus, Indianapolis, Louisville, and San Francisco,[3] a list which

[1] New York set up 1200 new lamp posts in the streets, San Francisco 1300; in Louisville the consumption of gas increased from 40,000,000 cubic feet in 1860 to 58,000,000 cubic feet in 1864.

[2] *Martin's Boston Stock Market*, Joseph G. Martin, Boston, 1886, p. 137; on the price of gas, see the *Banker's Magazine*, February, 1865, p. 648; the advance in Boston was from $2.25 to $2.75 per thousand, in Providence from $3 to $4, in Philadelphia from $2 to $3, in St. Louis from $3.33 to $3.50, in Pittsburgh from $1.50 to $1.60. The *American Gas Light Journal*, November 1, 1861, compares the gas systems of the North and the South. Although gas was discovered in the sixteenth century, it was first made practical by discoveries in Birmingham, England, in the last decade of the eighteenth century; London was first lighted by gas in 1814, Paris in 1820, Baltimore in 1816, Boston in 1822, New York in 1823, and Philadelphia in 1835.

[3] This list is probably incomplete; it is compiled from scattered but trustworthy references in newspapers, municipal reports, and town histories; in 1861, 2 lines were built; 1862, 4 lines; 1863, 13 lines; 1864, 7 lines; 1865, 1 line.

is impressive not only from its length but from the diversity of the sections represented. Everywhere franchises for the new roads were eagerly sought and generally readily granted, while in cities where the lines had been established when the war started, remarkable progress was achieved. The greatest mileage laid down, 45 miles, was in Philadelphia, but a close second was New York, where the laying of over 30 miles of track left the streets of hardly any section of the city undisturbed. Traffic in the latter city was practically doubled during the course of the war, 34,000,000 passengers being carried in 1860, and 60,000,000 in 1864.[1] Among the new lines in New York were the famous crosstown line and the belt line; in Brooklyn the Coney Island line began to carry people to that famous resort, then just at the outset of its popularity. "Projects for laying the streets of New York with railways are as plenty in the Legislature as blackberries," said a contemporary; but in one year so fierce was the rivalry that out of fifty such schemes only two or three succeeded in running the legislative gauntlet. The Broadway franchise was the one most hotly contested. A responsible company of capitalists, in imitation of similar undertakings in London and Paris, at a cost of $8,000,000 would have laid an underground railway, not then called a subway, under this great street if the veto of two different governors, based on the ground that the charters disposed of public interests and public property without adequate return, had not been interposed. The project was an old one, as were also the plans for an elevated road and for an East River bridge, but these latter proposals did not then reach the tangible form of successful bills in the Legislature. In Massachusetts the track mileage of the street railways and the number of passengers carried increased 100 per cent.

[1] The *Annual Report of the Institute of the City of New York*, 1865–1866, p. 612, contains many valuable statistics of the New York lines.

Inasmuch as this was but the natural continuation of the movement in favor of the new cars which began in the previous decade, it was doubtless not much affected one way or the other by the state of war. Horse cars were an American invention, introduced on Fourth Avenue, New York, for the first time in any city of the world in 1831; they began to run there permanently in 1852, in Boston in 1856, in Philadelphia in 1858, in Chicago, St. Louis, Baltimore, and Cleveland in 1859, and in Syracuse, Buffalo, and various other places in 1860; in the next five years the movement struck the smaller cities. As inducements to investors to place money in the new enterprise there were the easy conditions of franchise[1] and the generally accepted fact that the new cars had demonstrated their efficiency and had come to stay. Many points in the innovation appealed to the public. Though heavier and larger than busses, the cars were more convenient because of their numerous entrances and exits; their rates were lower, and as they were drawn on rails and thus confined to one section of the street, they were less liable to cause accidents; furthermore, the use of the smooth rails lightened the burdens of the horses. Busses, on the other hand, were disagreeable and in general disfavor on account of their noise, their jolts and jars, their irregularity, their hard wear on the streets, and finally the unprogressiveness of their proprietors, who, like the owners of ferries, exhibited a spirit too common to the possessers of a monopoly of public interests. None but the owners themselves of the old lines opposed the new order of things, and they were powerless.[2]

[1] See p. 178.

[2] In some cities experiments were made in the use of the dummy steam engine to run the cars; this was the beginning of the use of this engine for such purposes. Rates were commonly fixed by law at five cents; when prices were high the companies endeavored to get permission to charge higher rates, but this was never given; in defiance of law the New York companies began to charge six cents, and great public op-

In street improvements, so heavy was the special taxation arising out of the war, there was generally a decline, ranging from 25 to 50 per cent or even higher; many a city ordinance for street improvements was allowed to go unexecuted.[1] No money could be afforded for the streets. In Portland, Maine, the tax rate almost doubled in five years, while valuations increased one-third;[2] in Boston rates mounted 75 per cent, valuations 50 per cent; in New York rates rose 50 per cent, valuations 6 per cent.[3] It was in face of these heavy special exactions that Chicago accomplished so much for her streets,[4] and that San Francisco spent literally millions on her thoroughfares.[5] But these two cities were exceptions, and some cities in their disbursements did not go much

position was expressed, but the roads persisted. The busses raised their rates from six to ten cents, and in some cases to a higher rate, and consequently lost patronage. This account of the horse cars has been drawn from the newspapers, municipal documents, and local histories.

[1] Boston spent on her streets in 1860–1861, in gold, $205,000, in 1864–1865, $156,000 in paper; Cincinnati $93,000 in 1860, $78,000 in paper in 1864; considering the high rate of wages this was a heavy decline.

[2] $244,000 were assessed on the tax payers in Portland in 1860, $805,000 in 1865.

[3] The tax rate in Portland was $10.80 per thousand in 1860, $28 in 1865; total valuations in Boston mounted from $276,000,000 to $371,000,000, taxes from $2,600,000 to $5,000,000; in New York valuations in 1860 were $570,000,000, taxes $9,758,000, in 1865 valuations were $608,000,000, taxes $18,200,000. This high rate of taxation in New York led to much complaint of extravagance against the city government, and the Citizens' Association, the forerunner of the Citizens' Union of a later date, was formed.

[4] The tax rate in Chicago rose from $12 per thousand in 1861 to $20 in 1863, 1864, and 1865; in the same time the total valuations, both real and personal, went up from $36,352,000 to $64,709,000, and the amount of taxes from $550,968 to $1,294,183.

[5] San Francisco spent on her streets in 1860–1861 $308,168, which sum gradually rose year by year to $1,159,257 in 1864–1865. The tax rate mounted but little, from $28.50 per thousand to $29.80, but the total assessed values, real and personal, soared from $35,967,499 to $80,736,156. It must be remembered in connection with these figures that this city never got on the paper basis.

farther than to take care of the soldiers' families and to provide liberal soldiers' bounties; their streets they neglected.

Filthy streets became so common that the public health was menaced. Contractors, who had agreed to clean the streets at a certain figure with gold at a certain quotation, refused to carry out their contracts when gold and prices were higher, so that for weeks and months in the last part of the war, even during the hottest seasons, in New York, Philadelphia, and other cities the streets remained uncleaned; the tendency to disease, which was then very strong as the result of the presence of soldiers returned from Southern camps with their infections, was thus accentuated, whereas to combat the contagion arising out of the war the cities ought to have been in the very best sanitary condition. In New York there were 4000 more deaths annually than was usual in peaceful times, in Philadelphia 2000 more, and more in Providence and in all the state of Massachusetts.[1]

New York's sanitary conditions were generally bad. The 15,000 tenement houses, their stairways, closets, and cellars, their garbage cans and ash piles, were in very bad condition, overflowing with filth and breeding disease; many of the side streets were literally covered with manure with no attempt made to clean them, while to force the contractors to abide by their contracts was declared by the city officials to be impossible. There were 12,000 cases of

[1] In New York from 1855 to 1862 there were on the average annually 21,000 deaths, and 25,000 in both 1863 and 1864; in Philadelphia 17,000 in 1864 and 1865 respectively against a previous annual average of 15,000; 1200 in the last year of the war in Providence against a normal number of 1000; in the state of Massachusetts 28,000 in 1864; 22,000 in 1862. Conditions in New York were worse than in other American cities; the deaths there in 1863 represented 1 in 35.7 inhabitants, in Philadelphia 1 in 43.6 inhabitants, in Boston 1 in 41.2 inhabitants, in Newark 1 in 43.5 inhabitants, in Providence 1 in 45.3 inhabitants, in Hartford 1 in 54.8 inhabitants.

typhoid fever in one year; in the month of August, 1864, 1700 infants died, according to the reports of the Citizens' Association, double the number reported by the city officials, and in this same year 1500 cases of variola and varioloid were found by the inspectors of the association in a few days, together with 1200 cases of smallpox, of which only 2 cases had been visited by the city officials. One inspector "visited 5 domiciles in a single hour in which smallpox was prevailing within 50 feet of the largest dry-goods jobbing houses of the continent; and he saw children from whose faces the crusts of the pock had not fallen, passing back and forth through the narrow alley leading to their pestilential homes, and gathering unrestrained and apparently unnoticed about the entrance of the stores and offices of the vicinity, and upon inquiry at the time the fact was ascertained that smallpox had been constantly prevalent throughout that neighborhood for several months; that a succession of tenants, incoming and outgoing, had kept up a fresh supply of victims to the loathsome malady."[1] Public hacks and street cars were often used by smallpox sufferers; at death their clothing was frequently sold to second-hand dealers; there were many instances to show that victims of the disease often lived in rooms occupied by tailors at work on woolen clothing, who wrapped their children, sick with the disease, in the new garments, which were soon to be sold and scattered broadcast. In Washington there were over 1000 cases of the disease; a United States senator died of it, and the President of the United States was sick with it in a mild form. So absorbed, however, were the newspapers with other subjects that little was made of

[1] See the *American Journal of the Medical Sciences*, October, 1864, p. 423. The Committee of Hygiene and Health of the Citizens' Association of New York, which made the elaborate examination into the sanitary conditions of the city, published a very valuable report of its work through D. Appleton and Company, New York, 1865.

smallpox; it seemed to be a necessary evil, a result of the war that could not be avoided.

There were few public parks at this time. In her park system New York stood foremost, and in this she was getting a substantial return for heavy expenditures; her Central Park, the largest park in the country and one of the largest in the world, 843 acres in extent, a wilderness till the late fifties, was being rapidly and even lavishly developed at an average annual expenditure of $400,000 and was frequented by a rapidly increasing number of visitors.[1] Brooklyn also was lavish, spending $1,000,000 on her recently acquired Prospect Park, while Philadelphia, on the other hand, expended almost nothing on her new Fairmount Park. There were parks in Chicago, Boston, and Baltimore; none in St. Louis.

Building operations proceeded on an extensive scale in Chicago, Philadelphia, Brooklyn, and San Francisco, in the five leading cities of Ohio, and in such special centers as Springfield, Massachusetts, the seat of the government armory, and Lynn, the center of the developing shoe industry.[2] In New York and Boston, in the whole state of

[1] One million two hundred and nineteen thousand fifty-six pedestrians entered the park in 1861, and 3,219,056 in 1865; 467,849 vehicles entered it in 1861, and 1,425,241 in 1865. See *Reports of the Commissioners of Central Park.*

[2] In Brooklyn 1004 buildings were erected in 1864, and 1518 in 1865; see the *New York Sun*, January 11, 1865, and the *New York Tribune*, January 10, 1866. In 1864 and 1865 respectively there were erected in San Francisco 1000 buildings. From the reports of the *Ohio Commissioner of Statistics* the following figures are taken; they are for counties, and those counties are given which include respectively the cities of Cincinnati, Cleveland, Toledo, Columbus, and Dayton. In 1860 in Hamilton County 749 buildings were erected; in 1865, 549; in Cuyahoga County 185 buildings in 1860, and 548 in 1864, and in the same interval of four years in Lucas County the number increased from 102 to 308, in Franklin County from 220 to 306, and in Montgomery County from 236 to 418. For the record of Springfield and Lynn, see a Massachusetts State Document, *Aggregates of Polls, Property, Taxes,* etc.

Ohio, and in Massachusetts there was a decline, but in Illinois probably normal conditions.[1] From all available data the conclusion to be drawn seems to be that while building operations were very extensive in some centers, there was in the country as a whole a slight decline, though not a heavy one as has sometimes been maintained; and to this conclusion from the statistics in hand the unusual consumption of lumber, water, and gas lends weight, for much of the lumber, water, and gas must have been consumed in the construction of new buildings or used later in the processes of manufacture by the new manufacturing establishments. It is safe to say that if the men of this generation could walk the streets of the cities and towns of that day, they would not in general be impressed with evidences of suspended building operations.

A deterrent influence which seems to have made common the view that building then was largely suspended was the well-known high price of building materials; lumber and iron advanced 100 per cent or more, and soaring even above them were the prices of lead and other building materials. Pine clapboards at Albany, New York, December 31, 1861, were quoted at from $15 to $20, and three years later at from $55 to $60; while pig iron in New York, which in 1860 sold at from $20 to $27 per ton, reached $43

[1] In New York 2250 buildings were erected in 1860–1861; 1247 were commenced in 1863, 733 in 1864, and 1190 in 1865. See the *New York Tribune*, January 1 and August 3, 1861, and the *Reports of the Superintendent of Buildings* in the City Documents. In Boston 997 buildings were put up in 1860, 490 in 1861, 357 in 1862, 383 in 1863, 294 in 1864, 287 in 1865, and 414 in 1866; see *Reports of the Chief of Police* in the City Documents. In Ohio, roughly speaking, 26,000 buildings were erected in 1858–1860, 24,000 in 1861–1863, and 24,000 in 1864–1866. For the record of Massachusetts, see *Aggregates of Polls, Property, Taxes*, etc., referred to above. In Illinois 679 schoolhouses were erected in 1859, 557 in 1860, 382 in 1861, 321 in 1862, 349 in 1863, 528 in 1864, 510 in 1865, and 612 in 1866; see *Reports of the Superintendent of Public Instruction in the State of Illinois*.

to $80 in 1864.[1] Another important element, somewhat offsetting this and constituting a positive inducement to building, was the comparatively low price of land up to the very end of the war. Real estate was one of the last things to recover from the stagnation that resulted from the crisis of 1861; war taxes on land loomed heavy and forbidding, and this, together with the spirit of speculation that prevailed after gold began to advance, dictated that people should put their money, not into land, but rather into the stock market, where the returns would be large and quick and taxes not as heavy, and into railroad and bank stocks and government bonds. Every one wished to get rid of highly taxed land and to take up the better paying investments. Thus the real estate market was enlivened without any considerable increase in values; the land market was glutted. In the cities by the spring of 1865 on the leading business and residence streets there was an advance in land values from 1860 of only about 25 per cent, on the side streets none at all, and in the country only a little. This brought it about that the time was very favorable for the purchase of land by farmers, manufacturers, housekeepers, and all who would make use of the land themselves.[2] Valuations of real estate for the purposes of taxation, which made but little advance till after the close of the war, indicate the same situation in a general way.[3]

[1] On the Albany prices, see the *Merchants' Magazine*, May, 1865, p. 397. *The same*, February, 1866, p. 106, gives the quotations for lumber in Chicago. See the *Banker's Magazine*, October, 1865, p. 333, for pig iron in New York.

[2] On the prices of land, see the *Annual Review of the Commerce of Cincinnati*, 1864 and 1865; the *New York Spectator*, February 16, 1865; the *Chicago Tribune*, January 1, 1865; the *New York Herald*, March 7, 1864; the *New York Journal of Commerce*, May 6, 1864; the *New York Sun*, March 9, 1864.

[3] In Portland, Maine, valuations of real property rose from $14,400,000 in 1861, to $14,700,000 in 1864; in Cincinnati from $62,000,000 in 1861 to $67,000,000 in 1865; in Troy from $8,100,000 in 1861 to $8,900,000 in 1864; in the whole state of New York from $1,119,900,000 in 1860 to

Increase of incomes from rents was only moderate. For two years after the beginning of the war rents were lower than for many years; then increase set in, but by the spring of 1864 this had only succeeded in restoring the rates that had existed in the fifties; in New York City by 1865 the net advance from 1860 ranged only from 25 to 50 per cent. Bonds and stocks paid better than rents. This was another deterrent to building, but only for buildings to be rented. Everywhere it was in rentable property that building most declined, it persisted in property to be used by the owners themselves, namely, in factories, public buildings, business blocks, and dwellings. This was a common observation in every part of the country and probably is one explanation of the seemingly crowded condition of the cities. Rentable buildings were poor investments, and few were erected; therefore the cities with a growing population became crowded. After the war both land and rents went up rapidly.[1]

The number of new church edifices was conspicuous. In New York an "ecclesiastical stampede," a "migratory fever," was noted, affecting particularly the downtown churches, which were selling out and moving uptown; in three years 23 churches were built in the city, in two years 13 in Philadelphia and 15 in Chicago, and the religious newspapers bear ample testimony to the fact that this activity was common in all parts of the country. The *New York Observer*, commenting upon it, said: "An architect in this city told us the other day that he had 40 churches in hand to

$1,141,075,000 in 1864; in Ohio from $639,000,000 in 1861 to $655,000,000 in 1864. Valuations of personal property at the same time went up much more rapidly; for example, in Portland for the years indicated above, from $9,000,000 to $12,000,000, in Cincinnati from $30,000,000 to $63,000,000, in the whole state of New York from $320,000,000 to $388,000,000, in Ohio from $248,000,000 to $350,000,000.

[1] But the very undesirability of rentable property and the decline in the building of such property, by restricting the supply, finally tended to increase rents; and the property tax worked in the same way.

build, the drawings for which he was preparing, or was already superintending their erection. We were surprised to learn that so many houses of worship were going up under the direction of one man, and we naturally infer that the number must be very great in the hands of the others. This has been seized upon as a favorable moment for building, not because labor and lumber are cheap, for they were never higher, but because money is plenty, and people are easily induced to part with it for a good cause." [1]

City halls were erected in Portland, Lowell, Boston, and New Haven; courthouses in Brooklyn and Cleveland; many hotels and many bank buildings in all parts of the country. Almost every college secured one or more new buildings. In Washington the Capitol of the United States was completed; Lincoln was inaugurated in 1861, standing at the Capitol building amid piles of unfinished masonry, blocks of marble, and piles of iron casting; and while the war was in progress, the great bronze doors of the building were set up, the Senate and House wings, with their imposing porticoes, completed, and the great dome reared.

As a rule the dwelling houses were of frame, very similar in appearance to those of the present day, although generally lacking the modern exterior decorations; as it appeared to foreigners, they were usually on one model. Within there were many of the conveniences of to-day, bathrooms, lighting by gas and oil lamps, and heating by stoves, hot air, hot water, and steam furnaces. Business blocks were generally below six stories, and never over seven, and office buildings were yet without elevators, but were built rather about an open space for light and ventilation. The first hotel elevator was put up in the Fifth Avenue Hotel, in New York, in 1861.

The cities were gaining rapidly in population in spite of the absence of young men in the army; the extension of the

---

[1] The *New York Observer*, December 10, 1863.

public utilities, the growth of the schools, other statistics of population, and common report all point to the one conclusion. Chicago's record of growth from 109,000 to 178,000 was unique. San Francisco advanced from 78,000 to 103,000 in the first two years of the war, and continued progress in the last two years of the struggle was made evident at the spring election in 1865, when 3500 more votes were polled than in 1863; this increase could not be accounted for entirely by the return of soldiers. The number of children of school age in the city in five years increased by 7000.[1] Philadelphia, which in 1860 had a population of 565,000, increased her voting list by one-half during the war, the consumption of gas by one-third, that of water by one-fourth; the public school enrollment increased from 63,000 to 74,000.

The population of New York City, if the state census of 1865 may be relied upon, declined from 813,000 to 725,000; but there is evidence that the ignorant masses in the tenements of the city thought that the enumeration had to do in some way with conscription and hence evaded it, while others evaded it for fear that it involved taxation. The press, noting the city's great industrial and commercial strides, the presence of many Southern refugees, and the general tendency of the country districts of the state to lose population to the cities, believed that the total population of the city in 1865 could not have been much less than 1,000,000.[2] The number of children taught in the schools under the complete or partial control of the Board of Education increased by gradual yearly growth from 148,000 to 216,000 in the five years of the war.

In the entire state of New York, out of the 22 cities with a population of 10,000 or over, 20 gained in numbers in the course of the war, but of the 924 towns below 10,000 over

[1] From 13,316 to 20,581.
[2] By the census of 1870 the city's population was placed at 942,292.

one-half experienced a decline. Throughout the East this was the situation, the large cities growing, the smaller cities and the country declining; even the cities in agricultural Wisconsin, none of them very large, gained more rapidly in the five years than the country districts of the state. This is a change that is to be accounted for by the greater excitement of the cities, and by the ever increasing attractiveness of the business and professional careers there.[1]

Births declined both in the cities and in the country, while the absence of thousands of marriageable men reduced perceptibly the number of marriages, although in 1864, on account of business prosperity and the return home of soldiers, marriages suddenly began again to increase and in some places were greater in number than for many years.[2]

Proceeding in the time of prolonged war, the signs of municipal progress which have been described are of especial significance; they were the same as in normal times, and they give a peculiar emphasis to the fact that local interests

[1] *New York State Census*, 1865; *Massachusetts State Census*, 1895, Volume I; *Rhode Island Registrar's Report*, 1865; in New York in 1865 there were 946 towns; 505 showed a decrease over 1860, and of these 463 had shown an increase in 1860 over the next previous census; in Massachusetts, out of a total of 385 towns, 197 showed a decrease in 1865 over 1860, and 102 of these had shown an increase in 1860 over 1855; of 31 towns in Rhode Island 18 showed a decrease in 1865 of which only 7 had shown it in 1860.   In Wisconsin, 1861–1865, the agricultural population increased 6.3 per cent, while that of the 34 cities and villages increased 37.4 per cent. Boston increased only slowly, from 177,992 in 1860 to 192,324 in 1865; St. Louis still more slowly, from 162,179 in 1860 to 164,456 in 1864.

[2] There were 5765 births in Boston in 1860, 4992 in 1864; in the whole of Massachusetts the decrease was from 36,051 to 30,249; in Rhode Island from 4660 to 3995.   There was the same decline in Philadelphia. The increase of marriages in 1864 was very noticeable; for example, in Chicago there were 1693 marriages in 1860, but 2779 in 1864 and 3000 in 1865; in Providence 739 in 1864 and 707 in 1865, although in no previous year after 1856 had they exceeded 660; in the whole of Rhode Island there were 1000 more marriages in 1864 and in 1865 respectively than in 1860; the same was everywhere noticed.

were not swallowed up in national interests, and that municipal development and municipal pride, as well as war, politics,
and business, claimed a share of public attention.[1]

[1] It may be of interest to some to consider the experiences of the
Border cities. Louisville got its first horse street cars and its fire alarm
telegraph, laid 12 or 13 miles of water mains, increased its consumption
of water over 200 per cent, added almost 1000 people to the roll of gas consumers, increased the consumption of gas 50 per cent, and spent on public
works, including streets, bridges, wharves, sewers, public buildings, etc.,
$173,000 in 1860, $21,000 in 1861, $24,000 in 1862, $87,000 in 1863,
$122,000 in 1864, $243,000 in 1865. Baltimore, which in 1860 laid almost
10 miles of gas mains, each year thereafter laid a smaller amount, and in
1864 laid less than ½ mile; she laid 100,000 feet of water mains in 1860,
47,000 in 1861, 26,000 in 1862, 32,000 in 1863, 56,000 in 1864. On
street improvements she spent $41,000 in 1862, $42,000 in 1863, and
$132,000 in 1864. In St. Louis 5764 consumers of gas in 1860 consumed
113,000,000 cubic feet of gas, 4994 consumers in 1863 consumed the same
amount; water rent collections increased from $114,000 in 1861 to
$123,000 in 1862, $147,000 in 1863, $170,000 in 1864, $208,000 in 1865,
and $248,000 in 1866. Cincinnati laid 21,000 feet of gas mains in 1861–
1862, 12,000 in 1862–1863, 22,000 in 1863–1864, 14,000 in 1864–1865;
consumed 1,763,000,000 gallons of water in 1860, 1,982,000,000 gallons
in 1862, 1,819,000,000 gallons in 1863, 1,902,000,000 gallons in 1864,
1,983,000,000 gallons in 1865; spent on her streets $93,000 in 1860,
$78,000 in 1864, $110,000 in 1865; she also built a fire alarm telegraph.
Of the four cities Louisville seems to have made the greatest strides forward during the period.

CHAPTER IX

EDUCATION

INTEREST in the cause of popular education was everywhere manifested. Vassar College, the first institution of collegiate rank devoted exclusively to the interests of women, and the Massachusetts Institute of Technology dedicated their first buildings toward the close of the war, the one by the gift of over $400,000 from Matthew Vassar, the other by the munificence of the state of Massachusetts. Ezra Cornell, multi-millionaire, reputed to have amassed a fortune of $5,000,000 as one of the associates of Samuel F. B. Morse in the development of the telegraph, founded Cornell University by the gift of $500,000 in money and three hundred acres of land.[1] Judge Asa Packer gave $500,000 and a large tract of land for a college to be founded at South Bethlehem, Pennsylvania, ultimately to be known as Lehigh University, while gifts of Quaker philanthropists made possible Swarthmore College, at Swarthmore, Pennsylvania. Ten other colleges were founded, scattered in all parts of the country.[2]

[1] Cornell also presented the little village of Ithaca, New York, the seat of the new college, with a public library. See p. 235 for the land grant endowment exacted by Cornell as the condition of his own gift to the college. Andrew D. White, the first president of the institution, was chairman of the Committee on Education in the Senate of the state Legislature, which accepted the gift.

[2] Bates College, Lewiston, Maine; Manhattan College, New York City; Hope College, Holland, Michigan; Ripon College, Ripon, Wisconsin; Wallace College, Berea, Ohio; Wilberforce University, Wilberforce, Ohio; and University College, San Francisco, California, in 1863: Kansas State University, Lawrence, Kansas; and Boston College, Boston, Massachusetts, in 1864: Lane University, Lecompton, Kansas, in 1865.

Daniel Drew, merchant and owner of transportation lines, before the war was over formed the determination to found the theological seminary for the Methodist Church which now bears his name; two new divinity schools were opened in Philadelphia, one in Ohio, and one in Illinois. American generosity founded two missionary colleges in foreign lands — the Syrian Protestant College at Beirut, Syria, and Robert College in Constantinople.

Endowments of existing institutions, especially in the last two years of the war, were everywhere announced and were on a scale wholly unprecedented. In New England Yale College, which on the eve of the war received from Joseph E. Sheffield $100,000 for the founding of Sheffield Scientific School, received later the initial gifts for Battell Chapel, Farnam Hall, Durfee Hall, and the present buildings of the Divinity School; she added four new professorships and an endowment for the college pastorate, and through the generosity of a prominent New Haven citizen, Augustus Russell Street, in that day her most generous benefactor, the corner stone of the Yale School of Fine Arts was laid. All these gifts totalled $400,000. Harvard, which had just inaugurated her Museum of Comparative Zoölogy, received from James Lawrence, the son of Abbott Lawrence, the founder of Lawrence Scientific School, additional gifts for that school, and from George Sanders means to build a hall for Commencement and other exercises, to be known as Sanders Theater; Gray's Hall was finished, and the Bowditch scholarships endowed. Amherst raised $350,000, which was provision for three new buildings and four new professorships, and along with Tufts, Brown, and the Massachusetts Institute of Technology shared evenly in a fund of $1,000,000, left for educational purposes by Dr. William J. Walker.[1] Williams

---

[1] It was rumored that the whole of this gift was to have gone to Harvard, Walker's Alma Mater, but that that institution refused to accede to the conditions imposed.

and Bowdoin added largely to their endowments; Chicago University added $175,000 to its endowment and dedicated a new main building, and twenty other institutions raised on an average $100,000 each. Waterville College, Waterville, Maine, changed its name to Colby University, and Madison University, Hamilton, New York, to Colgate University, in honor of leading benefactors. Two colleges in Pennsylvania, Washington and Jefferson, united; two institutions that were burned, Rensselaer Polytechnic Institute and Andover Preparatory School, were speedily rebuilt.[1]

Hartford Theological Seminary was moved to its present situation from East Windsor, Connecticut, after a fund of $200,000 was raised in its behalf; $150,000 was easily raised for Union Theological Seminary by one hundred subscribers, as well as large subscriptions for the Unitarian Seminary, Meadville, Pennsylvania, and for the theological seminaries at Andover, Bangor, Newton, and Auburn.

It is doubtful if the world ever before witnessed such proof of a nation's devotion to education; voluntary contributions to the cause in time of protracted war amounted to over $5,000,000. More institutions, probably, in proportion had been founded in the decade from 1850 to 1860; but the list for 1861–1865, though short, is significant and surprising; the starting of new institutions and liberal endowment of others already established would not naturally be expected in such a crisis. There was scarcely an institution that was not benefited or one at which building operations were not

[1] In the long list of other institutions that were benefited were Wesleyan, Dartmouth, Trinity, Rochester, Lafayette, Western Reserve, Marietta, Antioch, Beloit, Allegheny, Iowa College Washington University, St. Louis, Rutgers, and Pennsylvania State College. Williston Seminary, Easthampton, Massachusetts, patronized by Samuel Williston, from whom it had already received $200,000, in 1865 was building a new gymnasium and a new dormitory, the gifts of the founder. William Robinson, dying in Exeter, New Hampshire, in 1864, left his fortune to the free academy for girls which he had already founded in that place at an expense of $300,000.

in progress, and in every community new institutions were appearing.[1]

Far greater and more evenly distributed than these private endowments was the agricultural college land grant act of Congress, by which epoch-making law the national government gave to each state, for every United States senator and representative in its congressional delegation, thirty thousand acres of public land for the benefit of colleges of which the "leading object should be, without excluding scientific and other practical studies, and including military tactics, to teach such branches of learning as are related to agriculture and the mechanic arts." For a government which had made grants for education only to each new state as it entered the Union, this was a distinct step in advance, the first time that Congress had ever assisted education in the older states; section sixteen had always been set off in each township in a new state for the purposes of general education, and from the admission of Ohio onward two whole townships for a state university; but, despite numerous petitions, never anything for education in the older states.[2]

[1] The sources of the statements in these paragraphs are the college catalogues, educational papers, and religious papers; the latter are especially good in that they give many accounts of Commencement exercises and the yearly progress of the colleges. The *New York Observer* and the *Congregationalist* of Boston are the most valuable.

[2] The agitation for congressional assistance to education in the older states began in the early part of the nineteenth century; finally, in the early fifties, the agricultural sections became interested in their own behalf. Europe had agricultural colleges, and Congress was disposing of the swamp land and was assisting the railroads and the old soldiers by grants of lands; why should not land be given for agricultural colleges? President Pierce was a strict constructionist of the Constitution, and it was known that he would veto any bill in favor of the agricultural colleges; the bill was passed under President Buchanan, but that President vetoed it, just as he did the homestead act, because of strict Construction ideas of the Constitution. When the act was passed under Lincoln, it was quickly signed.

Newspapers, educational journals, and state legislatures joined in an earnest discussion, as to whether the states should devote the bounty for the foundation of new institutions or should bestow it upon those already established; whether the institutions thus endowed should be predominatingly agricultural or devoted to general education, including the liberal arts as well as military training and agriculture. Massachusetts divided her lands between the Massachusetts Institute of Technology and Amherst Agricultural College; Rhode Island gave hers to Brown; Connecticut to the Sheffield Scientific School; New York to Cornell; New Jersey to Rutgers; in the West, generally, it was the state university that was the recipient of the bounty. The total grant to the loyal states represented an endowment of $10,000,000, which added to private endowments made the total outlay for education at the crisis still more marvelous. A new era was opened in the teaching of agriculture and military training, and the cause of the liberal arts was at the same time advanced. After the war the Southern states received their share of the new government endowment.[1]

The geographical distribution of the colleges was most unwise. Many more, comparatively, were situated in the sparsely settled West than in the more settled East; twenty-four in Ohio, thirteen in Indiana, fifteen in Illinois, and but

[1] As a rule when the lands came to be disposed of they sold for eighty cents per acre. States selling their lands late got large sums; North Dakota, which came under the provisions of the act long after the war, got $1,059,482 for only 130,000 acres; New York only $688,576 for 990,000 acres; Rhode Island only $50,000 for 120,000, or $.41 per acre; while Idaho got $10 per acre, or $900,000 for 90,000 acres. See *Report of the United States Commissioner of Education*, 1903, Volume I, p. 1179. On the history of the efforts to induce the government to help education in all the states, see *History and Management of Land Grants for Education in the Northwest Territory*, by George W. Knight, Ph.D., Papers of the American Historical Association, Volume I, No. 3, New York and London, 1885.

sixteen in all New England;[1] within a few miles of a certain small town in Illinois there were six institutions of collegiate rank. In this respect the West was suffering from the misguided zeal of the Eastern churches, as the latter worked to advance the cause of denominational education among new peoples. Every denomination sought to have a college in every state, and sometimes more than one, just as it sought to have a church in every town even if the town was small and was already well supplied with churches. The interests of the denomination were put ahead of the interests of the cause of education and of the church in general. In the East as well as in the West the majority of the institutions were both denominational and small; seventy had fewer than one hundred students.

With the war college attendance declined heavily in the small institutions and to some extent in almost every one. Yale, then the largest college, in the four years of the war fell from 521 to 438, Harvard from 443 to 385, Union from 390 to 294, Williams from 238 to 182, Amherst from 220 to 212, Princeton (in one year) from 312 to 221; Michigan alone of the larger colleges gained, advancing from 255 to 295; Beloit increased from 60 to 68; Dennison fell from 63 to 25, Western Reserve from 48 to 41, Lafayette from 87 to 51.[2]

The colleges of the Roman Catholic Church, though somewhat lower in rank than those of the Protestant churches and attended mostly by Irish, uniformly increased in numbers; Notre Dame in Indiana advanced from 111 to 364, St.

---

[1] There were twenty in New York, and twenty-one in Pennsylvania.

[2] Where the college included a preparatory school the attendance at the latter is not included in the above figures. Other colleges fared as follows: Rutgers fell from 124 to 75, Tufts from 53 to 51, Ohio Wesleyan from 157 to 119, Bowdoin from 199 to 132, Trinity from 70 to 51, Dartmouth from 275 to 146, University of Vermont from 101 to 40, Brown from 232 to 185, Columbia from 201 to 150, University of Pennsylvania from 140 to 111.

Francis Xavier, New York City, from 293 to 570. The first generation of the Irish, born and reared after the heavy immigration of the late forties, was just coming to maturity and thus naturally they were filling their schools in larger numbers than ever before; then as an industrial class the Irish were well employed, and they were known to be not very enthusiastic for the war.[1]

Professional schools generally flourished. At three medical schools in Chicago attendance rose from 234 to 411, at the medical department of the University of Michigan from 164 to 414, at that of Columbia from 260 to 465; young men were apparently drawn in unusual numbers toward medicine because of the opportunities offered for professional service in the army and navy.[2] The law school of the University of Michigan increased its attendance from 90 to 260, that of Columbia from 101 to 158. Theological schools held their own generally, although a few declined.[3]

One factor in bringing about the diminished numbers in the colleges was the withdrawal of Southern students. At Princeton, which was almost a Southern college, one-third of the 300 students were from the Confederacy and immediately left for home when the war broke out; out of 900 students in all departments at Harvard there were 63 from the South, 33 at Yale. For the best education Southerners before the war were forced to go to the North, the land of colleges, inasmuch as their own institutions were few in number and comparatively weak. While the North boasted of 184 colleges, the South contained only one-fourth

---

[1] It must be added that the figures for the Catholic schools included the attendance in preparatory departments, which figures are not included in the records of the Protestant colleges.

[2] Harvard Medical rose from 191 to 216, the medical school at Bowdoin from 50 to 101, Physicians and Surgeons in New York from 52 to 80.

[3] The seminary at Princeton grew from 180 students in 1860 to 186 in 1864, at Yale from 22 to 23; Union fell from 50 to 33, Oberlin from 35 to 13, New Brunswick from 57 to 48; Newton rose from 27 to 29.

of that number; in the one section there were 44 medical schools, and in the other only 9; in the one 76 theological schools, and in the other 14.[1]

Enlistment in the Northern armies, however, was the most important cause of the change. Harvard, from the college proper, graduates and undergraduates, enlisted 529 men, of whom 92 were killed or died of wounds; the class of 1860 sent 54 men and lost 12, 1861 sent 53 and lost 9, 1862 sent 38 and lost 10, 1863 sent 46 and lost 8, 1864 sent 40 and lost 6, 1865 sent 17 and lost 2, 1866 and 1867 each sent 6 and lost none. There were present at the Commencement exercises in 1865 250 of the survivors, discussing ways and means of honoring the memory of those who had fallen, and the present Memorial Hall is the result of the discussion. Yale, like Harvard, sent approximately one-quarter of her graduates and undergraduates.[2] In the West the hundred days' movement in 1864 drew especially heavily on the small colleges; practically all of the male students of Iowa College enlisted at this time, leaving only two or three behind, who with the girls of the institution carried on Commencement; the boys of the sophomore class went in a body. All but two students from Shurtliff College enlisted, and the institution was closed; the senior classes of Illinois and Beloit went in a body; from the state of Wisconsin there was a students' regiment. In all the war three colleges in the East and three in the West together raised 1862 soldiers, graduates and undergraduates, of whom over one-half became commissioned officers.[3] Fourteen colleges sent 4498 alumni and students; Oberlin 700, of whom 100 fell; Wabash 275;

[1] *National Almanac*, 1864, pp. 512 and 516.

[2] Seven hundred fifty-seven in all.

[3] This list included 9 major generals, 25 brigadier generals, 111 colonels, 15 lieutenant colonels, 68 majors, 171 surgeons and medical officers, 367 captains, 97 chaplains, 161 lieutenants, 21 paymasters, 6 naval officers, and 1 rear admiral.

Iowa 65; Beloit, with 88 alumni, 33; Bowdoin 248, of whom 44 were killed; Williams 200, of whom 22 were killed.[1]

In the anxious days preceding and attending hostilities the colleges were filled with the prevailing war spirit. Three months before Fort Sumter was fired upon, during the morning chapel service at Yale the Palmetto flag of the state of South Carolina was swung from the tower of Alumni Hall; discovered after the service, it was hauled down only after a fierce struggle. In every case the withdrawal of Southern students was an occasion of excitement; Princeton in this way in a few weeks lost one-third of her men, and other colleges and professional schools large numbers. Occasionally professors laid down their books to take up the sword and became officers of students' regiments and companies; at almost every institution drilling companies were formed, which carried on their daily drills on the college campus. College flag raisings were common. A popular student would enlist for the war and his classmates would gather about in a more or less formal manner and present him with a sword; more than a score of these presentations took place at Yale in four years, sometimes as many as two or three in a month. A student soldier would meet death, and his classmates would come together in solemn assemblage to pass resolutions of sympathy. Some members of the college classes, who had themselves seen service, were present among their fellows as veterans of war. Few Commencement exercises were held without the presence of veterans as guests of honor or as recipients of honorary degrees; one year Rear Admiral Foote and Major Anderson attended

[1] See the *Report of the Superintendent of Public Instruction in Illinois*, 1865–1866. The Boston Latin School sent 300 graduates, including 1 admiral, 11 generals, 47 colonels, lieutenant colonels, and majors, 10 captains and lieutenants, 3 surgeons and assistant surgeons, and 3 chaplains. Of the 275 sons of Wabash enlisting 3 were major generals, 3 brigadier generals, 9 colonels, 6 lieutenant colonels, 3 majors, 11 surgeons, 50 captains, and 40 lieutenants.

the Yale exercises, and later in the war Major General Terry received an honorary degree from the same institution. Harvard gave a degree to Major General Scott and was honored by the presence at her exercises of Major General Meade. In 1865 Union College gave degrees to Secretary of War Stanton and General Grant, to the latter with "three times three ringing cheers" and loud demands for a speech, but the general sat silent; in silence also the popular general and Major General Howard accepted the same degree from Bowdoin College, an honor that had been given shortly before the war by the same college to Jefferson Davis. Columbia in the first year of his administration granted to Abraham Lincoln, President of the United States, *in absentia*, the degree of LL.D. in token of "devotion to those principles of freedom, law, order, and union, which should always find their representative in the Chief Magistrate of the land"; Princeton bestowed the same degree on the President later, and it was reported that he was prevented from receiving the distinction from Harvard in 1864 only by the fact of his inability to leave official duties in Washington in order to receive the degree personally in Cambridge.[1] The spirit of war came home to the students in many ways, not only from letters and newspapers, but by actual contact with armies and camps and military life.

Yet with the war spirit the usual students' activities did not abate; there was boating, a crude form of the present game of baseball, and a rough and ill-organized form of football; gymnasiums were just coming into vogue. Every college supported rival literary societies, and many literary contests were held; there were students' publications, book stores, glee clubs, concerts, and dances. In many ways

---

[1] In 1864 American colleges granted 64 honorary degrees. Harvard gave an LL.D. to James Stuart Mill, Winfield Scott, and Governor Andrew; Yale honored Major General Terry, Charles Sumner and Secretary Seward; every Cabinet official was honored by some institution.

college life differed but little from that of the present day.[1]

Students' expenses were low, according to the estimates of the colleges themselves ranging from $100 to $300, and as a rule tuition did not advance during the war. At Dartmouth until 1867 this charge remained at $51, where it had been for some years; at Yale it was $45 throughout the period; among the few institutions that increased this charge was Harvard, which raised it from $75 to $104. From the standpoint of the students and of the fathers who paid the bills this failure of college expenses to advance with the general rise of prices was fortunate, but to the professors it meant wretched salaries. College teachers, when prices were highest, were forced to eke out their existence on the salaries they had been receiving in the fifties. Preachers of the gospel found added compensation in donation parties, the salaries of clerks in mercantile pursuits were finally increased, local boards of education by public opinion were forced to raise the salaries of the public school teachers; the wages of washerwomen and of laboring men went up; but college teachers were forced to see thousands of dollars spent on new buildings and scholarships, at a time when attendance was falling off, while their own salaries were utterly insufficient. Probably they and sewing women suffered more than other classes from the high prices of the war.[2]

The case of President Lord of Dartmouth brought the question of intellectual freedom in the colleges prominently before the public. Connected with the college either as trustee or president for over forty years, President Lord suddenly found himself unable to support the national administration on the question of human slavery; he believed that

[1] The author has collected a mass of material on this subject, but cannot here treat it in detail.

[2] College teachers may be taken as types of the vague class of those living on fixed incomes, the terms or amount of which were determined before 1861, before prices went on a paper basis.

slavery was upheld by the Bible, and in support of this view he wrote numerous campaign documents which were circulated by the New Hampshire and New England Democrats until he was finally accused of discouraging the enlistment of Dartmouth College men in the army and navy of the United States. This the ardent war men of New England could not endure, and strong representations were made to the trustees of the institution demanding the dismissal of their head; church conferences took up the subject, and finally after the trustees, in reply to certain of these resolutions, had practically censured the president as having become injurious to the college, the latter sent in his resignation. The action of the trustees was not taken on account of any malfeasance or delinquency in office, but, as the president said, "for opinions and publications on questions of Biblical ethics and interpretation supposed to bear unfavorably on one branch of the policy pursued by the present administration of the country." For his opinions and expressions of opinions on such subjects, he continued: "I hold myself responsible only to God and the constitutional tribunals of the country, inasmuch as they are not touched by the charter of the college or any express statutes or stipulations. And while my unswerving and never partisan loyalty to the government of my fathers, proved and tested by more than seventy years of devotion to its true and fundamental principals, cannot be permanently discredited by the excited passions of the hour, I do not feel at liberty, when its exercise is called in question, to resign my moral and constitutional right, nor submit to any censure nor consent to any conditions, such as are implied in the aforesaid action of the board, which action is made more impressive upon me in view of the private communications of several of its members. But not choosing to put myself in any unkind relations to a body which have the responsible guardianship of the college, — a body from which I have received so many tokens of confidence and regard, — and believing it to be inconsistent with Christian charity and propriety to carry on my administration while holding and expressing opinions injurious, as they imagine, to the interests of the college, and offensive to that party in the country which they here professedly represent, I hereby resign my office as President." [1]

Few regretted the incident, for even among the alumni of the college their president was unpopular. Academic freedom was undoubtedly valued by New Englanders, but the safety of the country in a time of peril was looked upon as of supreme importance and infinitely more valuable than freedom of speech and opinion in colleges. The president of Bowdoin was equally unpopular for the same reasons, but he retained his position.

Midway between the colleges and the public schools were the ladies' seminaries, sometimes called female colleges or female seminaries. The Methodist Church provided one hundred and twenty-six of these institutions, while in the state of Ohio alone there were twenty-three; although a few of them existed before 1837, the date of the graduation of the first class from Mount Holyoke Seminary, they were for the most part founded after that date and on the model of the famous Massachusetts school, frequently by Mary Lyon's pupils.[2] Changes, however, had begun; the founding of Vassar College started a succession of women's colleges that were destined soon to take higher education away from the seminaries to a great extent, while the growing high schools were to deprive them of their lower grades of work.[3]

---

[1] The *New York Observer*, August 13, 1863.

[2] As typical of the attendance at these schools during the war may be taken that of Mount Holyoke, which in 1860 had 42 graduates and 99 non-graduates; in 1861, 66 graduates and 91 non-graduates; in 1864, 51 graduates and 128 non-graduates.

[3] In every way the position of women was advancing. They were doing more work in industrial lines, and more in teaching and in clerical work; in charitable and religious lines their opportunities and achievements seemed boundless; they were pushing ahead in the professions,

The progress of the newly created high schools was temporarily retarded. Boys old enough for this grade, like college boys, in many cases at least, considered themselves old enough for the army or for places in the industrial and business world, and to these pursuits they tended to devote themselves rather than to school life; in Cleveland the number of pupils of this grade increased from 194 to only 200 in five years, in Baltimore from 204 to 205, in New Haven from 58 to 66, in Chicago from 312 to 369.

But the younger generation, growing to maturity, filled to overflowing the lower grades of the public schools. Enrollment at Chicago almost doubled, while in the whole state of Illinois it advanced more than 100,000, in New York City 70,000, in Philadelphia 11,000, in Brooklyn 4000, and with this progress the outlay of public money naturally tended to keep pace; relatively less than usual was being devoted to equipment, buildings, and repairs, and more than usual to salaries.[1] Attendance was voluntary and absenteeism very

especially medicine; and their education advanced. Extreme radicals were agitating for woman's rights, and some even had adopted the "American custom," — short skirts. The *Progressive Manual* for 1863 contains the names of 23 women, with Susan B. Anthony at their head, who were woman's rights reformers, also the names of 76 women habitually wearing short skirts. It was estimated in 1864 that there were then in the North between 250 and 300 women doctors of medicine, about one-half of them homeopathic, the rest eclectic, allopathic, hydropathic, and rational, all regular graduates of medical schools. There were at least five medical institutions receiving women, but there was great prejudice against such schools and their graduates. The State Medical Society in Pennsylvania and the Philadelphia County Medical Society refused its members the right to consult with women doctors.

[1] In Chicago the number enrolled increased, 1861–1865, from 16,000 to 29,000, the number of teachers from 160 to 240; in St. Louis enrollment rose from 12,000 to 14,000, in Philadelphia from 63,000 to 74,000, in Brooklyn from 51,000 to 55,000; in Philadelphia the number of teachers rose from 1097 to 1278, in Brooklyn from 486 to 581; in Illinois the number of scholars in the one year was 473,000, in the other 580,000, while the number of teachers in the state increased from 14,000 to 17,000; in New York State attendance mounted from 872,000 to 916,000; in New York City the increase in five years was from 148,000 to 216,000.

heavy; in New York the average daily attendance was 53 per cent of the total enrollment, in St. Louis 42 per cent, and in Chicago 53 per cent. This deplorable result must be regarded as natural, while labor in the industrial world was scarce, and while army camps and recruiting stations were scattered everywhere. The community was rare in which young boys did not run off to join the army or navy.

The teaching force changed rapidly. For some years women had been supplanting men in the work of the lower grades in the cities, and now this tendency spread to the smaller towns and to the country and amounted almost to a revolution; the men were going to the army, into business, and into better-paying professions. The Ohio state superintendent of schools, when the war was half over, estimated that 5000 Ohio teachers up to that time had enlisted in the army, one-half of the whole profession in the state; in Indiana, New York, Massachusetts, and in fact in every state there was the same tendency. In Illinois the number of women teachers increased 4000, and in a single year 1000 men left their positions.[1]

While low salaries constituted one of the causes of this change in personnel, these salaries were increasing. The advance was not uniform, but it was widespread and affected both men and women, in the country as well as in the city. In New Haven by the end of the war the pay of male teachers went up $150 a year, that of women $50; in Brooklyn $50 for both sexes; in Massachusetts the average salary of men rose $12 per month, and of women $5.[2] The salaries, however,

[1] In Illinois, in 1860, 8223 men and 6485 women were employed as teachers; in 1865, 6170 men and 10,843 women: in New York, in 1860, 8224 men and 18,139 women; in 1864, 4452 men and 21,181 women: in Michigan the number of men fell from 2599 to 1317, the number of women rose from 5344 to 7428: in Pennsylvania the number of men fell from 8170 to 5641, the number of women increased from 4843 to 8645.

[2] In Massachusetts the average salary per month for men rose from $47.71 in 1860 to $59.53 in 1865, for women from $19.95 to $24.36; in

at their highest were low. In Philadelphia 800 women teachers received 80 cents per day; 200 $1 per day; 200 $1.25; 100 less than $2; 100 were getting about the same as the washerwomen; and 800 just two-thirds of the washerwomen's wages.

In the organization of their profession teachers were in much the same position as at present. Normal schools were open for their training; there were teachers' agencies, teachers' institutes, and state and national teachers' associations.[1] Four states had normal schools when the war opened, and six established them during the war. Teachers' institutes, started at Hartford, Connecticut, in 1839 by Dr. Henry Barnard, were now common, especially in the West, where many states put a clause in the teacher's contract requiring attendance at the institute once or twice a month; in the East such a contract was not required.[2] State teachers' associations met regularly every year with but few exceptions, like that of the year 1864 in Massachusetts where the hundred days' movement prevented the

Wisconsin for men from $24.20 to $36.45, for women from $15.30 to $22.24; in Illinois for men from $28.82 to $38.89, for women from $18.80 to $24.89. Salaries had increased greatly from 1850 to 1860; for example, in Wisconsin the average salary of men teachers in 1850 was $15.22 per month, in 1860 $24.20; of women teachers $8.97 in the former year, $15.30 in the latter; the *Report of the State Superintendent* for 1865 gives these tables from 1849 to 1866. In Connecticut male teachers got on the average as monthly salary in 1856 $29, in 1860 $31.20, in 1865 $49; women $17.25 in 1856, $17.34 in 1860, $22.61 in 1865.

[1] There were 4 normal schools in Massachusetts, 2 in New York, 1 in Pennsylvania, and 1 in Ohio; Wisconsin, Maine, California, Kansas, Maryland, and Indiana established them, 1861–1865. The idea of such a school was very old, having existed in France as early as the seventeenth century; early in the nineteenth century they were discussed in this country, and in 1825 Governor Clinton, of New York, argued for them, but the first one was not founded till 1839 in Massachusetts. See *Journal of Education*, December, 1863.

[2] In New York, in 1860, 5913 teachers attended 54 institutes; in 1863, 9027 teachers attended 55 institutes.

meeting, and they were generally largely attended. Of the two national associations one was restricted to teachers only, the National Teachers' Association, with members in every state; while the other, the American Institute of Instruction, limited almost entirely to New England, included teachers and the friends of education in general. The latter was the older association and met uninterruptedly in every year of the war, in 1861 at Brattleboro, Vermont, where six hundred were present at its meetings, and in 1865 at New Haven, with five hundred present. The younger body, having for its leaders such men as Henry Barnard, Superintendent Philbrick of Boston, Professor Harkness of Brown, President Hill of Harvard, and President Woolsey of Yale, for two years held no meetings, but in Chicago in the middle of the war sixteen hundred teachers came together under its auspices in one of the largest and most enthusiastic gatherings of teachers that the country had ever seen. The National Association of School Superintendents was organized in 1865.[1]

Leading questions of the profession were physical education and military training; light gymnastics with wands, rubber balls, light dumb-bells, and light Indian clubs, then just coming into vogue in place of the former heavy weights, were introduced into the schools of a number of the leading cities, and military training was in the air. Outside of the government school at West Point this latter subject for many years had been of little interest, and in all the North there was scarcely a private military academy, although in the South there were several of considerable prosperity. To these private institutions the war brought sudden popularity and the military academies of the present day sprang up in large numbers. Many went a step further and urged the introduction of military drill in the public schools; the Americans were a military people, they declared. News-

---

[1] The National Teachers' Association was founded in 1857, and the American Institute of Instruction in 1830.

papers discussed the topic, and teachers' conventions took it up, but soon the war was over, and the warlike Americans characteristically forgot that they were a military people and forgot all about military training.

The school system was simply organized; at the top was the State Superintendent of Public Instruction, assisted in some states by a State Board of Education, and beneath, in a more or less loose relation, the local boards of education and local superintendents; an organized body of teachers, meeting frequently for mutual benefit; and free instruction; all supported by a public tax. Compulsory examination of teachers and compulsory attendance of scholars were almost unknown. Judged by its results, by the praise of intelligent foreigners, and by steady progress in the time of war, the system was good and justified itself. The North was proud of it, and when in the course of the war they saw it adopted by Kentucky, West Virginia, and Maryland, they rejoiced in the belief that their glorious institution of free public schools was taking the first steps in the triumphant conquest of the South, where education was backward.

The text-books and text-book writers of the day are a matter of interest to the present generation. In the college world among Harvard professors President Hill published a new geometry, Professor Francis Bowen a "Moral Philosophy," Professor Bôcher a "French Grammar" and a "German Grammar," Professor Sophocles a "Greek Grammar," ex-President Felton Latin and Greek texts, Professor Goodwin the "Syntax of the Moods and Tenses of the Greek Verb," and Professor Gray his "Botanical Series." At Yale President Woolsey was editing Greek texts; there were Professor Hadley's "Greek Grammar," which appeared in 1860, Professor Dana's "Manual of Geology," published first in 1862, Professor Silliman's text-books in physics and chemistry, Professor Olmstead's "Natural Science," and a new edition of "Webster's Dictionary," edited in 1864 by

Professors Chauncey A. Goodrich and Noah Porter. Professor Harkness of Brown University published the first edition of his "Latin Grammar," a book which immediately began to dispute the field with the old but popular "Latin Grammar" of Andrew and Stoddard, the standard for the previous twenty-five years, the ninetieth edition of which was then just out; the "First Lessons in Latin" of Andrew and Stoddard was in its fortieth edition. Harpers were publishing Professor Anthon's Greek and Latin texts, "The Students' History of France," "Greece," and "Rome," and Smith's "Classical Dictionary." A dozen new English grammars appeared in 1864, together with new editions of McGuffey's, Goodrich's and Sanders's readers, McGuffey's spellers, and almost countless arithmetics, algebras, and geographies. One publisher in 1863 sold 3,000,000 copies of a certain series of school text-books, of another series 2,500,000 copies were sold, of another 1,000,000 copies, and of still another 900,000. This enormous consumption of text-books in the free schools was without parallel in the history of the country, in fact in the history of the world; nor did patriotic Americans fail to note with pride that it was proceeding on so large a scale in a time of war.[1]

Night schools, organized in the industrial cities as early as 1842, first as a private charity and then under the supervision of the local school boards, were well patronized; 20,000 students were on their rolls in New York, 8000 in Philadelphia, and 1500 in St. Louis.[2] Of about the same age and equally popular, but more widely scattered, were the busi-

[1] The *American Literary Gazette and Publishers' Circular*, April 1 and September 15, 1864, and March 15, 1865. The Spencerian system of writing, perfected by an Ohio school-teacher, P. R. Spencer, in 1848, and first published in copy-book form in 1859, was very popular, and had a large sale, 1861–1865.

[2] These schools were first organized in Providence, Rhode Island, in 1842; they appeared in New York in 1847, in Philadelphia in 1850, and in Chicago in 1863.

ness colleges; in six cities these were established for the first
time after the war started. The Eastman Business College,
started in Oswego, New York, in 1853 and moved to Poughkeepsie, New York, in 1861, at the close of the war had 42
teachers and 1300 students. More popular than ever was the
business college after the return of the soldiers from the
field of war, eager for positions in the business world, but
without any especial training.[1] Roman Catholic schools
and convents existed in many places, attended by thousands of pupils. The kindergarten was introduced into
the United States in 1861, in Boston and New York.

The interests of education were fostered further by public lectures, popular magazines, learned societies, libraries,
and by the literature published. Almost every town had its
lecture course, drawing upon a magnificent array of talent,
and on account of the war topics for discourse were of unusual
interest. There were hundreds of lectures by such men as
Wendell Phillips, and Henry Ward Beecher, the foremost
orators of the country, by John B. Gough, George William
Curtis, Edward Everett, Ralph Waldo Emerson, and scores
of lesser lights. There was the continued publication of the
Youth's Companion, the *Atlantic Monthly*, *Harper's Monthly
Magazine*, *Harper's Bazaar*, *Harper's Weekly*, *Frank Leslie's
Illustrated Magazine*, and the *North American Review*.
Learned societies flourished, such as the Massachusetts His-
torical Society, the New York Historical Society, the Penn-
sylvania Historical Society, the Chicago Historical Society,
and many others; historical societies were founded in Brook-
lyn, New Haven, and Buffalo, as well as the Buffalo Fine Arts
Academy and the Buffalo Society of Natural Sciences.
The American Geographical and Statistical Society of New
York displayed unusual interest in expeditions to the North
Pole, two of which were absent from the country during the

---

[1] Boston had such a school as early as 1840, and Philadelphia in 1844.

progress of the war.[1]   The old American Association for the Advancement of Science, popular before the war, failed to meet;[2] but in lieu of its meetings and in imitation of the famous French Academy and the Royal Society of London, Congress incorporated the National Academy of Sciences, a close corporation of fifty men, which held a few secret meetings and then failed ignominiously, lacking entirely in popular support.   This was a striking illustration of one phase of American character, which seemed even in intellectual affairs to require the free and unfettered coöperation of all interested; a close corporation could not be classed as a free institution.   Senator Sumner was unsuccessful in his efforts to secure the incorporation of the National Academy of Literature and Arts and the National Academy of Moral and Political Sciences, and in a short time the old popular association was revived.[3]

Libraries, as a characteristic American institution, existed everywhere, private and public libraries, society libraries, college libraries, graded and district school libraries, academy libraries, and Sunday-school libraries.   The largest collections of books in the world were in Europe, in the Imperial Library in Paris and in the British Museum in London, in each of which there were approximately 1,500,000 volumes; in comparison with these the American libraries were small, but though small the latter were far more numerous than those in Europe, more diffused, more accessible to the

[1] C. F. Hall was absent on an expedition for the Pole from 1860 to 1862 and sailed again on the same mission in 1864.

[2] This association had met as early as 1854 and regularly thereafter; its annual meeting in Newport, Rhode Island, in 1860 was attended by 160 delegates; it was to have met in 1861 in Nashville, Tennessee, but the war prevented the meeting.

[3] The society, the popular name of which was the American Association for the Advancement of Science, was formally called in the fifties the American Association of Science.   There was a membership fee of $2, or $3 with the *Transactions;* there were 862 members in 1860.

people, and far more easily used.[1] New York City had 40
collections containing 4000 or more volumes each, and Boston
a large number; in the state of New York 200 academies
possessed almost 1000 volumes each,[2] while over 1,000,000
volumes were in the libraries of the district schools of the
state. This was typical of the district schools in all Northern states, especially in the Northeast; the South lacked
not only the district school libraries but also the schools
themselves. Of the more than 100 libraries in the nation
having over 10,000 volumes, 12 only were in the South, 92
in the North; 7 public libraries, all in the North, were included in this list.[3]

"As consumers of literature," wrote Anthony Trollope,
in his book on the Americans, in 1862, "they are certainly
the most conspicuous people on the earth. Where an
English publisher contents himself with thousands of copies
an American publisher deals with ten thousands. Every-
body in the States has books about his house." [4]

This national love of books and wide use of libraries was
very much stimulated by the state of war. Detroit,
Michigan, Lynn, Massachusetts, and Worcester, Massachusetts, founded new public libraries; the Boston Public
Library increased its annual loans with great rapidity, while

[1] In Great Britain and Ireland in 1856 there were 43 libraries of over
10,000 volumes each, in France 38, in the United States, in 1863, 104. This
represented a growth for the United States that was remarkable, for in
1837 the country had only 20 libraries of over 10,000 volumes, and in 1849,
40.

[2] There were 143,000 volumes in the libraries of the 201 academies of
the state.

[3] Twenty of the libraries of over 10,000 volumes were in Massachusetts,
16 in New York, 9 in Pennsylvania, 7 in the District of Columbia, 6 in
Ohio, Connecticut, and Maryland respectively. There were a number
of public libraries of less than 10,000 volumes.

[4] *National Almanac*, 1864, p. 58, has an interesting historical article
on American libraries. Printed catalogues were common in the larger
American libraries, whereas there was only one such catalogue in England.

such libraries as the Mercantile, and the Mechanics' and Tradesmen's of New York, and the Mercantile of Philadelphia, Brooklyn, and St. Louis more than doubled their loans.[1]

The epoch was a notable one in English literature, and many popular books, both foreign and American, were issued for the first time. Among the foreign books that were offered to the public for the first time by American publishers and were more or less widely read were George Eliot's "Silas Marner," Max Müller's "Lectures on the Science of Language," Volume V of Macaulay's "History of England," Volume II of Buckle's "History of Civilization," Herbert Spencer's "Education," Charles Reade's "The Cloister and the Hearth," Charles Dickens's "Great Expectations," and John Stuart Mill's "Considerations on Representative Government";[2] Volume I of Freeman's "History of Federal Government," J. G. Holland's "Bitter Sweet," Anthony Trollope's "North America," and Victor Hugo's "Les Misérables" (complete);[3] May's "Constitutional History of England," Huxley's "Man's Place in Nature," D'Aubigné's "History of the Reformation in the Time of Calvin," Lyell's "Geological Evidences of the Antiquity of Man," Tennyson's "Enoch Arden," Kinglake's "Crimean War," John Stuart

---

[1] The Boston Public Library in 1860 possessed 97,386 volumes and 27,381 pamphlets; in 1865, 130,678 volumes and 36,566 pamphlets; while its circulation increased from 151,020 books in the one year to 194,627 in the other; the Dana Library, in Cambridge, Massachusetts, loaned 7848 volumes in the one year, 11,005 in the other; the Mercantile Library in New York, for clerks in mercantile pursuits, possessed, in 1860, 56,788 volumes and 73,175 in 1865, and in the latter year had 6557 members, to whom were loaned 189,000 volumes compared with 5668 members in 1860, receiving 79,700 volumes in loans.

[2] These appeared in 1861. No attempt is here made to give the date of the first appearance of these books in Europe, only the date of their first appearance in the United States; in most cases the two dates would practically coincide.

[3] These appeared in 1862.

Mill's "Liberty," Bulfinch's "Age of Fable," Palgrave's "Treasury of Songs and Lyrics," Merivale's "History of the Romans under the Empire," Kingsley's "Water Babies," and Renan's "Vie de Jésus"; [1] Dickens's "Our Mutual Friend," Spencer's "First Principles," Browning's "Dramatis Personæ," and Volume IV of Carlyle's "History of Frederick II"; [2] the Emperor Napoleon's "Julius Cæsar," Forsythe's "Cicero," Matthew Arnold's "Essays in Criticism," and Volumes I and II of Froude's "History of England." [3]

There was likewise an interesting array of American books published and read for the first time; these included Holmes's "Elsie Venner" and "Songs in Many Keys," Parton's "Andrew Jackson," Aldrich's "Poems of a Year," and Motley's "History of the United Netherlands"; [4] Harriet Beecher Stowe's "Pearl of Orr's Island" and "Agnes of Sorrento," Parton's "Benjamin Butler" and Allibone's "Dictionary of Authors"; [5] Hale's "Man without a Country," Whittier's "Barbara Frietchie," Volume IX of Bancroft's "History of the United States," Longfellow's "Tales of a Wayside Inn," and Appleton's "New American Cyclopædia," sixteen volumes; [6] Kirk's "Down through Tennessee and Back by Way of Richmond," Bayard Taylor's "Hannah Thurston," J. K. Hosmer's "Color Guard," Bryant's "Planting of the Apple Tree," Winthrop's "Governor John Winthrop," Ticknor's "W. H. Prescott," Kirk's "Charles the Bold," Trowbridge's "Cudjo's Cave," Lyman Beecher's "Autobiography and Correspondence," Volumes II and III of Smith's "Dictionary of the Bible," Shedd's "History of Christian Doctrine," Parton's "Benjamin Franklin," and countless boys' books, such as "U. S. Grant, the Farmer Boy, and how he became Lieutenant General,"

[1] These appeared in 1863.
[2] These appeared in 1864.
[3] These appeared in 1865.
[4] These appeared in 1861.
[5] These appeared in 1862.
[6] These appeared in 1863.

"The Sailor Boy and how he became Rear Admiral, being an Authentic Life of Admiral Foote," "The Hero Boy, or Life and Deeds of General Grant," "The Pioneer Boy and how he became President," by such writers as P. C. Headley, T. S. Arthur, Oliver Optic, and others; [1] Thoreau's "Cape Cod," Volume III of Palfrey's "History of New England," and many more books for boys and girls by the writers of such books already mentioned, and by "Carleton," Louisa M. Alcott, "Pansy," Jacob Abbott, etc.[2]

The most popular book for several years was "Les Misérables," of which work one publisher within a year after its appearance sold one hundred twenty thousand copies; all the world was reading it and talking about it; but almost equally popular was "Enoch Arden," and Dickens's successive novels. The most popular American book was "The Man without a Country." [3]

Although a high standard of excellence was maintained in these current books, there was still a decline in the total number of books published; pamphlets increased in number. Before the war almost everything that came out in England was reproduced in this country, and this involved the publication of many vapid novels, all of which disappeared under the influence of high prices. With prices soaring publishers brought out only standard books of permanent value, for which there was an immediate and sure sale, and nothing was taken on speculation. This accounts for the surprisingly high tone of the new books. It was remarkably good literature that the generation of the war read, and largely foreign in origin. Far from suffering, publishers thrived; they stuck to good books and sold more of them than usual.[4]

---

[1] These appeared in 1864.   [2] These appeared in 1865.

[3] For information on new books, see the *American Publishers' Circular and Literary Gazette*, changed during the war to the *American Literary Gazette and Publishers' Circular*. A file of this is in the Harvard Library.

[4] In the United States 449 books were published in 1834, 2162 in 1855 (746 reprints), 3900 in 1862, 3800 in 1863. English publishers claimed

An interesting event in the literary world was a banquet given at the Century Club, New York, in 1865, in honor of William Cullen Bryant on the seventieth anniversary of his birth; five hundred people were present, including, besides Bryant himself, the élite of New York society and such distinguished literary men as George Bancroft, the president of the society, Bayard Taylor, Ralph Waldo Emerson, Oliver Wendell Holmes, and Mrs. Howe. Another literary event of considerable public interest was

that the Americans were pirates and stole their works; on this point there was an angry controversy. One English charge rankled in the hearts of all patriotic Americans. "Who reads an American book?" sneeringly asked Sydney Smith fifty years back, and then proceeded to show that there was no real American literature of the time. In 1860 this was rather tardily answered by a writer in the *Boston Post*, who seemed to think that quantity and quality were synonymous terms; up to 1860, he showed, 75,000 copies of Story's law books had been sold, 30,000 of those of Bouvier, 800,000 of Irving's works, 140,000 of those of the Artic explorer Kane, 310,000 of *Uncle Tom's Cabin*, 93,000 of *The Lamplighter*, 450,000 of Barnes's *Notes on the New Testament*, 1,000,000 of T. S. Arthur, 1,250,000 of Abbot's *Rollo, Lucy,* and *Jonas* books, 400,000 of Mrs. Williams's histories, 195,000 of *Appleton's Cyclopædia*, 80,000 copies of Benton's *Thirty Years'*, 45,000 of his *Abridgment of Congressional Debates*, 50,000 of Cooper's novels, 150,000 copies of Bayard Taylor, 186,000 of J. C. Headley, 70,000 of Ik Marvel, 600,000 of Mitchel's geographies, 110,000 of Goodyear's histories, 30,000,000 of Webster's spellers. The author of this defense claimed that he had access to the books of the publishers in all cases and that the figures given were accordingly accurate. See *American Publishers' Circular and Literary Gazette*, June 15, 1863. *Appleton's Cyclopædia*, begun in 1857 and completed in 1863, was the first original American work of the kind; there were 17,000 subscribers to it, 12,000 in the North and 5000 in the South. Lieber's translation of the German *Conversations Lexicon* had been the standard of these works for many years; *Chamber's Encyclopædia*, which was appearing in installments during the war, was based on the German work. Appleton's, after the appearance of their work, published an annual volume as supplement. The *Encyclopædia Britannica* was also in the market, and, up to 1865, 1800 sets of it had been sold. One man in New York was reported to have collected 3000 pamphlets on the politics of the war during the presidential contest in 1864, and it was estimated that 5000 in all were issued in this year. J. R. Bartlett, of Providence, Rhode Island, through a Boston house, published a catalogue of the literature of the war.

a reception to the visiting Oxford professor, Goldwin Smith, who was stanch in his native country in support of the cause of the North; leading American publishers made gifts to him from their best works, in order that Oxford might have a creditable collection of American books, while leading authors, such as Bryant, Bancroft, Holmes, Longfellow, Whittier, and Bayard Taylor, sent copies of their works with complimentary letters.   An attempt to make a national celebration of the three hundredth anniversary of the birth of Shakespeare failed utterly.[1]

In whatever way the term be construed, whether to include only colleges and public schools or broadly to include the lecture platform, periodicals, learned societies, libraries, and literature in general, it is evident that education did not materially suffer by the war.   College life went on with but few new manifestations; no matter how terrible the day on the Southern battlefield, no matter how great the excitement in the North, the public school bell rang out as usual in the first week in September, and day by day thereafter summoned the youth of the land in ever increasing numbers to their routine of study.   Intellectual leaders clung to their tasks with admirable fidelity and gave utterance to their thoughts with perhaps more zest than ever.   War was a stimulus to intellectual life.

[1] The corner stone of a monument to the great poet was laid in Central Park, New York, with hardly an item of notice in the public press.   The actor, James H. Hackett, made an address and laid the stone, but few besides theatrical people were present.

CHAPTER X

LUXURIES AND AMUSEMENTS

"THIS war," observed the correspondent of the *London Times*, "has brought the levity of the American character out in bald relief. There is something saddening, indeed revolting, in the high glee, real or affected, with which the people here look upon what ought to be, at any rate, a grievous national calamity. The indulgence in every variety of pleasure, luxury, and extravagance is simply shocking. The jewelers' shops in all these cities have doubled or trebled their trade; the love of fine dresses and ornaments on the part of the women amounts to madness. They have the money, well or ill gotten, and must enjoy it. Every fresh bulletin from the battlefield of Chickamaugua during my three weeks' stay in Cincinnati brought a long list of the dead and wounded of the Western army, many of whom, of the officers, belonged to the best families in the place. Yet the signs of mourning were hardly anywhere perceptible; the noisy gayety of the town was not abated one jot. Miss Laura Keene, the actress, did not draw a less full house. There may be a great deal of empty bravado, of bluster and swagger, in all this apparent indifference to undeniable suffering, but it makes no pleasing impression on a sensitive stranger." [1]

Again, the next year, the *New York Independent*, after describing the vast number of suddenly acquired fortunes, went on to say: "Who at the North would ever think of

[1] The *London Times*, November 3, 1863.

war, if he had not a friend in the army, or did not read the newspapers? Go into Broadway, and we will show you what is meant by the word 'extravagance.' Ask Stewart about the demand for camel's-hair shawls, and he will say 'monstrous.' Ask Tiffany what kind of diamonds and pearls are called for. He will answer 'the prodigious,' ' as near hen's-egg size as possible,' 'price no object.' What kind of carpetings are now wanted? None but 'extra.' Brussels and velvets are now used from basement to garret. Ingrains and three-plys won't do at all. Call a moment at a carriage repository. In reply to your first question you will be told, 'Never such a demand before, sir.' And as for horses the medium-priced five-hundred-dollar kind are all out of the market. A good pair of 'fast ones,' 'all right,' will go for a thousand dollars sooner than a basket of strawberries will sell for four cents. Those a 'little extra' will bring fifteen hundred to two thousand, while the 'superb' 2.40 sort will bring any price among the 'high numbers.'" [1]

A mass of details substantiates these general statements at every point.

Interest in horse racing underwent a pronounced revival. This sport before the sixties had been almost entirely given over to the Southern and Border states, and thither the breeders and turfsmen of Kentucky and the West sent their horses rather than to the North; but after the war arrayed section against section races could be held, if at all, only at the North, and successful efforts to arouse Northern interest followed. The Chicago Driving Park was now opened, a new race course in Washington was built and one in Boston, and to these as well as to the older courses, all united in a national circuit, the sportsmen with their horses traveled in succession, attending the races city by city. Twenty thousand dollars in stakes at the Laclede races in St. Louis, $5000 at the Hartford Driving Park, $10,000 at the Union course on

---

[1] The *New York Independent*, June 25, 1864.

Long Island, all in the great battle month of May, 1864;
$3500 in stakes again at Hartford in the fall of the year,
enormous stakes also in Louisville, Philadelphia, Paterson,
Saratoga, Chicago, Boston, and Washington furnish evidence of the popularity of the sport and of the free flow
of money. Enormous crowds were present throughout,
despite battle news, enlistment, the draft, and the excitement of politics during a great presidential campaign. The
masses seemed eager to spend their money for the amusement and the rich men eager to invest their money in a
"flyer." At the agricultural fairs, both county and state, the
same spirit was manifested; the farmers were complaining
that at all these gatherings the supreme interest which ought
to be bestowed upon the merits of cows, sheep, pigs, and
chickens was being diverted, under the reign of "King
Shoddy," to the horse race and to the side show.[1]

Grand opera enjoyed its share of prosperity. In the
winter of 1863–1864 four leading opera companies toured the
country, one singing in English, one in German, and two
in Italian; and while all were successful, the last two were
the most popular; English opera had not been attempted
for many years. One Italian company under the management of Maurice Grau, after a short season in New York,
visited the cities of the Middle West, Albany, Rochester,
Buffalo, Cleveland, Chicago, Louisville, and St. Louis,
presenting from six to twelve operas in each city. The
foremost company, Maretzek's Italian Opera Company,
during a most brilliant season performed for almost three
months in New York and for shorter periods in Boston,
Philadelphia, Baltimore, and Washington, everywhere be-

[1] This complaint is to be found frequently in the agricultural papers
of the time; on racing in general, see files of the daily papers, and the
contemporary sporting paper, *Wilkes' Spirit of the Times*, New York.
No trotting records were broken; this record was held by the horse Flora
Temple, which in 1856 trotted a mile in 2.24½, and in 1858 in 2.19¼;
but in 1865 the horse Dexter lowered this record to 2.18¼.

fore crowded houses, presenting such popular operas as "Les Huguenots," "Don Giovanni," "Il Trovatore," "Lucia," "La Traviata," and "Faust." The last-named was the most enthusiastically received, especially the soldiers' chorus, which never failed to elicit storms of applause. This recent work of Gounod, brought out in Paris in the fifties and later produced in London, was now introduced in America for the first time, with the young American singer, Clara Louise Kellogg, as Margherita, Signor Mazzolini as Faust, and Signor Biachi as Mephistopheles; the American girl by her superb acting and singing, by the purity of her voice, and her sweet, gentle sympathy, became very popular. It was in the same part that Patti was winning triumphs in Paris. People could not hear enough of Italian opera; it was wonderfully successful after many failures in the past. In their curls and crinoline, their swallow-tailed coats, white vests, and chokers, society turned out *en masse* and made of Miss Kellogg almost a national heroine. The next season the companies returned to their entertainments, greeted by the same crowds and achieving the same success.[1]

The pianist Gottschalk was giving concerts during these years with increasing popular favor, and associated with him for a brief time before her departure for Paris was Patti, whose singing recalled to all her hearers the days of Jenny Lind; Camille Urso was a popular violinist. Gilmore's band gave many concerts.[2]

In one branch of music there was no ostentation and no proof that the war was forgotten; this was in the popular songs, in which there was a magnificent reflection of the

---

[1] Summer opera by the Maretzek Company was rendered impossible in 1864 only by a strike of the musicians for higher wages.

[2] Important events in the musical world were the rendering of *Elijah* and other operas by the Beethoven Society of Hartford, various oratorios by the Handel and Haydn societies of Boston, Philadelphia, and other cities, and the inauguration of the great organ in the Boston Music Hall, by far the largest organ in the country.

popular heart as it was stirred by the war. At first, after
the flag was fired upon, these all resented the insult and
sang of the Union and love of the flag; then followed eman-
cipation songs and songs of home and family; enthusiasm
for the war was strong, but longing for home and the end of
the war became stronger and stronger until it finally burst
out in a widely popular song, entitled "When this Cruel War
is Over," which had an immediate sale of over five hundred
thousand copies; it touched the popular heart. Love songs
were almost entirely absent. Thus Americans unconsciously
paid a tribute to their national character; it did them credit
in the crisis, when the universal heart was pouring itself
out in song, that the light and frivolous love ditty, which
had been prominent among the songs of the French Revolution, was not popular; it was, rather, home and the family
that were prominent in their songs.[1]

The theater was never more crowded than in the very
height of the war. The initial depression here made itself
felt for but a brief time and by the second winter the play-
houses were filled, to remain crowded to the end. After
a defeat of the army in the field attendance fell off
slightly, a phenomenon that was particularly noticeable
after the battle of Fredericksburg. The same was true
during a period of suspense, while the issues of a battle
or a campaign were hanging in the balance; but a
great victory brought overflowing houses. Foremost among
the actors of the time was Edwin Forrest, then long
preëminent on the American stage; his Shakespearean

---

[1] Among the hundreds of songs and typical of them all were the following: "Bear this gently to my Mother," "Mother, when the War is Over,"
"Yes, I would the War were Over," "Mother Waiting for the News,"
"Brother, will you come Back?" "Will my Brother come Again?"
"When will my Darling Boy return?" The popular songs of the soldiers
were in a class by themselves. See the *Musical Review and World*, November 19, December 3 and 17, 1864; the tariff shut out imported sheet
music, and home publishers increased their sales rapidly.

tragedy, "Richard III," "Macbeth," "Othello," "Lear," etc., never failed to attract. Almost as strong was the tragic acting of Edwin Booth, less strong that of his brother John Wilkes Booth. Scarcely a town failed to see the raging play among the masses, "The Ticket of Leave Man," a story of English life. There was the Falstaff of James H. Hackett, the "She Stoops to Conquer" and other light comedy of Laura Keene, the acting of Mrs. John Drew and of Joe Jefferson. Negro minstrels were a "national amusement," everywhere popular; twenty-five negro troupes toured the country in the season of 1864, all playing to crowded houses. Three theaters in New York, two in Philadelphia, and a single one in several other cities were entirely given over to the "blackened comedians." A less popular favorite was Herman, the prestidigitateur.

Another diversion for the public was furnished by the exhibition of the four dwarfs, General Tom Thumb and his party of three, and finally by the marriage in Grace Church, New York, before a distinguished audience, including General Burnside, of the diminutive general and his bride, Miss Lavinia Warren; Barnum's Museum and Van Amberg's Menagerie contributed further to the gayety of the metropolis. Traveling in every direction, usually over the country roads rather than the railroads, and visiting almost every town, was the circus, and there were few towns that it did not visit. Four at least visited New Haven in one summer, while various small towns in Ohio were honored with three in one season; they reached the remote corners of Maine, the wilderness of northern Michigan, and the soldier camps of Nashville, — everywhere welcome.

Although not appealing to the refined classes, the prize fight was an event of great current interest, occasionally stopped by police interference, but on the whole proceeding with impunity. On the occasion of a championship match between the two Irishmen Coburn and McCool (almost all

the prize fighters came from Ireland), the *New York Sun* said :
"For weeks, in anticipation of the event, in the thousands of
bar rooms in the city, no topic was so common and so exciting
as the appearance, sayings, training, and points of excellence
of Coburn and McCool. Their muscularity, length of reach,
quickness, force of blow, wind, sparring, wrestling, height,
endurance, and a hundred other points about the past and
the present condition of the champions were excitedly
discussed by thousands of pugs, sports, gamblers, young
men about town, men on 'change, merchants, keepers of
public houses, solid men, mechanics, and many other sorts
of people." [1] Shortly after this fight the papers spent pages
describing an international prize fight in England for $10,000
a side between the Englishman King and the American representative Heenan, and it was a matter of almost national
regret that the American, after twenty-five rounds, lost the
fight.

The papers give us hints of other sports such as are popular now, championship billiard matches at $1000 a side, at-
tended by hundreds, championship chess matches carried
on by telegraph, and annual regattas of the yacht clubs in
New York, Brooklyn, Philadelphia, and some other cities.
There were no international yacht races. Baseball, although
twenty years old, was but little organized and received
little public attention. In fact, all sports of the time,
including prize fights and boxing matches, were accorded
much less space in the public prints than at present. [2]

[1] The *New York Sun*, May 6, 1863.
[2] In 1851 the New York Yacht Club sent the *America* to England,
which won the race for the Royal Yacht Squadron Cup, valued at $100,
against seventeen competitors. The *America* was later sold to an Englishman, who presented it to the Confederate States, and it was then turned
into a blockade runner, but was soon captured by the United States of
America at Fernandina, Florida, and put on blockading duty. Later it
was made a training ship for Annapolis. See the *New York Herald*,
July 4, 1863.

In the colleges, among the student body, baseball was a new sport; in fact, it was introduced at some institutions after the war began. Games of 31 innings, with scores of 70 to 40, were not uncommon, while the first game in the present Yale-Harvard series, won by Yale, resulted in a score of 36 to 33. Football was not the highly organized sport of the present day, but rather an annual free-for-all fight between the freshman and sophomore college classes at the opening of the term, the beginning of the hazing of the year in which the freshman class was abused collectively. Harvard and Yale had just done away with the custom, but it still existed in many colleges. The most popular college sport was boating. At Yale college boys had boats on the river as early as the forties, and when the war broke out the present Yale navy was nine years old; there were seven different boat clubs then in the college and over twenty boats on the harbor. A boathouse was erected in 1863 at a cost of $3000.

The first Yale-Harvard boat race took place in 1852 and was won by Harvard; later in that decade there were a few other matches; in 1859 Yale won, in 1860 Harvard, in 1861, 1862, and 1863 there were no races, but in 1864 and 1865 the race took place, won in each case by Yale. In the following words a Yale enthusiast described the contest of 1864: "*Ad gloriam Yalensiæ*. The great struggle of the great day of the regatta speedily drove even from one's recollection this prelude contest (the freshman race). Presently from the Yale tent, directly opposite the judge's boat, stepped six, tall, lithe, bronze fellows, with the slender, graceful shell as their burden, which soon in turn, with them as its burden, was to carry in them the confident hopes of six hundred men of Yale on a glad and glorious fruition. Slowly, and one would think carelessly, they pulled up close to the judge's boat. A few rods beyond them, and exactly in line, the Harvard crew took their place. Thus far the Yale men made no exhibit of any superior grace, strength, or skill whatever. They only promptly and slowly pulled up to their appointed place, and there sat quiet, calm, but ready. At the word 'go' the difference in distance gained by the two competitors was really wonderful. That two crews so nearly matched, and so carefully if not equally trained, should at the start exhibit no marked disparity was only to be expected; but in point of fact the crew of Yale at the first 'give way,' splash, and wild excitement of the start, darted full six feet, it would seem, beyond their adversaries; and that first stroke seemed the guerdon of victory, for from that moment, though the Harvard men worked determinedly, heroically, well, Yale constantly and perceptibly worked better, and gained so steadily that at the end of the first half-mile Harvard was directly in the wake of Yale, and victory, barring the interposition of Providence, was guaranteed. Two to one was forthwith offered on Yale with no takers. The confidence of betting men which was expressed so generously in ventures was echoed merrily from the opposite bank by moneyless enthusiasts with cheers. Fair creatures all along the shore gayly shook their blue ribbons, waved their handkerchiefs, and shouted with an exquisite little feminine earnestness 'Yale'; while seniors, freshmen and all waded into the water to catch the first glimpse of the winning boat and be the nearest to it as it dashed by. Tutors, one of Yale's most deservedly popular professors, the attorney general of Massachusetts, another graduate of fifty years, all shouted like boys, as they were once more for Yale and her victory. And so Yale took the champion flag for the first time in the history of college regattas, and so boisterously, if you please, she celebrated the achievement." [1]

[1] The *New Haven Palladium*, August 1, 1864. This victory of Yale was in no small degree due to the work of her trainer, Mr. Wood of New York. The Yale crew were Bacon, stroke, Seymour, Stoskop, Bennet, Coffin, and Scranton; Harvard: Curtis, stroke, Peabody, Nelson, Greenough, Perkins, and Farnham.

The dance, the card party, the reception, and the various social functions in a little while regained the popularity which had been somewhat shattered by the outbreak of war. "War and high prices could not terrify the Gothamites," said the *New York Herald*, early in the war; "as long as life remained in them they would keep up their reputation for jollity and good fellowship." [1] Immediately after the rebellion began there were no balls or parties in the city, the theaters were deserted, and zest for amusements was gone; but after two years the war became an old story and amusements were as popular as ever. Frederick W. Seward, assistant secretary of state, late in 1863, in a private letter, wrote as follows: "Gayety has become as epidemic in Washington this winter as gloom was last winter. There is a lull in political discussion; and people are inclined to eat, drink, and be merry. The newspapers can furnish nothing more interesting to their readers than accounts of parties, balls, and theaters, like so many court journals. Questions of etiquette are debated with gravity. People talk of 'society' who never before knew or cared about it. A year ago the secretary of state was 'heartless' or 'unpatriotic' because he gave dinners; now the only complaint of him is that he don't have dancing. It is a sign of a changed state of feeling everywhere, that all the Northern cities have given up mourning and grumbling and are devoting themselves to festivities and fairs." [2] A correspondent in the *Springfield Republican* wrote as follows: "I have been deeply afflicted over the sufferings of our boys, but have come to the conclusion that a soldier in the Army of the Potomac does not endure a severer strain on his constitution than a woman in 'society' in Washington. I don't believe that he

[1] The *New York Herald*, February 1, 1863.
[2] *Seward at Washington as Senator and Secretary of State. A Memoir of his Life, with Selections from his Letters*, by Frederick W. Seward, New York, 1891, III, 207.

is as utterly worn out at the end of a march as she at the close of a week of the 'season.' Think of it, shopping, dressing, calling, all day; parties, dancing, late suppers, late sleep, repeated week after week. If she is a good woman, trying to satisfy the demands of her conscience as well as the claims of society, she visits hospitals, works for the fair, collects money for the soldiers, devotes at least some time to husband and children. Is it any wonder that at the close of a season she is thin, and yellow, and sick, and thinks Washington a horrid place? At present Washington is mad with gayety, reeling in the whirl of dissipation, before it sits down to repent in the ashes of Lent. There are three or four grand parties a night; theaters, operas, fairs, everything to make its denizens forget that war and sorrow are in the land." [1]

The strange experience of war, the excitement, and the commercial depression at first kept people away from the popular watering places, Saratoga, Nahant, and Cape May, and from the many places of less importance on the Hudson, at Lake George and Lake Champlain, on the Great Lakes, on the Maine coast, and in the White Mountains. Even during the second year of the war, along with slowly increasing attendance there was yet a cast of seriousness over all the resorts, and many a hotel had its society of belles for the making of bandages, lint, etc., but within another twelve months frivolity reigned supreme, unattended by any tokens of war. One correspondent thus described Saratoga: "Of fashions here there is no end. Indeed it makes one's heart sick to see the folly which reigns triumphant. Dancing, dressing, and flirtation are the chief diets of men, women, and children (if there be such creatures as the latter nowadays). One would hardly think after gazing on a $4000 dress ' just from Europe,' on a woman professing to be a patriotic American, that the Sanitary Commission was in

[1] The *Springfield Republican*, February 20, 1864.

need of stores and that the country's heart was being torn asunder. Girls, none too young to be in the nursery, make their three or four toilettes a day, having hats and gloves for each dress, and assume affectations that would disgrace an actress at the Bowery. In flirtation the married women are decidedly the most *au fait;* in fact, from the manner of a certain set of New York fashionables, one would suppose that he had dropped into one of the Spas of Europe. Shoddy seems to be preëminent, and there are government officials here who are doing their best to aggravate the evil that is now cursing the land. Honest men may make money out of the government, but no man who has any respect for himself or regard for his country will revel at Saratoga when the times demand sobriety and economy. What the women spend in dress, the men spend in 'liquoring up,' until they can't stand, in horses and in gambling. The 'Hell' here is very elegantly kept up and patronized by gentlemen. We heard of several young men in society who 'fought the tiger' so persistently as to be (using the elegant vernacular of the place) entirely 'cleaned out,' and obliged to borrow of the bank to get home. One gentleman lost $1000 in one evening with the greatest nonchalance. Surely we are improving on the morals of our Puritan fathers. The races attracted nearly all the sporting community of the country." [1]

The *New York Journal of Commerce* in the middle of the war found picnics in full blast in the groves and parks of that city; there were Sunday-school picnics, church picnics, and charitable society picnics; picnics everywhere and of every kind were the rage. "There is real moral heroism in the way some people attend picnics. They rise early and take their household flock with them. They carry enormous baskets. They pack themselves into the stages three deep, or wedge themselves into cars, or stand in the burning sun on the decks of the crowded steamboats. During the after-

[1] The *Boston Journal*, August 16, 1864.

noon a shower sets in and drives the party to the shelter of the largest tree." [1]

Reigning fads, innocent and relatively unimportant, but characterized by a strong hold on the masses, were croquet, a new game introduced from England, *tableaux vivants*, New Year's calls, winter ice skating, easily the most popular amusement of the winter time, a favorite diversion of the Americans, according to the *London Times* correspondent,[2] and flower shows. Photographs were a novelty that enjoyed much popularity; a call for new troops and subsequent enlistments filled the photograph galleries with the young soldier boys and their friends, just as in the army the traveling photographer was overwhelmed with business at the rumors of an advance. Photograph albums, introduced from Paris, were instantly popular, and every young lady expected one as a present and upon receiving it besieged her friends for photographs.[3]

When the cause of the sudden outburst of extravagance is sought, there seems to be but one answer that can be given; namely, extraordinary prosperity and a plentiful supply of money in the hands of both the rich and the poor. Thousands of poor people had more money than ever before, gained through constant employment, wages as soldiers, immense bounties to soldiers and sailors, and immense charities for the support of soldiers' families; thousands of men who had never been rich before now suddenly acquired wealth. It was this class of the newly rich more than that of the older rich families which so easily parted with their money; money easily and quickly made was as easily and quickly spent.

[1] The *New York Journal of Commerce*, June 27, 1863.

[2] The *London Times*, January 19, 1864; ice skating had been indulged in before 1861, but during the war assumed unusual prominence; in the winter of 1862–1863 six new skating ponds were opened in Brooklyn alone.

[3] The *Scientific American*, February 25, 1861, and April 5, 1862; *Humphrey's Journal of Photography*, July 15, 1864; the *Springfield Republican*, December 28, 1864.

It may be said that one cause of the reckless expenditures was the mad desire to escape sorrow, to banish temporarily, as far as possible, all thought of the war with its horrors and responsibilities. Undoubtedly this motive existed, but to what extent it exercised a controlling force over the minds of the people it is impossible to determine; if the crowd at the theater, the races and the opera, at the watering places, parties and balls, on skating parties and picnics, were partly bent on covering up sorrow, they had strange, almost suspicious success in their endeavor. Their hearts they certainly did conceal, and there is little evidence that war-time pleasure parties differed from such parties of the present peaceful times. But while there is so little in the contemporary records to lend credence to this theory of pleasure indulgence to drown grief, the theory may yet be a true one; perhaps it reflects one of those rare popular characteristics during a state of prolonged war which eludes the written records, and must be deduced from a general knowledge of human nature.

One thing is plain; many of the leaders of the time were shocked at the popular taste and cried out against it. They believed that a state of civil war, when the foundation principles of the republic were on trial, was no time for indulgence in pleasure and amusement. Leading women of the national capital, among them the wives of cabinet ministers and of senators and representatives, united in forming a Ladies' National Covenant and subscribed to the following pledge: "For three years, or during the war, we pledge ourselves to purchase no foreign article of dress." An appeal to the country was issued setting forth the purposes and needs of the movement, calling attention to the non-importation societies aimed against Great Britain in colonial times, and inviting all women to join in one concerted effort to curb extravagance; prominent newspapers gave their encouragement and sympathy, and a large meeting of two thousand five hundred women assembled in New York in Cooper Union to further the movement; on all sides it was looked upon as a saving sign of the times; but apparently all praised, while none practiced the covenant, and little was effected. The failure is as significant as the very fact of the movement itself.

There were countless appeals for economy and plain living. The editor of the *Providence Journal* called a halt on those "who have suddenly found themselves in receipt of unwonted sums, who have made more in a week or in a month than they are accustomed to gain in a year, whether the sum be a thousand dollars or a million, as well as those who have had large fortunes in their control; it is such men and women that are in especial danger of rushing into extravagance as unbecoming the state of our country as it is injurious. It is too often forgotten that extravagance is relative. The poor soldier's wife who spends two-thirds of her husband's bounty in jewelry is really more extravagant than many a rich man would be in buying a three-thousand-dollar shawl." [1] William Cullen Bryant, in the *New York Evening Post*, was another voice lifted up in opposition. In his paper he wrote: "Extravagance, luxury, these are the signs of the times; are they not evidence of a state of things unhealthy, feverish, threatening to the honest simplicity of our political life; and threatening not less evil to the ideas and principles of which that life has hitherto been a fair exponent? What business have Americans at any time with such vain show, with such useless magnificence? But especially how can they justify it to themselves in this time of war? Some men have gained great fortunes during the past two or three years, but that does not excuse their extravagance. Is there nothing worthier than personal adornment in which to invest their means? Are there no enter-

[1] The *Providence Journal*, May 4, 1864.

prises open to these men of fortune which would benefit the country and their fellows as well as themselves? One man spends two hundred thousand dollars on a dwelling house; but he might build with this sum a long row of decent cottages to rent to people in moderate circumstances; he might enable fifty or one hundred families of working men to live cleanly and respectably in New York, and thus make himself a public benefactor, and that without sinking his money where he can never recover it. Or instead of dressing a few children in silks and jewels, and robbing them of the freshness and charm of youth by these vanities, why not spend the money in sending the homeless children of the city to comfortable farm houses in the West, where they will be trained to industry and virtuous conduct, and grow up good citizens?" [1]

[1] The *Scientific American*, May 21, 1864, quoting the *New York Evening Post*.

CHAPTER XI

CHARITY

ONE of the agencies of the time that served to draw all sections of the country into closer bonds of union was the common interest in national charities. Never before in the history of the United States had such great charities existed; there had been local funds for the assistance of fire sufferers or for the victims of some great epidemic or other visitation of Providence. Now for the first time charitable organizations extended the length of the Union. While narrow state interests were being replaced by a national feeling through the fraternization of soldiers from different states as comrades in a common cause, citizens at home of every state and in every class of society were finding union through the bonds of common sympathy and charity for the soldiers in the field. The army and the navy made a national appeal. When regiment after regiment passed through the Northern cities, traveling homeward, wounded and hungry, in need of care and food, the men of Maine, of Dakota, of Michigan, and of Pennsylvania were welcomed alike; resting in camp or wounded on the field of battle, it was as soldiers of the Union and not as men from any particular state that the "Boys in Blue" were ministered to. The United States Sanitary Commission and the United States Christian Commission were national and not state organizations. The heart of the whole nation was appealed to, further, by the pitiful condition of the wives, mothers, children, and dependents left at home by the soldiers, and by the wretched-

ness and misery of the emancipated negroes and of other
sufferers of the war; and all these special claims, although
nobly supported, did not cause any diminution in ordinary
charities. Home and Foreign Missionary Societies, Bible
and Tract Societies, those for the aid of the seamen, homeless
children, and the poor in general, all prospered. Never
before had charity taken such a hold on the national heart;
it afforded a common ground on which all sections might
meet in common sympathy.

As soon as men began to go to war, women all over the land
began to come together to make bandages, lint, shirts,
drawers, towels, bedclothes, etc., organizing themselves into
Ladies' Aid Societies. In New York fifty or sixty women
extended their work by organizing the Women's Central
Association for Relief, and within a few months the government at Washington, after much importunity, approved the
creation of a national society to care for needy and injured
soldiers under the name of the United States Sanitary Commission, which was to work by way of supplement to the
Medical Department of the United States Army, and was to
receive no financial aid from the government but depend
entirely on private means. With this society most local
societies immediately affiliated, although some remained
independent to the end of the war and devoted their energies
to local troops only.[1]

The work of the commission, under the presidency of the
noted divine, Dr. H. W. Bellows, who with the other officials
gave his services gratuitously, was on a comprehensive scale;
there were two hundred, and sometimes five hundred, agents,
including clerks, depot keepers, wagon drivers, and relief
agents; storehouses of the commission were located in
Boston, New York, Philadelphia, Cincinnati, Cleveland,

[1] Some states had a state agent, a special officer, in the field to look
after the needs of the soldiers of the one state alone, and many gifts were
sent to these agents.

Chicago, and Louisville, and contributions were received amounting in the whole course of the war to $7,000,000. Railroads and express companies gave their services free of charge; and all the services rendered by the commission were estimated to be worth $25,000,000. Expenses were three per cent of the value of the goods distributed.

The battlefield service was the most important. In anticipation of battles immense quantities of stores were accumulated where it was thought that they would be of the most benefit, ready for an emergency. In the Gettysburg campaign the government made preparations for 10,000 wounded, but the number proved to be 25,000, and trains were so clogged that little could be sent in from a distance to be of immediate benefit. Of great value, therefore, was the work of the commission, which in a few days distributed $75,000 worth of food supplies and clothing. These included 11,000 pounds of fresh poultry and mutton, 6430 pounds of fresh butter, 8500 dozen eggs, 675 bushels of fresh garden vegetables, 48 bushels of fresh berries, 12,900 loaves of fresh bread, 20,000 pounds of ice, 3800 pounds of concentrated beef soup, 12,500 pounds of concentrated milk, 7000 pounds of prepared farinaceous food, 3500 pounds of dried fruit, 2000 jars of jellies and conserves, 750 gallons of tamarinds, 116 boxes of lemons, 46 boxes of oranges, 850 pounds of coffee, 831 pounds of chocolate, 426 pounds of tea, 6800 pounds of white sugar, 785 bottles of syrup, 1250 bottles of brandy, 1168 bottles of whisky, 1148 bottles of wine, 600 gallons of ale, 134 barrels of biscuit crackers, 500 pounds of preserved meats, 3600 pounds of preserved fish, 400 gallons of pickles, 42 jars of catsup, 24 bottles of vinegar, 43 jars of Jamaica ginger, 100 pounds of tobacco, 1000 tobacco pipes, 1621 pounds of codfish, 582 cans of canned fruit, 72 cans of oysters, and 302 jars of brandied peaches.[1]

---

[1] See an article in *Johnson's Universal Encyclopædia* on the "United States Sanitary commission," by H. W. Bellows. In ten days after the

In the battles of the Wilderness in Virginia in 1864 the work was even more laborious; two steam barges and four hundred forty wagons conveyed over two hundred tons of stores, which were distributed by two hundred agents. In May and June in Virginia in this year the commission spent in the battlefield service alone $515,000.

There were twenty-five soldiers' homes maintained by the commission in the leading cities, North and South, where passing soldiers received meals, lodging, rest, advice, and comfort; in July, August, and September of 1864 in the home in Cincinnati 76,322 free meals were served, and 13,150 lodgings furnished, in Louisville 65,578 meals and 19,188 lodgings, and in all the cities in all the war 4,500,000 meals and 1,000,000 lodgings. Somewhat different from this were the impromptu receptions and meals furnished to passing soldiers at the railroad station, as their train stopped for a few minutes; many cities won everlasting gratitude of strangers for generosity on these occasions. The following is an account of such a reception in Cleveland, Ohio, one of many given in that hospitable city: "Yesterday afternoon, at four o'clock, the long-expected regiment (4th Massachusetts) arrived. There were nearly a hundred sick, and all in very worn condition. The preparations so long made proved ample, and after two hours' merciful work among the hospital cars and a full feast set out for the well, the ladies

battle the following articles were distributed by the commission in addition to the list of things given in the text: 5310 woolen drawers, 1833 cotton drawers, 7158 woolen shirts, 3266 cotton shirts, 2144 pillows, 264 pillowcases, 1630 bed sacks, 1007 blankets, 275 sheets, 508 wrappers, 2659 handkerchiefs, 3560 pairs of woolen stockings, 2258 pairs of cotton stockings, 728 bed pans, 10,000 towels and napkins, 2300 sponges, 1500 combs, 200 buckets, 250 pounds of castile soap, 300 yards of oiled silk, 7000 tin basins and cups, 110 barrels of oil linen, 7 water tanks, 46 water coolers, 225 bottles of bay rum and cologne, 3500 fans, 11 barrels of chloride of lime, 4000 pairs of shoes and slippers, 1200 pairs of crutches, 180 lanterns, 350 candles, 300 square yards of canvas, 648 pieces of netting, 237 quires of paper, 189 pieces of clothing, and 16 rolls of plaster.

had the satisfaction of sending the brave boys on their way in a much better condition than that in which they came to us. Another regiment was telegraphed to be here in two hours from the departure of the first, and you may imagine the commotion in which the whole town was thrown; messengers were sent everywhere to notify the housekeepers, and to hasten their gifts, and such excitement and hurry of preparation at the depot! Cleveland people are equal, you know, to any good work, and so at eight o'clock, when the 28th Maine came in, there was an abundant meal spread for them, and a fully organized committee of ladies to attend to the sick. The hospital cars, five in number, were crowded with bad cases. All our ladies were down there and worked like heroines. At ten o'clock at night we left the depot, only to go home to make fresh arrangements to meet a third regiment, at five o'clock in the morning. This last regiment, the 47th Massachusetts, has occupied us all the morning of this beautiful Sabbath, and our hearts have been sorely tried by the dreadful state in which the men were found. We had very good provision for their reception. Believing cleanliness next to godliness, we organized a new department and set long tables at the entrance of the depot, and upon them put rows of tin wash basins, with a cake of soap and towel at each, and had plenty of fresh water ready. Such a splashing and scrubbing and cheering you never saw. I believe this was the most welcome part of the program. From their bath the soldiers passed to a really bountiful breakfast, soft bread and butter, cold meat, pickles, herring, salmon, plenty of onions and cucumbers, tomatoes, apples, coffee, and tea. So the well men were abundantly fed. Meanwhile the ladies carried hand basins and towels into the hospital cars. Each sick man was refreshed by having his face and hands bathed, and then the tea, coffee, warm gruel, bread and jelly, dried beef, sponge cake, egg and wine, and stimulants were dispensed with lavish hand. A sad scene indeed was the death of one poor fellow this morning in our little hospital. He was sinking fast when the train came in. Everything was done for him that kindness and experience could suggest, but he was too far gone with the exhaustion following a long fever and died almost within sight of his home and family. How hard he tried to speak, and to send some word home!"[1]

Similar in nature, but sometimes entailing even greater exertions on the part of the citizens of the home communities, was the care devoted to train loads of wounded, sent to the cities of the North after battles; almost whole cities would turn out and give themselves to such a work.

Claim agencies were maintained by the commission, where soldiers who had lost their papers and records and who therefore might be cheated or otherwise suffer loss, were assisted in getting their bounties and pensions.[2] Back-pay agencies were established, many convalescent camps set up, through one of which, at Alexandria, Virginia, two hundred thousand soldiers passed and received benefit, such as clothing, dainties, paper, stamps, assistance in writing, rest, and medicine; a hospital directory was made, containing the names of over six hundred thousand patients, from which one could easily obtain information concerning any patient in any of the sixty-nine government hospitals; hospital cars were furnished; escorts were sent to accompany home the sick and wounded; surgeons were hired to inspect the hospitals, to spy out unsanitary conditions there and report on possible improvements; a statistical department gathered and tabulated various statistics of the soldiers; and finally there was a department of publication, which sent broadcast to surgeons the latest results of science.

---

[1] The *Sanitary Reporter*, Louisville, Kentucky, September 1, 1863 (Boston Public Library).

[2] Fifty-nine thousand seven hundred seventy-three claims were thus settled.

Most strenuous efforts were made to gather supplies for this work; there were the appeals of the regular agents, private appeals, the work of the local societies, countless church fairs and suppers, and the sanitary fairs. Vegetables were in especial demand to enable the men to ward off the dread scurvy and other diseases; the first telegram sent north by the commission after its agents arrived in Atlanta, Georgia, September, 1864, ran as follows: "We are established in this place. Hurry on large quantities of vegetables." After one call a certain small town in Illinois sent to the front five hundred bushels of potatoes; the school boys and girls of New Haven, invited to devote their Fourth of July firecracker money to oranges and lemons for the soldiers, collected for the purpose $543.33.[1] Oftentimes the public schools had "onion days" and "potato days" for the army. Newspapers collected special funds; the *New York Evening Post* opened an "onion fund," July, 1864, and in a few weeks acknowledged the receipt of $8633.70. The captain of the 104th Illinois, in the dead of winter, sent home a letter which was read on Sunday in the churches of a small town in that state, saying that one-half of the regiment were without socks, and on Monday morning two hundred seventy-five pairs of socks were dispatched by mail. In one winter Ward School 46 in New York City gave an entertainment, netting $117, by which 408 pairs of stockings were purchased for men in the Army of the Potomac. In far-off Nevada, in a mining town, a flour sack was sold at auction for $5300, the proceeds to be sent to the soldiers, and other near-by towns, bidding for the same sack, raised this unique contribution to $25,000.

The sanitary fairs were the leading means employed in raising funds, especially in the last part of the war, by which time the private homes, through direct contributions, seemed to be depleted of their extra unnecessary articles, and

[1] This was in 1864.

voluntary gifts began to dwindle. Lowell, Massachusetts, had the honor of originating the idea and of holding the first fair, followed soon by Lawrence and other towns in eastern Massachusetts, and later by all the leading cities and towns of the nation. New York and Philadelphia netted in their fairs $1,000,000 each; $3,000,000 in all was thus raised.[1] At the fairs there was an admission fee, sales of articles at special booths, always a New England Kitchen, and generally, though not always, a lottery wheel for the disposal of special articles; an art gallery was sometimes an additional attraction. New York went "fair mad."[2] The parade there opening the fair was two miles long and was participated in by eight thousand soldiers and many civilians; for days the metropolitan papers printed pages in description of the occasion. Commodore Vanderbilt, offering to give as much as any one else, was forced to give $100,000 to match the gift of A. T. Stewart. The public schools of the city by their concerts, exhibitions, and small gifts raised $24,600; the wholesale dry-goods merchants of the city contributed $131,000 in money and $9000 in goods, the wholesale grocers $20,000, the wholesale dealers in fancy goods $20,000, while leading theaters contributed $14,000 as receipts from special entertainments. At the sword contest, in the award of which individuals after purchasing a ticket were allowed to cast a vote, General Grant received 30,291 votes, and General McClellan 14,509 votes. These sword contests at the fairs were common. Frequently, also, the

[1] Brooklyn raised $300,000, Boston $50,000, Albany $80,000, Cincinnati $235,000, Chicago $80,000, Cleveland $60,000, Buffalo $40,000, Honolulu $5500.

[2] The question of lotteries in the fairs was hotly debated; the following places had lotteries, or raffling: Boston, St. Louis, Madison, Wisconsin, Albany, and Brooklyn; there was none in New York City. Most states had laws against lotteries and the sale of lottery tickets, and yet the sale of the tickets was common, not only at the fairs but to the public in general by the agents of the lottery companies.

street railways of the city presented the proceeds of one day's traffic.

In Baltimore and St. Louis, lukewarm cities in lukewarm states, so far as loyalty to the United States army was concerned, fairs were held only after much exertion; in hostile Louisville none was held. The fair was looked upon not only as a great charity but also as a great school of patriotism in Northern as well as in Border states, and was of especial value, therefore, in the Border cities. At Baltimore and at Philadelphia the President of the United States attended the fair on the opening day, and made appropriate speeches in praise of the women of the land, the organizers and directors of the great movement.[1]

The Thanksgiving dinners sent to the army were supplies of a special nature. In the first three years of the war New York City sent such dinners to New York soldiers and in 1864, in response to an appeal to all the United States by a committee of the Union League Club of that city, a fund of over $70,000 was raised and forty thousand turkeys with "fixin's" sent off to the army of Sheridan in the Shenandoah Valley and as many to Grant on the Potomac and to Butler on the James; other smaller bodies of troops were supplied; none, however, were sent to the army of Sherman, which was then lost to view in its march to the sea. The effective public appeal for this charity ran in part as follows: "The undersigned appeal to the people of the North to join them in an effort to furnish our gallant soldiers and sailors a good Thanksgiving dinner. We desire that on the twenty-fourth of November there shall be no soldier in the Army of the Potomac, the James, or the Shenandoah and no sailor in the

[1] There is a mass of source material on the Sanitary Commission. The most valuable source is the newspapers, with references too numerous to mention; the *Sanitary Reporter* was a paper of the commission and is very valuable. Then there were the special documents of the commission; further, the commission published in New York the *Sanitary Commission Bulletin.*

North Atlantic Squadron who does not receive tangible evidence that those for whom he is perilling his life remember him. It is hoped that the armies of the West will be in like manner cared for by those nearer to them than we. It is deemed impracticable to send to our more Southern posts. To enable us to carry out our undertaking we need the active coöperation of all loyal people in the North and East and to them we confidently appeal. We ask primarily for donations of cooked poultry and other proper meats as well as for mince pies and fruit. If any person is so situated as to be unable to cook the poultry or meat, we will receive it uncooked. To those who are unable to send donations in kind, we appeal for generous contributions in money. Will not every wife who has a husband, every mother who has a son, every sister who has a brother, serving in the armies or navies of the Union, feel that this appeal is to her personally, and do her part to enable us to accomplish our undertaking? Will not all who feel that we have a country worth preserving do something to show those who are fighting our battles that they are remembered and honored? Will not the press and the clergy lend their aid to the movement?" [1]

The United States Christian Commission, while not neglecting the physical and material wants of the soldiers, had for its primary object their spiritual welfare, just as the Sanitary Commission attended mainly to the physical, though not entirely neglecting the spiritual. The Christian Commission originated in the first year of fighting in a small convention of the Young Men's Christian Association in New York, and while the war lasted was one of the leading works of that young organization, though patronized by the religious world in general. For a thousand young men, constantly exposed to injury and death, in enforced idleness, and a prey, therefore, to loose habits and vices, in whose higher welfare, too, the home people were tenderly interested, one Christian

---

[1] The *New York Observer*, November 17, 1864.

shepherd, the army chaplain, was not sufficient; furthermore, many regiments had no chaplain at all. The services of volunteers were therefore needed. This call the ministers of the home churches heard; and few Northern pastors failed at some period of the war, for a few weeks or a few months at a time, to visit the army camps for Christian work, loaned temporarily by their churches and commissioned for the occasion as delegates of the Christian Commission. At the camp of the Army of the Potomac in the winter of 1863–1864 fifty-four wooden chapels and fourteen tents were erected by the soldiers themselves for the purpose of religious services, and three other buildings were used for the same purpose, making seventy-two churches in all dedicated to religious work within a radius of twenty miles in the confines of the great army. In every church there was daily preaching, and sometimes two and three times a day, while in the seven months preceding the spring campaign of the army in 1864 ten thousand public meetings were held; many of the men were converted and added to the roll of church membership. This is but an example of what was done for many armies and for many camps. Among the men the work was very popular.

Besides these meetings the delegates distributed copies of the Bible, religious tracts, and good literature in general; they attended the hospitals and after a battle were active in caring for the sick and dying. After Gettysburg $70,000 worth of supplies were thus distributed, almost as much as that dispensed by the Sanitary Commission, and in addition to it.[1]

[1] In the year 1864 the society had 2217 delegates in the field, who rendered 78,869 days of service; 47,103 boxes of stores and publications, worth $1,169,000, were distributed, also 569,594 Bibles, Testaments, and other parts of the Bible, 489,245 hymn and psalm books, 4,326,676 knapsack books, 93,872 bound library books, 346,536 magazines and pamphlets, 7,990,758 copies of religious papers, 13,681,342 pages of tracts, and 3601 "Silent Comforters."

The total receipts of the commission were over $6,000,000. Of this sum the army committee of the Boston Young Men's Christian Association raised $160,000; special collections in the churches netted $83,400; after Gettysburg Boston in a few hours raised $35,000 for the work; Philadelphia in a few weeks during the battles of the Wilderness raised $50,000, Pittsburg $35,000, and Boston $60,000.

Many missionary, charitable, and religious societies, tract societies, and publication societies expended a part of their energies for the soldiers and sailors. The American Tract Society of New York in one year distributed in the army and navy 63,000,000 pages of free literature, about one-half of its total activities, which included work in many fields at home and abroad; the Tract Society of Boston was likewise engaged. The American Bible Society, which in one year gave away 800,000 volumes, bestowed 686,000 of them on the soldiers and sailors of both the United States and the Confederacy, for the Washington government allowed Bibles to pass through the lines to the South. The American Temperance Union sent to the army and navy 2,000,000 tracts on temperance, for which work hundreds of Sunday schools devoted $2.50 each, thus becoming responsible for the distribution of 1000 pamphlets. The Red Cross Society, originated at Geneva, Switzerland, in the middle of the American war, did not play any part in this war inasmuch as the United States did not subscribe to the convention till after hostilities closed.[1]

Soldiers' homes, soldiers' orphan asylums, pensions, and the employment of veterans in the civil service became uppermost subjects in the public mind. Before the war the government had acted in the matter of soldiers' homes and had established one at Washington for the regular army and one at Philadelphia for the navy; but provision was needed for the disabled volunteers. William Cullen Bryant, Henry W.

[1] See the reports of the societies named.

Longfellow, Horace Greeley, John A. Dix, and U. S. Grant petitioned Congress for a national home for the volunteers, and thus began the movement which has resulted in eight fine government institutions scattered in all parts of the country from Maine to California.[1] Governor Yates of Illinois early moved in this matter to secure state institutions; France and Germany had such institutions, and it was the due of our volunteers to have them here. Massachusetts was the first state actually to secure a state home and was quickly followed by New York, Illinois, and other states. The Jews, of whom there were over forty thousand in the army, established five homes for the men of their race. The effort to build soldiers' orphan asylums was just as insistent, and many state and local institutions of this nature were built, while Admiral Dupont bequeathed his prize money of $150,000 for such a home in Washington. Acts of Congress extended the pension laws, so that in five years the number of pensioners rose from eight thousand to eighty-five thousand.[2] Congress also passed a law to the effect that soldiers "discharged by reason of disability resulting from wounds or sickness incurred in the line of duty" should "be preferred for appointments to civil office, provided they are found to possess the business capacity necessary," and immediately in pursuance of this law veterans began to secure places in the local post-offices. In the states there were movements having the same objects in view. Nothing in the popular mind was too good for the soldiers; the politicians saw this; and it was easy to pass laws for homes, pensions, and for the preferment of the veterans in the civil service. The people called for these things, and both political parties gave their aid.

[1] These are located in Montgomery County, Ohio; Milwaukee, Wisconsin; Elizabeth City, Virginia; Leavenworth, Kansas; Los Angeles, California; Grant, Indiana; Danville, Illinois; and Togus, Maine.

[2] In 1861 the 8000 pensioners received $1,000,000; in 1865, 85,000 received $16,000,000; in 1907, 967,371 pensioners received $139,309,514.

In its admiration and gratitude the public often made gifts to popular military leaders and sometimes to their families. Chicago subscribed for a home for the widow of Colonel Mulligan; Boston raised $10,000 for the widow and family of General Reno, killed in battle; Philadelphia presented a furnished house to General Grant, and another to General Hancock, and citizens of Ohio presented General Sherman with a home in that state; the New York Chamber of Commerce gave $50,000 in bonds to Admiral Farragut, and General McClellan, before sailing for Europe in 1865, received from friends $30,000.

Next to the soldiers themselves the greatest sufferers from the war were their dependent families and friends, to whom millions were dispensed. In the first months of war excitement the newspapers, chronicling the enlistment and the departure to the war of the local company, detailed long lists of names with the contribution of each to the support of the soldiers' loved ones left behind. So it was throughout the war. Philadelphia disbursed in this way in one year $600,000, in another year slightly more; at one time there were as many as 9000 beneficiaries on the rolls of the city. Individuals constantly contributed. At Dayton, Ohio, a great procession, headed by a band, entered the city from the country, bearing the contributions of the neighboring farmers to the families of the soldiers: 225 wagons heavily laden with firewood, 20 wagon loads of flour, and 60 wagons of farm produce. In the winter time the farmers were constantly urged to give of their stock of wood and the response was always generous. There was state aid and in many cases county aid, but in most cases the available records do not distinguish the amounts given in this way to the dependent families by the states and the counties from the amounts paid to the soldiers themselves in bounties. However, a very large part of the bounty money, undoubtedly over half, was turned over by the soldiers to their needy relatives and may be looked upon as a form of relief. Six hundred million dollars was disbursed to the soldiers in bounties by the national government and by the state and local authorities; at least $100,000,000 more was paid by individuals.[1] In two years municipal bounties in Philadelphia totalled $5,800,000, distributed to 20,000 men; county bounties in New York State probably equaled $30,000,000.[2] For both bounties and charitable support of families the city of Hartford, Connecticut, expended $270,000, all the cities and towns of the state $5,200,000; the state of Vermont and its cities and towns $8,500,000, Maine and its cities and towns $14,000,000.

It was these vast payments that made local taxes[3] so high and left the large debts. The three states of Vermont, Rhode Island, and Connecticut, which had no debts at all at the outbreak of hostilities, were burdened by the war with $16,000,000 of obligations, while the debt of New York State advanced $15,000,000.[4] Bounties themselves reached their high figures, many declared, largely because of the abounding material prosperity. When all had joined the ranks of the army who would do so for reasons of pure patriotism, without these payments men could not be induced to forego business opportunities for the military service; life at home was too attractive, and new incentives to leave it had to be supplied after the first flush of patriotism had spent its force.

Thus upon soldiers' families a great charity was lavished; more novelty and excitement attended the ministrations to the soldiers themselves and to the negroes and Southern refugees, but vastly less was spent on these classes than upon the dependent families.

[1] Estimate of the provost marshal general of the United States. Individual bounties by the end of the war in many places reached $1000 to $1200.

[2] In 1865 the counties of the state had a debt of $38,000,000 for bounties and other war purposes.

[3] See p. 221 for these taxes.   [4] From $34,000,000 to $49,000,000.

U

Negroes constantly found their way into the military lines of the United States as the troops penetrated farther and farther into the Confederacy. In the first year of fighting the new dependents began to fasten themselves on the care and bounty of the Northern generals, first along the Atlantic coast, in Virginia and North and South Carolina, and later in the valley of the Mississippi and elsewhere; and finally they were concentrated in four leading localities, the conditions in each of which were distinctive from those in all the rest. At Arlington Heights, opposite Washington, at Fortress Monroe and at neighboring points the negroes, fugitives from their masters, were gathered in farms and villages, where they maintained themselves by a system of free labor at regular wages. Sanitary conditions were wholesome. The large cotton plantations in and about Port Royal, on the islands off the coast of the Carolinas, abandoned by their masters in all their luxuriance, were another center of refuge for the blacks, and here the first experiment of free black labor in a slave state during the period of the war was tried; except for the rebel owners, everything remained as of old, the plantation, the negroes, and the buildings; even the disturbing element of war did not intrude. The plantations themselves were confiscated by the government for the non-payment of taxes and allowed to pass into the hands of Northerners, some into the hands of negroes. There was governmental supervision of work, regular wages, and pay to the blacks for all cotton produced; and no great suffering resulted. Another community for contrabands was on the lower Mississippi in Louisiana, where there was a big city, a populous state, and large plantations from which the resident planters refused to flee; the latter, though rebels at heart, preferred to take the oath of allegiance to the United States and be called loyal, and thus remain at their houses undisturbed. These planters, largely of French extraction, had a better opinion of negroes than did Anglo-Saxons, and treated them accordingly; moreover, a considerable degree of skill was required for sugar making, so that the negroes here were of a type superior to that of the Carolina negroes. There were also in Louisiana numerous free negroes.

There was, lastly, the upper valley of the Mississippi from the Red River to Cairo, with many abandoned plantations and many hastily constructed concentration camps, in which were gathered together more runaway negroes than in all the other centers combined.[1] Both here and in Louisiana the free black labor was strictly regulated under the famous system elaborated by General Banks in Louisiana.[2] As many confiscated plantations as possible were leased to Northern speculators, who would carry on the work of the plantation by a system of free black labor. The negro was permitted to choose his employer, for whom he must work faithfully for one year on pain of being swept to the government plantations, he could not pass freely from one plantation to another, and he was paid wages arbitrarily fixed by the government at $8 per month for first-class hands and smaller sums for those of less ability; the employer, on his part, guaranteed never to resort to flogging his men, never to give them liquor, to supply them clothing and medicine, to support the weak and infirm, to furnish free schools, to give each laborer an acre of land to hold and work as his own. This was the plan in theory, but a sudden military crisis arising in 1864, all the able-bodied blacks, five thousand in number, were forced by conscription into the army.[3]

[1] In 1864 there were 183,000 negroes in the four centers, and 113,000 in the Mississippi Valley alone.

[2] There were minor differences in the application of the system in the two places, but the essentials in each case were the same.

[3] The *National Intelligencer*, February 4, 9, and 11, 1864; the *Springfield Republican*, October 5, 1864; the *American Missionary*, November, 1864; the *Liberator*, November 11, 1864; this last reference contains a great speech of General Banks in Boston in defense of his labor system. See *Official Records of the Rebellion*, Series III, Vol. IV, p. 166, for the regulations in detail.

Of these government plans for furnishing substitutes for slavery and for encouraging self-help among the emancipated negroes, those in practice about Arlington and in the Carolinas were on the smallest scale and relatively the most successful, and they aroused but little Northern opposition; but these in the West were bitterly attacked as worse than failures. They were hardly better than slavery, it was charged; under them the negro had but little real freedom, he was forced to work, his wages were arbitrarily fixed and very low, he had no freedom of movement, and in a most outrageous and unjustifiable manner he was forced to do military service; the camps of the helpless ones were a disgrace to civilization. On the other hand, the Northern speculator as lessee was protected and had his labor practically guaranteed to him by the government.

Of the actual conditions of these Western negro quarters there is ample evidence. Late in 1863 James E. Yeatman, president of the Western Sanitary Commission, investigated the conditions along the Mississippi, and from his report the following extract is taken: "At Young's Point are now some twenty-one hundred in miserable huts, tents, and hovels. There appears to be more squalid misery and destitution here than in any place I have visited. The sickness and deaths were most frightful. During the summer from thirty to fifty died in a day, and some days as many as seventy-five, during the latter part of June, July, and August. Most of the medicines received were from the Western and United States Sanitary Commission. At De Sota, immediately opposite Vicksburg, there are about two hundred seventy-five old men, women, and children, to whom the government furnishes rations but from some cause or other none had been received for more than two weeks preceding my visit, and great destitution and dissatisfaction existed. At Natchez is a camp of twenty-one hundred freedmen, all in cabins which are without proper light and ventila-

tion, overcrowded and most prolific sources of disease.
Seventy-five had died in one day. I was informed that some
had returned to their masters on account of the suffering.
Physicians are greatly needed. Thousands must die for
want of medicines and medical attendance this winter.
There are already teachers, missionaries, and chaplains
enough in the field; without physicians there will soon be
no scholars for the teacher to teach or souls for the missionary to save. This camp had numbered four thousand at
one time, now it is reduced to twenty-one hundred — a sad
tale to tell, but nevertheless true. The same, I doubt not,
can be said of other camps." [1]

Said President Jefferson Davis in his annual message to
the Confederate Congress in the late fall of 1863, undoubtedly
appealing to the world in condemnation of the United
States, through whose fault, he charged, the terrible situation had come about: "Nor has less unrelenting warfare been
waged by these pretended friends of human rights and liberties against the unfortunate negroes. Wherever the enemy
have been able to gain access they have forced into the
ranks of their army every able-bodied black that they could
seize; and have either left the aged, the women, and the
children to perish by starvation, or have gathered them into
camps where they have been wasted by a frightful mortality.
Without clothing or shelter, often without food, incapable,
without supervision, of taking the most ordinary precautions
against disease, these helpless dependents, accustomed to
have their wants supplied by the foresight of their masters,
are being rapidly exterminated, wherever brought in contact with the invaders. There is little hazard in predicting
that in all localities where the enemy have gained a temporary foothold, the negroes, who under our care increased

[1] The *Springfield Republican*, January 13, 1864; this report in full
in pamphlet form may be found in the Massachusetts Historical Society
Library, Boston.

sixfold in number since their importation into the colonies by
Great Britain, will have been reduced by mortality during
the war to not more than one-half their previous number."
A Union official reported in 1864 that the mortality
in the negro camps was "frightful"; "most competent
judges place it at not less than twenty-five per cent in the
last two years." [1]

In the North profound sympathy was aroused. Philanthropists rushed in to supplement the work of the government and to accomplish that which the latter either could
not or would not perform. Northern arms had freed the
blacks, it was argued, and had placed them in a position of
great peril before their old masters; many of them were
fighting and dying in the Northern armies; protection and
care seemed their only due. They were helpless wards, from
whom the light of society, of education, and almost of conscience and religion had been withheld by cruel customs. But
now that the light was beginning to dawn, everything that
could be done for them ought to be done. A wave of missionary enthusiasm swept over the churches. It was universally
recognized in the religious world that one of the greatest
opportunities for missionary work in the world's history had
come. The immense population of the freedmen needed to
be taught how to receive and profit by their freedom.

The missionary societies of the churches directed their
energies southward, and many local freedmen's aid societies
were organized, which united themselves into various
larger organizations, such as the National Freedmen's
Relief Association of New York, the Friends' Association
for the Relief of Colored Freedmen of Philadelphia, the Western Freedmen's Aid Commission in Cincinnati, and others,
all of which in 1865 were united into the American Freed-

[1] *The Emancipated Slave, Face to Face with his Old Master* (*Valley of
the Lower Mississippi*). *A Supplementary Report to the Honorable E. M.
Stanton, Secretary of War*, by James McKaye, Special Commissioner, 1864.

men's Aid Commission. Missionaries and teachers hurried to the new charges, and throughout the North collections for the negroes were taken, and slates, pencils, spelling books, readers, blackboards, chalk, shovels, hoes, medicine, and old clothing of every variety and description were sent to the South. In the last year of the war at least one thousand Northern young men and women were teaching and caring for the ex-slaves. Slave owners were exceedingly angry, but the Northerners, fired with religious enthusiasm, persisted in their course. Every religious paper was filled with the most enthusiastic, rosy, but hasty and ill-advised, accounts of the great desire of the negroes for education and of their wonderful ability and quickness in learning. One almost doubts the English language and his own senses in perusing these letters; they are in the language of the most extreme optimism. In this spirit, at the first opportunity, the religious spirit tendered its services to the down-trodden; in the jubilation of the moment excess of enthusiasm was perhaps natural. The commission of the teachers can only be compared to the sending of the American teachers forty years later to the brown races of the Philippines; there is nothing else in the world's history like it.

It is not necessary to set forth the stirring appeals made for the contrabands, the countless collections of old clothes, etc. One speaker, said to have been a former coachman of President Davis, was extremely effective. The mansion of Ex-president Tyler was used for a contraband school, and later that of Jefferson Davis himself in Mississippi; it was General Grant who suggested making the home of the Southern President a "negro paradise," and who made this possible by the Vicksburg campaign. It may be noted, in concluding this part of the account of the national charities, that there was no success in the attempt to colonize the negroes in Africa or in other places. They liked American manners and customs, the American climate and language, and would not give them up. The American Colonization Society took out of the country fewer negroes during the war than in some previous years.[1]

Another charity to war sufferers was that given to the Southern white loyalists, either refugees in the North or still languishing in the South. In 1864 over fourteen thousand of these people came to Nashville, Tennessee, thousands to Cairo, Illinois, to Louisville, Cincinnati, and other points. The wretches were mostly women and children, poor and forlorn in the extreme, in need of clothing, rations, hospital service, and direction in finding employment. In the frequented places refugee committees sprang up among the loyal people, and finally the American Union Commission was formed to harmonize the work of the local societies. The larger organization was ready to assist all loyal Southerners to reëstablish themselves "on the basis of industry, education, freedom, and Christian morality"; its objects were set forth in 1865 at a meeting in the House of Representatives in Washington, and a stirring appeal made to the nation for funds. This appeal read in part as follows: "One year ago the American Union Commission appealed to the churches for means to relieve the suffering refugees. The war was still progressing. The Christian and Sanitary Commissions were still in the field. No governmental provision had been made for the freedmen, who were entirely dependent upon public charity for relief. But numerous as were the calls, you generously responded to our request. And your liberal contributions given to us last Thanksgiving Day enabled us to relieve thousands from starvation and death. We procured barracks for their temporary shelter in Chicago, Cairo, Cincinnati, Baltimore, New York, and other

---

[1] In this account of the negro charity the religious papers and the reports of charitable societies have been relied upon, especially the *Freedmen's Advocate* and the *American Missionary;* all religious papers of the time have much material on the subject.

points, gave them the clothing you sent us, obtained homes
for the orphan children, and provided the adults with
employment upon the farms and villages of the North.
Thus you have enabled from seventy-five to a hundred thousand persons to procure a livelihood and saved the country
from the evils of a gigantic pauperism. The work is now
ended. These refugee barracks are now all closed. But another and greater work the providence of God lays upon us.
Half the continent has been devastated by war. In many
portions of the South, especially in the track of Sherman's
army, the distress is great and constantly increasing. Official reports received at our office tell us of women and children who walk from ten to forty miles for bread and then
obtain a morsel, frequently nothing; of naked beings crouch-
ing down by the side of their once happy homes, now reduced
to nothing save the roots of an old brick chimney; of tens
of counties in northern Georgia in which there is not as
much food growing for man or beast as can be found in a
respectable Northern farm. In this distress the innocent
suffer with the guilty; children with their parents, freedmen with their former masters. The greatest sufferers are the
families of Union volunteers from southern Tennessee and
northern Georgia, whose homes have been ravaged by
guerillas or rebel armies. The Union Commission is an-
swering their appeals for help. It has given assistance to not
less than twenty thousand suffering poor in middle Tennessee,
and to an incalculable number in east Tennessee, through
the New England branch; has given food and clothing to
fifteen thousand in Richmond; through the Baltimore
branch has distributed nearly two thousand school books and
Bibles, and over three thousand dollars of supplies, chiefly
in the valley of the Shenandoah, and has sent in less quantities to various points from Little Rock in the West to
Fernandina in the South." [1]

[1] The *New York Observer*, October 12, 1865.

Edward Everett was chairman of a committee in New England which quickly raised $100,000 for the suffering loyalists in east Tennessee; in other places large sums were raised for the same purpose. No sooner was Savannah entered by the Northern army than committees were formed in various places in aid of that city; Philadelphia in a few days raised $25,000 for provisions; New York sent two shiploads of food.[1]

This record of effort to relieve pain and suffering during the progress of a great war is a most remarkable one; millions upon millions of dollars were freely spent, the devoted services of thousands of willing hands as freely offered, to care for the exposed, wounded and dying soldiers, to succor their families at home, to protect and nurture the emancipated but abject and helpless blacks, to sympathize with and assist the innocent non-combatants, North and South. In all its manifestations it was the greatest charity that has ever swept over the nation, sudden and extraordinary but prosperously supported.[2]

Yet how was it with the ordinary charities of the nation, those that had been practiced before the war? Did they decline? It is a tribute to the nobility and the prosperity of the nation that in general they did not but that they flourished as formerly. Deaf and dumb asylums, blind asylums, and insane asylums continued their work.[3] The

[1] One contained 8000 barrels of flour, 500 barrels of salt meat, 600 barrels of vegetables, 25,000 pounds of salt meat, 25,000 pounds of beef and mutton, 100 sacks of salt, and 100 barrels of molasses.

[2] Nine million five hundred thousand dollars were raised in a few days for the relief of the fire and earthquake sufferers in San Francisco in 1906; the *New York Sun*, December 28, 1908.

[3] The first deaf and dumb asylum was founded at Hartford, Connecticut, in 1817, another in New York in the same year, one each in Pennsylvania in 1820, in Ohio in 1829, Kentucky in 1830, Virginia in 1839. In 1860 there were 23 of these asylums in the United States, and 130 teachers and 2000 pupils. Boston built the first blind asylum in 1833, and one was built in New York and another in Philadelphia in the same year. In 1860

peaceful tribes of Indians were cared for as usual.[1] In the cities free medical dispensaries and hospitals were maintained, the former in New York City annually helping one hundred fifty thousand people. The generosity to colleges and to all institutions of learning may here be recalled; gifts to churches were unusual, scores of them celebrating the happy event of getting out of debt.[2]

The Children's Aid Society in New York, founded in 1853, went forward in its work as never before. In 1861 its annual receipts amounted to $20,000, but four years later to $60,000. Homeless newsboys were received into its Newsboys' Lodging House, homeless girls sheltered in its Girls' Home, thousands of children instructed in its Industrial Schools, while many children, saved from the streets of the city, were taken in large companies to the West, where they were adopted into private homes. This last phase of the work was most interesting. In one year, 1864–1865, over one thousand children were thus rescued and sent to the country by this society, and in all the war by the work of all similar societies in the city over eight thousand homeless children were rescued and given a new start in life. The adopted homes were mainly in the agricultural sections of Ohio, Indiana, Illinois, and Michigan, where labor was scarce and where therefore all newcomers of whatever age were gladly welcomed. The same work was carried on in almost

there were in the United States 23 blind asylums and 1000 pupils. The first insane asylum in America dates from 1751 in Philadelphia; 5 were built between 1820 and 1830, 7 from 1830 to 1840, 10 from 1840 to 1850, 18 from 1850 to 1860. *U. S. House Executive Documents*, 37 Congress, 2 Session, No. 116.

[1] There were 5098 Indians in the army of the United States; the total Indian population was put in 1860 at 294,574. There were 48 Indian schools, with 2165 scholars.

[2] Boston built a magnificent hospital, another was erected in Philadelphia; in New York James H. Roosevelt left $900,000 for the erection of a new hospital in that city.

every city. From the hundreds of entries in the *Monthly Record of the Five Points House of Industry* the following typical ones indicate the nature of the work: "Ann S——, sixteen years old; a remarkably smart, bright girl; is an orphan. Father was killed in the war. Mother was a drunkard, and has been dead for several years. Has a brother married; has no other friends. The brother is now in the army, and she does not know where his family lives, and has no place to stay. Had been with a family and came away from them because the woman tried to make her go to a Catholic church, and because the woman was frequently intoxicated. Ann's stay was short with us; a gentleman from a fine town in New Jersey took a fancy to her, and she went with him, with the understanding that she was to be instructed, clothed, and at the end of two years to receive twenty dollars in money, if she was a good girl." "John, Ellen, Thomas, and Delia ——, brothers and sisters, ten, eight, six, and four years old; are children in our schools, and are now brought by their mother, with a babe in her arms, saying that she has no shelter for herself or them. She has been lodging in a room with a poor widow whom we are aiding; making eleven persons occupying a very small room and bedroom. The father of the children is a drunkard and neglects his family; has done nothing for them for several weeks. We consented to take the children for a little time, on condition that the mother would go to a magistrate and make complaint of abandonment, which would cause his arrest, and compel him to support his family; he is a mechanic, obtaining good wages." "John McG——, thirteen years old; came from Yonkers; mother recently died; father has been dead for some time; has no home or friends; came to the city to obtain employment; could not find any one to employ him, as he had no recommendation; slept on cellar steps on Fulton Street; met a gentleman on Nassau Street, who brought him here. Is very rugged, and with right usage will make a first-rate boy on a farm, where we shall doubtless be able to place him when his quarantine expires." [1]

The increase in the work of the children's societies does not indicate any increase in poverty and misery in the cities; the societies were young and were just beginning fairly to cope with the evil which was one of the first and the most natural results of heavy immigration. General charity to adults declined, not from any inability on the part of the public to support such work, but because there were fewer people to be relieved. On this point there is an abundance of evidence. The Howard Benevolent Society made such a report for Boston, the city missionary of Lowell, Massachusetts, the same for that city, the New York Association for the Improvement of the Condition of the Poor, and the Commissioners of Public Charities, Corrections, and Prisons, the same for New York. None of these societies complained of a lack of funds; they had as much money as was needed, while their disbursements declined for the simple reason that there was less need for their services. The New York Society for the Improvement of the Condition of the Poor relieved eight thousand families both in 1860 and 1861, but four thousand in both 1863 and 1864, and the total number of individuals relieved fell in the same proportion. Sixteen hundred fewer persons were received into the almshouse of New York in 1864 than three years earlier, and three thousand fewer into three Massachusetts state almshouses. [2]

The continued activity of church missionary societies must not be overlooked. The receipts of the American Bible Society almost doubled, while the number of Bibles

[1] *Monthly Record of the Five Points House of Industry*, July, 1864, p. 55.

[2] The New York Society for the Improvement of the Condition of the Poor in 1858 made 48,173 visits, received $66,578, and disbursed $67,094, relieved 13,842 families, and 54,268 individuals; in 1864 it made 18,106 visits, received $47,788, disbursed $47,416, relieved 4696 families, and visited 20,810 individuals.

and Testaments distributed more than doubled.[1] The receipts of the American Tract Society increased slightly and its circulation of tracts many fold;[2] the American Seaman's Friend Society, devoted to the social and moral elevation of seamen, prospered and finally relieved itself of a long standing debt.[3] The work of the American Sunday-school Union was but little interrupted, and at the close of the war it was annually establishing more than one thousand new schools, and organizing and aiding many more.[4] There were Bible societies, tract societies, and publication societies and Sunday-school societies connected with the various churches, and all were flourishing.

The American Home Missionary Society of the Congregational Church maintained eight hundred missionaries in the field at the close of the war, two hundred fewer than five years earlier, while its receipts were about stationary; over a half of its force were at work in the Western states. The American Baptist Home Missionary Society doubled both its receipts and the number of its workers.[5] The

[1] This society was formed in 1816; in 1859 it split on the subject of slavery into an antislavery society resident in Boston and a society in New York which was not pronounced and decided in opposition to slavery; the New York society was the larger and is the one referred to in the text. Receipts in 1860–1861 were $389,000, in 1864–1865 $677,000; the number of Bibles and Testaments issued increased in this interval from 700,000 to 1,500,000.

[2] This society was formed in 1824 and was a union of local societies which began in 1803 with the Massachusetts Society for Promoting Christian Knowledge. During the war there was still a large society flourishing in Boston. The New York Society referred to in the text employed, in 1864, 134 regular colporteurs in the United States, besides 37 students. It received in donations in 1861 $93,000, in 1865 $126,000; in the one year it issued 6,700,000 pages of tracts, in the other 109,000,000 pages.

[3] This society was formed in 1828.

[4] In 1859 the American Sunday-school Union established 2091 new Sunday-schools, and visited and helped 3701; in 1864 its missionaries established 1124 new schools, and organized and aided 5236.

[5] The receipts of the Home Missionary Society of the Congregational Church were $183,000 in 1860–1861, and $186,000 in 1864–1865. The

Methodist Episcopal Church widened its home missionary efforts with constantly growing receipts, and at the end of the war it had over three hundred missionaries laboring among the foreign classes of the country alone, eight hundred among all classes, while the Protestant Episcopal Church, the Old School and New School Presbyterian Churches, and others kept up their activities. Under all denominations approximately four thousand home missionaries were at work throughout the North in the last part of the war. In some cases this was a little less activity than usual, but in most cases more, and the general complaint was constantly for more men rather than for more money. Men to serve as missionaries were more scarce than the money to pay them. Salaries of the missionaries advanced but little, so that a slight advance in the receipts of the societies easily enabled them to maintain the usual scale of their operations or even to enlarge them. According to the figures of a leading society the average expense of a year's labor in the home field during the war advanced only twenty per cent, and if this may be taken as the average of all denominations in the same field of work (and there is no reason why this may not fairly be done), then the receipts of all the societies in general needed to advance only twenty per cent in order that the work might not be curtailed. For many of the societies the advance was much more than this.[1]

At the meeting of the American Board of Commissioners for Foreign Missions of the Congregational Church, held in

receipts of the American Baptist Home Missionary Society in the one year were $55,000, in the other $93,000, while its force in the latter year was 250.

[1] These are the figures of the American Home Missionary Society of the Congregational Church. This yearly expense of one man in the home missionary field in 1826–1827 was $127, $169 in 1835–1836, $166 in 1845–1846, $180 in 1850–1851, $241 in 1855–1856, $220 in 1860–1861, and in the next four years respectively $259, $240, $248, and $299. See the reports of the society. Donation parties as aids to salaries must be held in mind in this connection.

Worcester, Massachusetts, in 1864, one of the most enthusiastic meetings of the kind ever held, six hundred members,
fifteen missionaries, and from four thousand to six thousand
strangers were present, and it was ascertained that the receipts of the society in the previous three years had increased
more than fifty per cent; not only were the past year's expenses met and a deficit wiped out, but a surplus was created.
The total force of workers in the field at the end of the war
was slightly more than at the beginning, although the number of new missionaries annually devoting themselves to the
work fell off greatly; twenty-one sailed under the auspices
of the society in 1863, ten in 1864, and fourteen in 1865,
whereas the number in 1860 was twenty-eight. Not enough
men could be found to fill the places desired; here also men,
not money, constituted the greatest need. Few ill effects
of the war mar this record. It was the same with the foreign missionary societies in most of the churches. Receipts
sufficiently increased to maintain in gold their expenses in
foreign countries, and although fewer new missionaries
sailed from the country than were desired, in the year 1864
at least fifty sailed. Interest in the cause nowhere flagged.
Thus enthusiasm for missions, home and foreign, in fact for
all charities, was perfectly consonant with a state of prolonged war. Both extraordinary and ordinary charity
were dispensed with equal prodigality.[1]

The question arises whether war and crime raged together
and whether the passions of war caused an unusual outburst
of crime. It was commonly believed and stated at the time
that these two phenomena accompanied one another. The

[1] The missionary receipts of the Methodist Episcopal Church, domestic
and foreign, rose from $270,000 in 1860 to $607,000 in 1865, the receipts
of the New School Presbyterian Church for foreign missions rose from
$80,000 to $112,000 in the same interval, of the Old School Presbyterian
Church from $137,000 to $180,000, and of the Baptist Missionary Union
from $88,000 to $153,000. Twenty-six national missionary societies,
home and foreign, in 1865 collected $3,000,000.

newspapers noted a "carnival of crime," "crime on the increase"; Governor Fenton, of New York, in an annual message to the State Legislature spoke of "crime's startling increase." But had these contemporaries concerned themselves to look into the actual records and statistics, they would have realized that their generalizations were not founded on fact. Year by year the penitentiaries of New York held fewer and fewer prisoners than previously, over 2600 in 1860 and 1900 in 1865; commitments to the county jails of the state as well as to the city prison in New York City fell off; the number of prisoners in the Massachusetts state prison was 509 in 1860, but in 1864 was only 376, while in the county prisons of the state the number fell from 1700 to 1100. The same was true of the penitentiaries of Rhode Island, Pennsylvania, and of other states. The Philadelphia county prison held 21,585 prisoners in 1860, but only 14,000 in 1864. This falling off in the number of criminals convicted was general, whereas the population in the cities was on the increase, and the only possible conclusion is that the infractions themselves of the rules of civilized society were also less; many of the particular individuals in the growing centers of population who were liable to fall into crime were gone to the army. It was a natural decrease. There may have been some laxity in the enforcement of the law; possibly judges imposed lighter sentences than usual or no sentence at all, on the promise of the prisoner to enter the army; but if this were done, it could be only a partial explanation. The nature of the crimes committed doubtless grew more bestial, a result that would naturally come from the prolonged state of war, and this probably led to the popular impression that the number of crimes committed was increasing. It was when the soldiers got home from the war, and before they had all succeeded in finding places for themselves in the industrial world, that the prisons filled up. In New York City in 1865 the number of

x

arrests was 14,000 greater than in the previous year; 700 more prisoners entered the state penitentiaries in 1866 than in 1864; in Pennsylvania the inmates in these institutions in the later year were almost twice the number of the last year of the war.[1]

Diminution in crime could hardly have been due to the increased influence of the church, for in the first two or three years of the war the people were little interested in spiritual things; there were but few revivals, and church services seem to have lost their hold on the masses. The excitement of the war and interest in its progress and the very newness and strangeness of these appeals to the public attention weakened the hold of the church. Missionaries in the country districts of the West noticed this as well as the pastors of the city churches. One of the former wrote: "The mustering and the drilling of soldiers, the suspense of the public mind, the exciting intelligence from time to time received, indeed the very idea of war, all tend to obliterate seriousness, and to close the ear and the heart to the appeals of the Gospel of Christ." Another said: "The sound of the drum calling for volunteers, the training of soldiers, companies leaving for the seat of war, are but scenes of every day's occurrence. Amid the excitement consequent upon such a state of things, you can readily understand the difficulty of sustaining the institutions of religion. In fact, the pastor and his church are continually in danger of having their feelings more deeply interested in the fearful conflict between the North and the South than in their own growth in grace, or in winning soldiers for Christ." Another: "I am sorry that I have no more pleasing intelligence to communicate; but it is all wars and rumors of wars. Scarcely anything else is talked of, and it is very difficult to call people's minds to anything else." A fourth: "The war excitement seems to absorb the attention of the great

[1] See the reports of the institutions referred to in the text.

majority of the people, to the exclusion of everything of a religious nature. Instead of having the effect that it should, to bring Christians nearer to God in prayer and humiliation, for our personal and national sins, I fear it has had the opposite result, begetting in some instances a bitterness of feeling toward the people of the Southern states that is unfavorable to a spirit of prayer." Lastly: "The all-absorbing topic is the war, by the side of which politics, business, and even religion stand no chance. War in all its fearfulness is stamping anxiety on every brow, is bringing desolation to every family. Mothers will stay you as you pass through the country, eagerly inquiring about the last fight, and old men with gray hairs will question you respecting the young man."[1]

The following observation was made in regard to the churches of Albany, New York: "Of the general state of religion in this city and neighborhood, I regret to say that our worst fears in regard to the effects of the war are realized. Ever since the calamitous conditions of the country became the all-engrossing subject of thought and conversation, the higher interests of Christ's spiritual kingdom have been thrown proportionately in the background. The additions to most of our churches have been few; the interest in our week-day meetings has been diminished; the preaching of the gospel has not excited the accustomed power; in short, the humiliating confession must be made that the church and the world seem, to a great extent, to have fallen into a common slumber. And the saddest thing is that our condition in this respect seems to be but too faithful a representation of the conditions of nearly the whole church."[2]

A change began to be felt in the early months of 1863. The missionary letters then ceased mentioning martial

---

[1] For these extracts from missionary letters, see the *Home Missionary* for the years 1861–1862, pp. 125, 240, 266, and 268; 1862–1863, pp. 14 and 220.

[2] The *New York Observer*, December 25, 1862.

excitement and spoke rather of revivals, the activity in building new churches, the receipt of the missionary barrel from the East, etc. Notices of revivals in the cities began to appear in the religious papers from month to month. Every section seemed to be affected by the change. In the next winter, that of 1863–1864, there were numerous strong revivals. Under the leadership of a successful evangelist there were particularly large revivals in Haverhill, Massachusetts, in Detroit, Michigan, and in Newark, New Jersey, as the result of which thousands were added to church membership. A strong movement was disclosed in Springfield, Massachusetts. "Yesterday was a memorable day in the history of the first church in this city," wrote a correspondent from that place to the *New York Observer*. "At its communion service one hundred nine were admitted to membership, fourteen by letter, and ninety-five by baptism. One hundred five have been baptized since the revival began."[1] Manchester, New Hampshire, was stirred; here the days of the revival of 1857 were recalled. Out of 200 students in Phillips Academy, Andover, Massachusetts, 50 joined the church in two weeks, 40 at Williams College out of 180 students, 30 at Mount Holyoke Seminary out of 175 students. In 1864 throughout the nation the new spirit and interest manifested itself. Revivals which added 50 to a church were very common, and while this may not seem a large number, it was still noteworthy in comparison with the lack of interest in such things which had characterized all classes for the previous two or three years of the war. Numerous new branches of the Young Men's Christian Association were formed; for example, in Detroit, Newark, Springfield, Worcester, and Poughkeepsie; many new church buildings were erected; and the annual gatherings of the churches were large and enthusiastic. But the size of the movement is not the point of greatest interest, for there have been many

[1] The *New York Observer*, April 14, 1864.

larger revivals in the country's history. Sin was not driven
out; frivolity and selfish indulgence seem even to have increased, and crimes, if less numerous than usual, were more
brutal and fiendish than ever, while frauds on the government were ghastly in the extreme. The important point
rather is the very fact of the revival itself, its universality,
and the evidence it affords of the changed condition of the
public mind.

The change was apparently accomplished without excitement and hysteria of any kind. It was the natural reaction
from the experiences of the first two years of the war; the
state of war was now usual, the first impressions of its novelty,
excitement, its physical power and awfulness, that had earlier taken such a hold on the popular heart, had passed away,
giving place to a more passionless and more profound state
of mind. Men could not always live at the high tension of
feeling which had characterized them in the opening years
of the struggle; there was bound to be a reaction to the
common things of everyday life, a psychological readjustment due to the very prolongation of the war. With the
change religion appealed to men. The real nature of the war,
its underlying principles, the great charities and ministrations
necessarily springing from it, once understood in the calm
light of reason, drove men to religion. The first blows of
fighting had stunned men's finer sensibilities; hospitals
filled with the wounded, countless funerals at one's very door,
the anguish and the suffering at first filled men with that
feeling which has been voiced by the present generation in the
cry, "Remember the *Maine*." It was then: "Remember
Colonel Ellsworth," "Remember my son," the utterance of a
spirit of revenge that plainly was not compatible with a
spirit of prayer. Then the readjustment came and the spirit
of religion asserted itself.[1] Revivals of religion appeared,

[1] These changes of public spirit are of slow growth, but the war was
long.

education took a new hold on the public mind, charities at home and abroad were maintained with greater munificence than ever, the churches added to their numbers, schools and colleges were endowed, suffering was relieved, and the missionary spirit reached out to all the world. The heart of the nation was touched in spite of commercial prosperity, which usually has a tendency to draw men's minds away from the thoughts of religion.[1]

This readjustment of the public mind after the first depression was one of the most important results of the state of prolonged war, for it affected not only educational, charitable and religious life, but industrial activities as well, and contributed toward bringing about the widespread prosperity which, it must be concluded, characterized the period. There were extraordinary agencies at work arising from the war, and contributing to the same prosperity, such as the heavy demands for war supplies and the rapid increase in prices, but with this readjustment to the new circumstances the ordinary influences of peaceful times were allowed to operate. The increase in the supply of the precious metals and other mineral products, the tariff, immigration, the

[1] As a growing charitable and religious organization the Young Men's Christian Association deserves mention. Founded about 1854, it held annual conventions from that date up to 1861, the largest convention being that of 1859, when 259 delegates were present; the war broke up the meetings of 1861 and 1862, but 150 delegates met in 1863 in Chicago, 136 in Boston in 1864, and 222 in Philadelphia in 1865. The association grew fast after the revival of 1857, and deserves great credit for its part in the organization of the work of the United States Christian Commission and of the work for the negroes. The society was then equipped and organized much as at present; in the local association there were library and reading rooms, educational classes, lectures, an employment agency, a boarding house committee, Bible study classes, prayer meetings, and the army committee and its work for the soldiers. It is noticeable that the same society took the lead in Christian work for the American soldiers in the war between Spain and the United States in 1898.

opening of new lands, and the growth of the crops were factors that would tend to progress just as they had in the previous decade; war exercised but little check upon them. High prices also were a result of these same tendencies as well as of the paper standard of money.

Again, the circumstances of war, the tariff, the immediate demand for both supplies and laborers, and perhaps to some extent the aroused national spirit accelerated wonderfully the development of the country as a self-sufficient industrial unit. Dependence on foreign markets was being shaken off, a home market developed, and reciprocal interests created, in short the "American system" of Henry Clay was suddenly set up, and a new epoch in American industrial life introduced, involving a reorganization of industry into larger and more harmonious units in place of the smaller units of the past. The new régime worked for greater efficiency and economy as well as for greater harmony. It met the needs of the time and was welcomed by the business world, with little of the questioning of a later period as to the desirability of a purely American system.

In spite of the high prices the prosperity was shared by the laboring classes with but few exceptions as well as by the capitalists. [1]

[1] The diminished needs of the charitable societies, the progress of the savings banks, and the lavish expenditure upon popular amusements furnish a body of evidence as to the well-being of the laboring classes that cannot be gainsaid. For a partial explanation of the possession of money by the poorer classes, see the treatment of soldiers' bounties and wages, pp. 125 and 289.

INDEX

Agriculture, crops, **1–4**; agricultural conditions, 4–17; foreign demand and its influence, 17–21; prosperity, 22–23.

Alcohol, manufacture of, 82.

American Bible Society, 302.

American Board of Commissioners for Foreign Missions, 303–304.

American Home Missionary Society, 302–303.

American Seaman's Friend Society, 302.

American Sunday School Union, 302.

American Tract Society, 302.

Apprentices, 188.

Arbitration, 210.

Atlantic and Great Western, new railroad, 54–57.

Atlantic cable, 158–159.

Attendance at schools, colleges, and preparatory schools, 237–240; ladies' seminaries, 244; high schools, 245; grammar and primary schools, 245; night schools, 250.

Bankruptcy, arguments for and against a national law, 141–143.

Banks, national, general nature, 115–116; arguments for and against, 116–117.

Banks, savings, progress, 124–125; army as source of deposits, 125–126; interest paid, 127.

Banks, state, in the panic of 1860–1861, 109–110; wildcat banks in the West, 110–112; expansion, 112–113; prey to counterfeiters, 113–114; evils of bank notes, 115; reforms by the banks, 115, 152–154; progress and profits in cities, 123–124.

Baseball, 265, 266.

Beer, increased consumption, 82.

Billiard matches, 265.

Birth rate, 230.

Blacklist, 209.

Blanchard, Rev. Jonathan, 36.

Boat building, 46.

Boat races, Yale and Harvard, 266–267.

Books published, European, 254–255; American, 255–256; encyclopædias, 257, note.

Border cities, progress in public improvements, 231, note.

Boston, volume of grain exportation, 47; general position as transportation center, 47; previous disregard of Western trade, 61; efforts to improve communication with the West, 61–65; banks, 124, note; building, 225; tax rate and valuations, 221.

Bounties to soldiers, totals paid, 125; evidence of sums saved, 126; details, 288–289.

Boycott, 210.

Bridges, over Mississippi, 68; at Cincinnati, 65; at Havre de Grace, 59; at Albany, 58.

Bryant, William Cullen, seventieth anniversary, 257.

Buffalo, lake commerce, 45; position in transportation rivalry, 47; relation to canal at Niagara Falls, 53.

Building, statistics, 224–225; high prices as a deterrent, 225; low price of land as an inducement, 226; declines most in rentable property, 227; church building, 227–228; public buildings, 228.

Business blocks, 228.

Business colleges, 250–251.

Camden and Amboy Railroad, its monopoly, 169–170; effect of the war, 171–172; action in Congress, 173–175; attitude of New Jersey, 173–174.

Canals, tonnage on Erie Canal, 46; agitation to improve Illinois and Michigan Canal, 48; influence of *Trent* Affair, 48; agitation to improve Erie Canal, 50; Chicago canal convention, 50–52; other canal projects, 52; around Niagara Falls, 53; end of canal agitation, 54.

313